Roy Ward Baker

Published in our
centenary year
~ **2004** ~
MANCHESTER
UNIVERSITY
PRESS

BRIAN MCFARLANE, NEIL SINYARD *series editors*

ALLEN EYLES, PHILIP FRENCH, SUE HARPER,
TIM PULLEINE, JEFFREY RICHARDS, TOM RYALL
series advisers

already published

Jack Clayton NEIL SINYARD

Lance Comfort BRIAN MCFARLANE

Terence Davies WENDY EVERETT

Terence Fisher PETER HUTCHINGS

Launder and Gilliat BRUCE BABINGTON

Joseph Losey COLIN GARDNER

Michael Reeves BENJAMIN HALLIGAN

J. Lee Thompson STEVE CHIBNALL

Roy Ward Baker

GEOFF MAYER

Manchester University Press
MANCHESTER AND NEW YORK

distributed exclusively in the USA by Palgrave

Copyright © Geoff Mayer 2004

The right of Geoff Mayer to be identified as the author of this work has been asserted by him in accordance with the Copyright, Designs and Patents Act 1988.

Published by Manchester University Press
Oxford Road, Manchester M13 9NR, UK
and Room 400, 175 Fifth Avenue, New York, NY 10010, USA
www.manchesteruniversitypress.co.uk

Distributed exclusively in the USA by
Palgrave, 175 Fifth Avenue, New York NY 10010, USA

Distributed exclusively in Canada by
UBC Press, University of British Columbia, 2029 West Mall, Vancouver, BC, Canada V6T 1Z2

British Library Cataloguing-in-Publication Data
A catalogue record for this book is available from the British Library

Library of Congress Cataloging-in-Publication Data
A catalog record for this book is available from the Library of Congress

ISBN 13: 978 0 7190 6355 8

First published by Manchester University Press 2004

First digital paperback edition published 2011

Printed by Lightning Source

Contents

LIST OF PLATES	*page* vi
SERIES EDITORS' FOREWORD	vii
ACKNOWLEDGEMENTS	viii
Introduction: a classical director working in a melodramatic force-field	1
1 'A pre-war man': a career overview	13
2 'Realism' – *Flame in the Streets* and *A Night to Remember*	69
3 'A morbid sensibility': 1947–61	95
4 'Roy Ward Baker': Hammer and Amicus	152
5 Conclusion: *The One That Got Away*	186
FILMOGRAPHY	190
SELECT BIBLIOGRAPHY	212
INDEX	217

List of plates

1	Dirk Bogarde in *The Singer Not the Song*	page 140
2	Mylene Demongeot and Dirk Bogarde in *The Singer Not the Song*	140
3	Dirk Bogarde and John Mills at the climax of *The Singer Not the Song*	141
4	John Mills in *The Singer Not the Song*	141
5	Poster for *The Singer Not the Song*	142
6	Poster for *The Singer Not the Song*	142
7	Poster for *The Singer Not the Song*	143
8	Press book for *The Singer Not the Song*	144
9	Press book for *The Singer Not the Song*	145
10	Ava Gardner visits Dirk Bogarde on the set of *The Singer Not the Song*	146
11	Lobby card for *Asylum* featuring Herbert Lom	147
12	Lobby card for *Asylum* featuring Babara Parkins	147
13	Lobby card showing Ian Ogilvy in *And Now the Screaming Starts!*	148
14	The American poster for *Operation Disaster*, which was released in Britain as *Morning Departure*	149
15	Poster for *The Singer Not the Song*	150
16	Poster for *The Vampire Lovers*	151
17	Poster for *Inferno*	151

Series editors' foreword

The aim of this series is to present in lively, authoritative volumes a guide to those film-makers who have made British cinema a rewarding but still under-researched branch of world cinema. The intention is to provide books which are up-to-date in terms of information and critical approach, but not bound to any one theoretical methodology. Though all books in the series will have certain elements in common – comprehensive filmographies, annotated bibliographies, appropriate illustration – the actual critical tools employed will be the responsibility of the individual authors.

Nevertheless, an important recurring element will be a concern for how the oeuvre of each film-maker does or does not fit certain critical and industrial contexts, as well as for the wider social contexts which helped to shape not just that particular film-maker but the course of British cinema at large.

Although the series is director-orientated, the editors believe that reference to a variety of stances and contexts is more likely to reconceptualise and reappraise the phenomenon of British cinema as a complex, shifting field of production. All the texts in the series will engage in detailed discussion of major works of the film-makers involved, but they all consider as well the importance of other key collaborators, of studio organisation, of audience reception, of recurring themes and structures: all those other aspects which go towards the construction of a national cinema.

The series explores and charts a field which is more than ripe for serious excavation. The acknowledged leaders of the field will be reappraised; just as important, though, will be the bringing to light of those who have not so far received any serious attention. They are all part of the very rich texture of British cinema, and it will be the work of this series to give them all their due.

Acknowledgements

My thanks to Roy Ward Baker for allowing me into his home and sharing his keen insights into the British film industry in general and his films in particular. I also wish to express my appreciation to Lady Astor for providing a splendid lunch and entertaining company. To Dean Brandum, one of my Cinema Studies students, I wish to convey my gratitude for acquiring the Warner Bros press book for *The Singer Not the Song*. This press book was a valuable resource as it included an unpublished interview with Roy Ward Baker. Dean's ability to locate and purchase film posters, lobby cards and 'lost' films is truly mystifying. Finding a copy of *Paper Orchid* was a particular coup, as this film seemingly disappeared after its trade screening in London in 1949.

Thanks also to La Trobe University for the financial assistance that enabled me to visit Roy Ward Baker in Kensington and spend many hours at the British Film Institute. Brian McFarlane's knowledge of, and passion for, British cinema assisted the book in many ways, and I also wish to convey my gratitude to Neil Sinyard, Kate Fox, Matthew Frost and the staff of Manchester University Press for facilitating its production. Finally, my wife Lesley provided assistance well beyond proof-reading the manuscript.

Introduction: a classical director working in a melodramatic force-field

> Anybody, working in whatever medium, who believes that technique can be disregarded, is simply no artist[1]

In 1962, Roy Ward Baker, at the time of the release of *The Singer Not the Song* in the United States, claimed that the 'most important attribute of a director is ruthlessness'. The producer–director said that there 'was too much compromise in the world today. A director must be fully conscious of everybody's problem but he must not let his knowledge of those problems override his idea of how the scene should look on the screen'.[2] Yet Baker's career was, in one sense, a series of compromises. *The Singer Not the Song* (1960) was not a film he wanted to direct. Dirk Bogarde, the star of the film, was cast as a Mexican bandit in the film because Rank desperately wanted him to renew his contract. Baker – with the possible exceptions of *Inferno*, *The One That Got Away*, *A Night to Remember* and *Two Left Feet* – did not actively seek or develop his films. They were, generally, chosen by Rank or Twentieth Century Fox or Hammer or Amicus and he was asked, or told, to direct them. When he developed a series of projects in 1958, including *Saturday Night and Sunday Morning* and *The Long and the Short and the Tall*, Rank rejected them and they were made elsewhere.

Yet within the aesthetic, institutional and cultural parameters of the popular film, Baker directed a number of outstanding and better-than-average films. His contribution, however, can only be fully appreciated within the constraints, or parameters, of the classical mode of film-making. Baker's best films display those qualities of 'classicism' that, as David Bordwell demonstrates,[3] are characteristic of this mode. They are elegant, poetic, 'realistic' and coherent. They also display a high level of craftsmanship. And, within these constraints, a number of them are 'odd',[4] or, at least, contain 'odd' moments.

At the end of *Passage Home* (1954), Ruth (Diane Cilento), Vospers (Anthony Steel) and Captain 'Lucky' Ryland (Peter Finch) attend a party to commemorate Ryland's retirement. Ryland, a gruff martinet, tells the group that he plans to spend his remaining years alone in a cottage by the coast. He then leaves the function to catch a taxi. After he walks down the stairs to the dock Ruth, now married to Vospers, follows him outside and stands at the top of the stairs looking down at the man who tried to rape her twenty years before. As the film is clearly about to end, this is an interesting moment – will the film conclude in a conventional, upbeat manner by showing Ruth with her husband? Or will Ruth confront the man who attacked her? Baker, however, rejects both possibilities and closes the film in a strange way. Vospers, the man who saved Ruth from Captain Ryland, does not appear. Instead, there is an exchange of glances between Ruth and Ryland. Her reaction is not one of satisfaction at his torment but of pathos. This presentation of sadness for, perhaps, lost opportunities is an odd way to end a nautical melodrama.

It is these odd moments that make Baker's films so fascinating. His films do not confront the basic tenets of popular, or classical, filmmaking. Nor do they repudiate the moral norms of the period in which the films were produced. But they often unsettle or surprise the viewer. For example, the ending in the classical film traditionally consists of two phases of action. The resolution shows the overcoming of the obstacle and the achievement of the narrative goal, or goals, while the epilogue reassures the audience that the 'characters' futures are settled'.[5] *Passage Home* challenges both phases. While Ryland is shown to be villain (attempted rapist) and hero (the ship's saviour), the film refuses to reassure us that the characters' futures are settled. Why, for example, would Ruth express concern for a man who attempted to rape her? It is, for Baker, a characteristically pessimistic, moving – and odd – moment.

Such moments permeate Roy Baker's films.[6] He worked for most of his career within strict institutional and formal contexts – both in film and television. The need to emotionally involve the audience, through the use of conventional techniques such as action and suspense, was expected. Pathos became a key device in many of his films, especially those with downbeat endings such as *Paper Orchid* (1948), *Morning Departure* (1950), *Night Without Sleep* (1952), *A Night to Remember* (1958), *Flame in the Streets* (1961) and *The Vampire Lovers* (1970). Its use in *The Singer Not the Song* is less clear while still powerful. In *Passage Home* it disturbs the conventional ending, while the printed epilogue in *The One That Got Away* (1957) suddenly threatens, or even reverses, the 'triumphant' climax to the film.[7] Baker's weaker films, such as *The Weaker Sex* (1948), *Jacqueline* (1955) and especially *Moon Zero Two* (1969) do not share these qualities, where the sentimentality (*The Weaker Sex* and *Jacqueline*) and action (*Moon Zero Two*) appear perfunctory and predictable.

Except for *Paper Orchid*, *The Valiant* (1962) and *Two Left Feet* (1962), Baker's 29 feature films were made for four film companies: Rank, and Rank-owned associate companies such as Two Cities, Twentieth Century-Fox, Hammer and Amicus. After a thorough apprenticeship at Islington from 1934 to 1940, and his first experience as a director during the war, he entered the industry at a time when directors were motivated to introduce expressive[8] or distinctive elements into their genre films – providing they did not violate the overall dramatic logic of the work. Hence, there was a 'space', within the constraints of the classical cinema and the dramatic and moral parameters of melodrama, for genre directors such as Baker, John Guillermin and J. Lee Thomson to craft more than just formulaic films. This 'space' disappeared after 1958.

His chance to break away and work in non-melodramatic, non-genre films, and also extend his career as an A-list director, came in late 1958 when Rank purchased the rights to Alan Sillitoe's novel *Saturday Night and Sunday Morning*. Baker was excited by the prospect of a film version. However, when Rank's production committee rejected his proposal in December 1958, and J. Arthur Rank returned the rights to the author, Baker's career stalled and he never regained his status in the industry. Worse was to follow with the failure of two independently produced films in the early 1960s, and with the decline of the medium-budget genre film there were no more feature films until 1967 when Hammer offered him *Quatermass and the Pit*. In the intervening years he worked on British television shows such as *The Saint*, *The Human Jungle*, *Gideon's Way*, *The Avengers* and *The Baron*. His return to feature films as 'Roy Ward Baker' was at the less prestigious, although commercially successful, end of the industry.

No longer did he have the same sort of creative 'space' that was available to a director at Rank or Twentieth Century-Fox. Rank's demise as the most prolific film-producing company in Britain severely affected his career. Hammer, with their policy of genre and exploitation films, suffered from financial problems during Baker's tenure at the company and this affected his output. Amicus, his last film company, offered even less creative 'space', as their portmanteau films were tightly controlled, especially with regard to the script and the editing, by the company's co-founder, Milton Subotsky. Baker's status in the industry was reflected in the way newspaper critics often approached these films. 'Hokum in the nuthouse' – even 'well-made hokum', as one reviewer described *Asylum* (1972) – was symptomatic of his post-1967 period.

From 1934 to 1940 Baker was employed as a 'gofer', production assistant and location manager at Gainsborough's Islington Studios. Many of the films he worked on during this period were low-budget comedy films, including four 'Aldwych farces' with Tom Walls. These 'performative' films, a term used by John Ellis to distinguish such films from the classical cinema, were prominent in the British film industry in the 1930s and 1940s and they were distinguished by their inclusion of 'non-classical' elements that encouraged an 'interactive' relationship with the audience.[9] As part of his argument that these films were the dominant mode of British filmmaking at this time, Ellis compares a 'performative' film, *Radio Parade of 1935*, with a classical example, *Brief Encounter*. He notes that although David Lean's film received a harsh reaction when it was previewed in the 'rough naval dockyard town' of Rochester, it is seen today 'as a perfect example of post-war British narrative film construction, a classic text that strives towards completeness'.[10]

Baker never directed a 'performative' feature film and distinguished between these films and what he calls 'proper' films, such as Carol Reed's *Night Train to Munich*.[11] He was less influenced by Tom Walls and his 'tight 15', and other 'non-classical' techniques, than the processes and practices utilised by classical directors such as Alfred Hitchcock, Carol Reed and especially Robert Stevenson, who also made films at Islington in the 1930s. This mode of filmmaking allowed a certain degree of individual choice within an overall narrative and stylistic paradigm. It does not, as David Bordwell points out, 'determine every minute detail of the work, but it isolates preferred practices and sets limits upon invention'.[12] Although standard practices have coalesced into a system of priorities and constraints over the years, thereby establishing 'rules' of acceptable and unacceptable methods, this system permits 'functional equivalents'. Hence, a cut-in may replace a track-in, as both devices fulfil the same role.[13]

Change within the classical system is less likely if it violates the system of narrative logic and the conventional presentation of cinematic time and cinematic space. Its techniques are designed to promote narrative clarity so that the spectator knows not only where he or she is in relation to time and space but also his or her position within the logic of the plot. It is a system that tries to deflect audience attention to the story and away from the processes of narration.[14] Yet it allows creative 'spaces' for expressive moments that don't violate its fundamental principles.[15] For example, Baker shot the *Tiger in the Smoke* (1956) with the camera set-up on a baby crane so that he could keep it on the move, in any direction, throughout he film.[16] Also in *The One That Got Away* (1957) he staged everything so that Von Werra moves from right to left and the other characters from left to right.[17] Both examples are 'permissible' within this system because, as he acknowledged with regard to his staging of the action *The One That Got Away*, nobody noticed them because *'they weren't suppose to notice'*.[18]

In early 1961 Baker[19] outlined his approach to filmmaking. He maintained that whilst a good knowledge of the 'technique' of filmmaking was a necessary prerequisite to a successful film, other facets were also important:

> There is a great deal of talk about the technical aspects of film-making. Technique, surely is A B C – something to be mastered, then forgotten, and then deliberately abused. Of course one has to be very careful to be sure that you do know technique well enough to start to abuse it. Anybody who is ignorant of technique is at a disadvantage because it's only knowing what you can get out of the medium that you can start putting something into it.[20]

In this interview Baker cites an example from his current production of *Flame in the Streets* (1961) of how he was able to explore the advantages of the Cinemascope format without violating basic classical principles:

> At first it was maintained that you couldn't use it [Cinemascope] for close-ups. Now the only value of a close-up is that it isolates someone or something, and he, she or it is on the screen alone. Its value is not that it is closer but that it gives singularity. Nowadays with clever staging in Cinemascope you can do exactly the same thing to achieve the same object, but somehow you will retain a sense of the background.[21]

Thus, Baker argues, while Cinemascope offered a better means of delivering the effect of the close-up, it did not change the *function* of the close-up. Similarly, he rejected the notion that Cinemascope changed the way directors staged their scenes:

> I don't believe you can stage scenes with a large group and play it off as you would in the theatre ... your cuts remain the same: they must do because the only thing we really have is a control of time and space, and if you chuck that overboard you might as well not make pictures at all. You can still cut as quick as you like, from close-up to long-shot and back in again to close-up in Cinemascope if you want to ... It's a front-office argument that with Cinemascope you don't need as many cuts and so therefore you can make a picture quicker. This is absolute nonsense.[22]

Baker concluded the interview with a summation of the attitude to filmmaking:

> I think that some people tend to try and make out of films a lot of things

they are not. But really a motion picture only consists of a succession of animated photographs. If they are not photographed and not animated then you haven't got a film. This is why the Western is the classic motion picture, simply because it is an action picture.

We're governed by the fact that action is character and action is movie, so let's tell the story in terms of action, and a story that does not naturally expose itself to an audience is not a valid motion picture story.[23]

This attitude is evident in his first film, *Home Guard Fighting Series* (1943), an 80–minute instructional film he directed for the Army Kinematograph Service Film Production Unit. As the film was shot silent, with commentary and sounds added later, it gave him the chance to tell the story in images. It was, in his words, a 'golden opportunity' as it 'was all action'.[24] Similarly, his last film for Twentieth Century-Fox, the outdoor melodrama *Inferno* (1953), offered him the best chance to put his ideas into practice, as much of the film is concerned with Robert Ryan alone in the desert. This delighted Baker as he 'could return to the most effective presentation that a film can offer'.[25] Similar, if briefer, opportunities to indulge himself in 'pure cinema' include the opening scenes in *The October Man* (1947), *Night Without Sleep*, *Tiger in the Smoke*, *The One That Got Away* and *The Vampire Lovers*.

Because Baker worked mainly in these 'spaces' within the classical system, and because he was a director of genre films for much of his career, he did not receive enormous coverage, or credit, from the British critics. The exception to this pattern was his 'realist' films such as *Morning Departure* and *A Night to Remember*. Here the subject matter proved less of a distraction and the critics could appreciate his expertise unsullied by generic conventions. This is evident in the reaction of the *New Statesman* (6 September 1947) to Baker's first, and arguably best, film, *The October Man*, when the critic compared Baker's film with RKO's *Journey Into Fear*, which was produced in Hollywood in 1942. This comparison, designed to distinguish between an 'artist' (Orson Welles) and a 'craftsman' (Baker), was motivated by the fact that *The October Man* was scripted by Eric Ambler while *Journey Into Fear* was based on one of Ambler's novels. The reviewer concluded that Baker failed to match the flair of the American: 'Mr Roy Baker, with a better story in *The October Man*, has taken no such liberties of style and decoration and the result is almost too unpretentious'. The difference, in the reviewer's mind, was due to the fact that Orson Welles directed *Journey Into Fear* and was able to make something more from 'that piece of wonderful bluff'.[26]

The superiority of *The October Man* to *Journey Into Fear* is not difficult to sustain in terms of both the narrative and formal presentation –

especially the scenes of John Mills contemplating suicide on a railway bridge. Yet Baker's ability to integrate such expressive moments within the overall narrative failed to impress the *New Statesman* reviewer, who was seeking a filmmaker who would rupture rather than amplify the story.

The *Tribune* (5 September 1947), on the other hand, was prepared to overlook the film's generic basis, which was described as a 'psychological thriller', as it was 'characterised and motivated with such care that it rises ... into the class of serious drama'. Much of the credit for this, however, went to the writer, Eric Ambler, and not the director. It was, the *Tribune* argued, 'creatively his [Ambler's] film'. Fred Majdalany, in the *Daily Mail* (5 September 1947), on the other hand, was more to the point when he emphasised the significance of the film's dramatic mode – melodrama – and he praised the film as 'another of these Grade One English melodramas which the Rank producing companies are now turning out with gratifying frequency'. Baker was never to leave this mode for the rest of his career as a feature film director.[27]

As he was a studio director this is hardly surprising, although it is important to clarify what exactly constitutes a melodrama – a question that has occupied film, literary and theatre scholars for many years. Prior to the early 1970s there was some consistency across the various disciplines as to its meaning, but with the publication of Thomas Elsaesser's article 'Tales of Sound and Fury: Observations on the Family Melodrama'[28] in 1972 film studies took a different path. This article was based on a small number of films – *Written on the Wind* (1956), *Bigger Than Life* (1956), *Rebel Without a Cause* (1956), *Imitation of Life* (1959) and *Home From the Hill* (1960) – and a limited number of directors such as Douglas Sirk, Nicholas Ray and Vincente Minnelli. Elsaesser showed how colour, editing rhythms, camera movement and various aspects of the mise-en-scène were able to expose discordant elements in American culture in the 1950s. Although he was less interested in the historical development of melodrama, he did note that it 'was a form which carried its own values' and functioned as a 'historically and socially conditioned *mode of experience*. Even if the situations and sentiments defied all categories of verisimilitude ... the structure had a truth and life of its own, which an artist could make part of his material.'[29] Subsequent film writers focused only on one aspect of the article – the ironic subtext of the small, unrepresentative selection of family melodramas – and for the next two decades 'melodrama' in film studies was often conflated with, and reduced to, a sub-genre, the domestic or family melodrama, or, in some cases, the woman's film.[30]

Fortunately this is no longer the case as Steve Neale, Christine Gledhill, Linda Williams, Ben Singer, and others, have restored its meaning by examining the historical relationship between nineteenth-century theatrical and literary melodrama and twentieth-century film melodrama.[31] Film studies has now, in most cases, converged with literary and theatre studies in providing a more comprehensive, and accurate, account of the development of film melodrama from its literary and theatrical antecedents. A critical publication, although one that was ignored in film studies for many years, was Peter Brooks's 1976 account of the melodramatic imagination employed by nineteenth-century novelists and its basis in French theatrical melodrama following the French Revolution.[32] Although the main aim of Brooks's study was to establish the centrality of melodrama in the novels of Henry James and Honoré de Balzac, his more lasting effect was to demonstrate the significance of melodrama to film and television in the twentieth century. His greatest advantage in formulating his ideas, as Linda Williams points out, 'may have been his ignorance of film theory and criticism. Unlike film critics who have seen melodrama as an anachronism to be overcome or subverted, Brooks takes it seriously as a quintessentially modern (though not modernist) form arising out of a particular historical conjuncture.'[33]

Brooks shows that melodrama is not a 'set of themes', nor a genre, but 'a mode of conception and expression, as a certain fictional system for making sense of experience, as a semantic field of force ... a sense-making system'.[34] It carries, he maintains, the burden of expressing the 'moral occult', the 'domain of operative spiritual values which is both indicated and masked by the surface of reality'.[35] Williams, and others, argue that this 'quest for a hidden moral legibility is crucial to all melodrama'.[36] As a dramatic mode it should not be seen as exceptional to classical cinema but as a pervasive mode with its own rhetoric and aesthetic.[37]

This aesthetic is characterised by a range of devices and elements, although the polarisation of morality and the use of action, spectacle and pathos to render the world morally legible is central to this dramatic mode. Williams, in particular, is very decisive as to the importance of pathos and action and the relationship between these two attributes:

> To study the relation between pathos and action is to see that there is no pure isolation of pathos in woman's films nor of action in the male action genres. If, as Peter Brooks argues, melodrama is most centrally about moral legibility and the assigning of guilt and innocence in a post-sacred, post-Enlightenment world where moral and religious certainties have been erased, then pathos and action are the two most important means to achieve moral legibility.[38]

INTRODUCTION 9

Melodrama, it should be noted, is not *necessarily* an excessive mode. Nor should it be seen as the antithesis of realism. Nor is it an aberrant, 'unmotivated' moment in the classical cinema. Nor is it subservient to the linear chain of psychologically based causes that Bordwell, Staiger and Thompson claim as the basis of the classical cinema. As melodrama transferred from the theatre to the cinema, and as the cinema developed throughout the early twentieth century, it 'frequently instituted more realistic causations and techniques for the display of pathos and action'.[39]

Melodrama functions, as Christine Gledhill shows, as an 'early cultural machine for the mass production of popular genres capable of summoning up and putting into place different kinds of audience' and as a 'culturally conditioned mode of perception and aesthetic articulation'.[40] It is time then, as William argues, to realise that melodrama is not a 'submerged, or embedded, tendency, or genre within classical realism, but that it has more often itself been the dominant form of popular moving-picture narrative'.[41]

For a studio director working within popular genres, it is hardly surprising that the vast majority of Baker's films are melodramas. Pathos and action are his staple ingredients as both enhance audience involvement through the 'emotion of sympathy engaged in the pathetic spectacle of suffering and the emotion of suspense engaged in action sequences'.[42] Emotional gratification is paramount and pathos and/or action are key elements in *The October Man, The Weaker Sex, Paper Orchid, Morning Departure, Night Without Sleep, Passage Home, Jacqueline, Tiger in the Smoke, A Night to Remember, The Singer Not the Song, Flame in the Streets* and *The Vampire Lovers* – although not necessarily in equal proportions in each film. Some, however, use both very effectively such as the final moments in *The October Man* and *A Night to Remember*. Others are more reliant on pathos (such as *Night Without Sleep* and *Jacqueline*) or action (*Inferno* and *Tiger in the Smoke*).

Sometimes, pathos is employed to upset audience expectations, as in the epilogue in *Passage Home*, or the final moments in *The Vampire Lovers*, where it subverts the cathartic 'pleasure' of the vampire's destruction by shifting the focus to Emma's sense of loss following Carmilla's staking. As for *The Singer Not the Song*, the use of pathos is anything but simple and plays a substantial part in evoking audience curiosity in this delirious film, which has intrigued audiences and critics since its release in 1960.

Regeneration often accompanies pathos in Baker's films, although it is used in a number of different ways. In *The October Man*, for example, Jim Ackland is both psychologically and socially redeemed. Richard

Morton in *Night Without Sleep* is morally regenerated but socially condemned, while Donald Carson in *Inferno* is socially and emotionally regenerated. Father Keogh not only fails to save the soul of the bandit Anacleto but jeopardises his own soul in *The Singer Not the Song*, while the social reality of 1961 British attitudes to sexual intercourse between Kathie Palmer, a white English schoolteacher, and her Jamaican colleague, Peter Lincoln, is sufficient to prevent a fully determined ending in *Flame in the Streets*. Regeneration, as the film's final image indicates, is not yet complete for Kathie's mother and father.

Throughout the book I have tried to place Baker's films in a number of contexts, including comparisons with the approach adopted by other directors working with similar material within the same time period. Hence Anthony Kimmins's *Mine Own Executioner* is briefly compared with *The October Man*, Guy Hamilton's *Manuela* with *Passage Home*, Peter Sasdy's *Hands of the Ripper* with *Dr Jekyll and Sister Hyde* (1971), and Terence Fisher's *Dracula* and *Dracula – Prince of Darkness* with Baker's *Scars of Dracula* (1970).

'Realism', Baker argued, was his strength and even his fantasy films for Hammer and Amicus were approached from the point of view of making the characters 'real'. When interviewed on the set of *And Now the Screaming Starts!* in 1972 he explained that the 'more outrageous it is, the harder you've got to work on the characters so that the audience can accept them as real people'.[43] Chapter 2 explores his conception of 'realism' through a comparison between two of Baker's 'realist' films, *Flame in the Streets* and *A Night to Remember*, with the one of the key New Wave 'realist' films, *Saturday Night and Sunday Morning*, a film that Baker desperately wanted to direct.

Despite a number of impressive films and a long career Baker has attracted little critical attention.[44] An exception is Raymond Durgnat's brief, but masterly, analysis of Baker's pre-1961 films. Durgnat detects 'elements of doubt, disgust and despair'[45] in his films and he concludes that Baker is an 'auteur whose spiritual attitude, a kind of fair-minded pessimism, precludes open revolt and it precludes acceptance'.[46] Chapter 3 examines the mixture of morbidity and pathos in most of his pre-1961 films.

Baker has expressed mixed feelings about his post-1967 career. He resents the fact that as a result of his name change some critics are unaware that he directed films such as *Morning Departure*, *The One That Got Away*, and *A Night to Remember*. Instead they remember him as a 'horror director' and this, he argues, is misconceived as he directed very few horror films: 'I don't want to be and don't like it'.[47] Chapter 4 examines his films at Hammer and Amicus: *Quatermass and the Pit, The Scars of Dracula, Dr Jekyll and Sister Hyde, Asylum, The Vault of Horror* (1972), *And Now the Screaming Starts!* and, especially, *The Vampire Lovers*. The next chapter provides an overview of his career in the British and American film industries and I have included the critical reaction to *The Weaker Sex, Jacqueline, The Anniversary* (1967), *Moon Zero Two, The Valiant, Two Left Feet* and *The Legend of the Seven Golden Vampires* (1973) as they do not receive detailed analysis in chapters 2, 3 and 4.

Notes

1 Roy Ward Baker, *The Director's Cut*, London: Reynolds & Hearn, 2000, p. 20.
2 The Press Kit for *The Singer Not the Song*, distributed by Warner Bros. in the United States.
3 See David Bordwell, Janet Staiger and Kristin Thompson, *The Classical Hollywood Cinema: Film Style and Mode of Narration to 1960*, London: Routledge, 1985, p. 4.
4 I am indebted to Peter Hutchings for the term 'odd' as it seems to capture the tenor of such moments in Baker's films. See Peter Hutchings, 'Authorship and British Cinema: The Case of Roy Ward Baker', in Justine Ashby and Andrew Higson (eds), *British Cinema, Past and Present*, London: Routledge, 2000.
5 See David Bordwell, 'Happily Ever After, Part Two', *the velvet light trap*, Number 19, 1982, p. 4.
6 I use the name 'Roy Baker' for much of the book, not 'Roy Ward Baker', which he adopted in 1967, as 18 of his 29 feature films were credited to 'Roy Baker'.
7 See the Conclusion.
8 See Peter Hutchings, 'Authorship and British Cinema', pp. 186-7. Hutchings also cites the example of John Guillermin and J. Lee Thompson.
9 John Ellis, 'British Cinema as Performance Art: *Brief Encounter, Radio Parade of 1935* and the Circumstances of Exhibition', in Ashby and Higson (eds), *British Cinema, Past and Present*.
10 Ibid., p. 101.
11 Baker, *The Director's Cut*, p. 36.
12 Bordwell, Staiger and Thompson, *The Classical Hollywood Cinema*, p. 4.
13 *bid.*, p. 5.
14 Through devices such as goal-oriented protagonists, character-centred stories and an omniscient narration style – derived largely from late nineteenth-century aesthetic norms – are supported by characteristic narrative techniques such as repetition, retardation and redundancy of information.
15 This is noticeable, for example, in the endings in films such as *The October Man, Paper Orchid, Passage Home, Flame in the Street* and *The Singer Not the Song*.
16 See Baker, *The Director's Cut*, p. 93.
17 Ibid., p. 98.
18 Ibid., my italics.
19 Roy Baker, 'Discovering Where the Truth Lies', *Films and Filming*, Number 7, May 1961.
20 Ibid., p. 17.
21 Ibid., p. 38.
22 Ibid., p. 38.
23 Ibid.

24 Baker, *The Director's Cut*, p. 82.
25 *Ibid*.
26 See Chapter 1. Welles was not credited as the director on *Journey Into Fear* although he did contribute to the film.
27 I have seen all of Baker's feature films except the two films he directed in the early 1960s after leaving Rank – *The Valiant* and *Two Left Feet*.
28 Thomas Elsaesser, 'Tales of Sound and Fury: Observations on the Family Melodrama', *Monogram*, Number 4, 1972.
29 *Ibid.*, p. 5.
30 See *ibid*. Also Barbara Klinger, *Melodrama and Meaning, History, Culture, and the Films of Douglas Sirk*, Bloomington: Indiana University Press, 1994.
31 Steve Neale's intensive study of American trade journals revealed that the film industry, in most cases, reserved the term 'melodrama' for the action genres, and not the 'woman's film'. See Steve Neale, 'Melo Talk: On the Meaning and Use of the Term "Melodrama" in the American Trade Press', *The Velvet Light Trap*, Number 32, autumn 1993. See also Ben Singer, 'Female Power in the Serial-Queen Melodrama: The Etiology of an Anomaly', *Camera Obscura*, Number 22, winter 1990. See also Christine Gledhill's excellent chapter, 'Rethinking Genre', in Christine Gledhill and Linda Williams (eds), *Reinventing Film Studies*, London: Arnold, 2000. See also Geoff Mayer, 'The Liberation of Virtue: The Cinema, Melodrama and Lizzie Borden', *Metro*, Number 95, spring 1993.
32 Peter Brooks, *The Melodramatic Imagination: Balzac, Henry James, Melodrama, and the Mode of Excess*, New Haven: Yale University Press, 1995.
33 Linda Williams, 'Melodrama Revised', in Nick Browne (ed.), *Refiguring American Film Genres: Theory and History*, Berkeley: University of California Press, 1998, p. 51.
34 Brooks, *Melodramatic Imagination*, p. xvii.
35 *Ibid.*, p. 5. Linda Williams prefers Brooks's more secular term 'moral legibility' to identify the ethical basis of melodrama. See Linda Williams, *Playing the Race Card: Melodramas of Black and White from Uncle Tom to O.J. Simpson*, Princeton: Princeton University Press, 2001, note 17, p. 315.
36 Williams, 'Melodrama Revised', p. 52.
37 *Ibid.*, p. 48.
38 *Ibid.*, p. 59.
39 Williams, *Playing the Race Card* p. 25.
40 Gledhill, 'Rethinking Genre', p. 227.
41 Williams, *Playing the Race Card*, p. 23.
42 See *ibid.*, note 29, p. 318.
43 Chris Knight, interview with Roy Baker, *Cinefantastique*, Volume 2, Number 4, summer 1973, p. 6.
44 See Robert Murphy, *Sixties British Cinema*, London: BFI Publishing, 1992, p. 48, and Peter Hutchings, 'Authorship and British Cinema', p. 179.
45 Raymond Durgnat, *A Mirror for England: British Movies from Austerity to Affluence*, London: Faber & Faber, 1970, p. 239.
46 *Ibid*.
47 John Brosnan, *The Horror People*, London: MacDonald & Janes, 1976, p. 224.

'A pre-war man': a career overview 1

Roy Horace Baker was born in Hornsey in 1916; his father was a salesman in the Billingsgate Fish Market where he eventually owned his own business. When Roy was twelve his father, who frequented the same pub in St Martin's Lane as workers from the nearby MGM office, bartered goldfish in exchange for tickets to the gala opening, on 9 November 1928, of MGM's newly renovated Empire Theatre in Leicester Square. This lavish spectacle had a profound effect on Roy as he watched his first sound film, a Movietone short. The silent feature – *Trelawny of the Wells*, starring Norma Shearer, Ralph Forbes and Owen Moore – followed this and it was accompanied by a 90-piece orchestra. This moment changed his life: 'I was rooted to my seat, movie-struck. I made up my mind then and there that I must get into films as soon as I could get out of school'.[1]

It took Roy another five years to achieve this aim, but in the interim his interest in the cinema continued to grow. An only child, he regularly accompanied his parents to the Rialto Cinema in Coventry Street and he was allowed to watch films from the projection box – sometimes the same film two or three times. As the Rialto often screened European films, Roy's film education extended beyond just the British and American movies and he developed an interest in the films of René Clair. Later, in 1930, he met the director and the stars of *Sous les toits de Paris*, Annabella and Albert Préjean, at the London premiere of the film.

In July 1933, at the height of the depression, Roy left school and began writing, without success, to the British studios in search of a job. Later, a housemaster at Roy's ex-school, the City of London School, encouraged the seventeen-year-old to apply for a vacancy in the mailroom at the Columbia Graphophone Company in Farringdon Road. After eight months in the mailroom, Roy was offered a job with Gainsborough Studios, at 30 shillings per week. He began his film career in February 1934.

Islington: February 1934–February 1940

Roy was sent to the Islington studio, which had been converted from a railway power station into a two-stage film studio by the American company Famous Players Lasky in 1919. The studios were subsequently purchased by Michael Balcon and his associates in 1924 and Alfred Hitchcock began his career there as a sign-writer. Gainsborough, however, produced most of their 'prestigious' (i.e. large-budget) films at Shepherd's Bush, while Islington was normally the home of low-budget comedies – starring Tom Walls, Will Hay and Jack Hulbert – as well as cheaply produced musicals and thrillers.

There were only two stages and one was up on the second floor. Everything was shot on sets owing to the poor quality of sound recording and perennial problems with the British weather. Location work, as Baker noted, was

> frowned upon. It cost too much money. And that was a great pity; we boxed ourselves into the studios early on, and we never really got out of the habit, and everything looked 'setty'. It was a free and easy life, though, in a way, because there were no unions ... It was only a tin-pot industry anyway, at the time. So you could do what you liked on the floor; you took whatever job needed to be done.[2]

In the cramped conditions at Islington Baker was a 'gofer' and one of his first tasks was to sort out the 'dirty, ragged old gowns' for a crowd of beggars in a bazaar scene in the musical *Chu Chin Chow* (1934).[3] While this position as a jack-of-all-trades was poorly paid, it had the advantage of letting this inquisitive young man 'poke ... [his] nose into everyone else's business, until – sometimes – told to bugger off ... I lived for the job, enjoying myself no end'.[4]

Roy Baker's second film was the sentimental musical comedy *My Old Dutch* (1934) and his main duty was to make sure that veteran director Sinclair Hill had his pipe. As there was a temporary halt in production after his next film, *The Camels Are Coming* (1934) starring Jack Hulbert, Baker asked if he could work in the editing room at Shepherd's Bush. However, after assisting Charles Frend on a Leslie Henson and Frances Day musical *Oh! Daddy* (1935), he 'saw no future for myself as a film editor'.[5] He returned to Islington in September 1934 as assistant director on the musical comedy *Heat Wave* starring Les Allan. This was followed by his first Aldwych farce, *Fighting Stock* (1935) starring Tom Walls, Robertson Hare and Ralph Lynn. Baker worked on four of these films and enjoyed the relaxed atmosphere and Walls's idiosyncratic approach to filmmaking. After exercising his horses at Epsom, he would arrive at the studio 'around elevenish' and then 'rehearse a three or four page dialogue scene and set up the camera on an all-embracing shot to include all the actors and most of the set – a set-up still known to most of us as a Tom Walls tight 15'.[6] Baker enjoyed the experience but he had little respect for this approach as he described it as 'merely photographed theatre', not 'proper films'.[7]

The Clairvoyant (1934) was an exciting melodrama starring Claude Rains and American Fay Wray, but Baker's next film, Boys Will Be Boys (1935), was more typical of the low-budget films produced at Islington, and it was the first of nine films starring popular comedian Will Hay that Baker worked on. The importance of this film to his subsequent career was that he was able to observe veteran Hollywood filmmaker William Beaudine. At the end of a take Beaudine would shout, '"Cut! Prinnit! Over here with a fifty!" This greatly impressed producers ... they thought, this director really knows what he wants; he's got the next set-up all worked out. Of course, nobody ever checked whether the next set-up was in fact over there with a 50mm lens'.[8] Later, in the 1960s, when Baker was directing television series that required the same speed and efficiency he would use Beaudine's words to impress producers.[9]

Baker was not overly impressed by the standard of filmmaking at Islington as, generally speaking, 'our pre-war world was full of actors who fluffed their lines and missed their marks, were hopelessly inefficient about their wardrobe, make-up, props, etc and spent most of their time wandering off the set'.[10] Thus, when actors of the calibre of Claude Rains, Fay Wray and Boris Karloff[11] came to Islington they were 'eye-openers to us. They had an instinct for the camera and they weren't afraid of it. They always knew where it was and what it was doing without having to look. More importantly, they had an elementary understanding of editing, sensing how the set-ups would cut together'.[12]

Baker was promoted to second assistant director in 1936 with an increase in salary to five pounds a week, and he worked on Tudor Rose, a film that was to remain in his memory for many years. It was about 'real people', with a strong cast including Nova Pilbeam, Cedric Harwicke, Sybil Thorndike, Felix Aylmer and a young John Mills. It also allowed Baker to study the methods of the director, Robert Stevenson, who became his hero. 'This was when I began to nurture a tiny ambition to be a director.'[13] The basic plot of Tudor Rose – and the machinations that installed Henry VIII's niece, fifteen-year-old Lady Jane Grey, on the throne for nine days before beheading her in the Tower of London – remained with him for many years. In the 1970s and 1980s he worked on a screenplay for another version. After directing the six-part mini-series The Flame Trees of Thika in 1979 he decided to cast Holly Aird, a young actress in that series, as Lady Jane Grey. As Aird was still too young he had to wait two years until she was the right age. In the meantime he continued to work on the script, which he called *Jane the Quene*. However, as he was about to propose the film, he discovered that Paramount already had a version in development[14] and Baker was forced to abandon his plans. This was, he later declared, 'undoubtedly the biggest disappointment I ever had'.[15]

Before *Everybody Dance*, starring Cicely Courtneidge, began production in 1936 Baker became location manager at the studio and this brought him into direct contact with directors, as he had to show them photos of possible locations. He began seeing things 'from the director's point of view: why one setting was right for the scene and another would be wrong'.[16] On Carol Reed's *Bank Holiday* (1938), for example, he was sent out with a small camera to film the opening sequence, which showed an assortment of people leaving work prior to the holiday break ('My cup ran over that day, I can tell you'[17]).

In Baker's transition from assistant director to (potential) director, the arrival of Hitchcock at Islington to film *The Lady Vanishes* (1938) was a pivotal moment. During the ten-week shoot he learned 'as much about film direction as I did in all the rest of my time at Gainsborough'.[18] He was especially impressed by the control Hitchcock exerted over the entire production and his economy of effort on the set.[19] This was due to meticulous pre-planning – a lesson the aspiring director never forgot. As second assistant director, one of his duties was to collect copies of a small-scale plan of the set from the art department and take them to Hitchcock's office before lunch. After lunch he had to collect the plans Hitchcock had prepared for the next day. Baker was impressed by the amount of detail contained in these plans and, in some cases, Hitchcock had even specified the lens he intended to use and 'he never double-crossed you by changing his mind'.[20] Watching Hitchcock film the action, most of which takes place aboard a (studio) train in cramped compartments, was invaluable and, in 1957, Baker was able to directly employ some of this knowledge when he staged the train sequence in *The One That Got Away*.

Baker's experience at Islington provided a solid basis for his subsequent career although he never worked as a first assistant director. In 1939 he registered for national service and then accompanied the production of *Band Waggon*, starring comedian Arthur Askey, when it was moved from Islington to Shepherd's Bush. War with Germany was declared during this production, and he was working on Carol Reed's *Night Train to Munich* when he joined the army on 15 February 1940.

War

Jeffrey Richards argues that film historians have underestimated the effects that the war had on British filmmakers.[21] Baker, William MacQuitty and Eric Ambler – the director, producer and writer of *A Night to Remember* – made films after the war that reflected this period, Richards maintains, in that they 'often displayed a mood of bleak realism, a total absence of triumphalism and gung-ho heroics, and a stress on the realities of pressure, determination and duty'.[22] The war, Richards continues, also affected the style of their post-war films as they emerged from the 'wartime documentary movement into commercial feature film production and shared a commitment to values nurtured by that movement: authenticity, emotional restraint, the idea of duty, concern with the predicament of ordinary people under stress'.[23]

Obviously a traumatic event, such as a world war, will affect its participants but this is not the whole story. Baker was primarily influenced by his pre-war experiences, especially his six-year 'apprenticeship'[24] at Islington, where he formed his ideas as to what constitutes a 'proper film' while working with Alfred Hitchcock, Carol Reed, Robert Stevenson, William Beaudine and others. In terms of his values and outlook Baker describes himself as a 'pre-war man'.[25]

After a year as Acting Lance-Corporal, Baker was posted to Pwllheli in North Wales, then on to Bedford and Cromer where he spent his time erecting barbed wire defences on the coast. In 1942 the War Office repeated its call for people who had worked in the film industry to assist in the making of training films, so he volunteered. He was sent to the old Fox-British Studios at Wembley Park to work with the Army Kinematograph Service Film Production Unit (AKS), headed by filmmaker Thorold Dickinson. His first job was as production manager on a film directed by Jay Lewis, a man who was to have an influence, both positive and negative, on his film career. Baker also met Eric Ambler at this time, when he attended a church service.

As there was a shortage of directors in the AKS 26-year-old Baker offered to direct *Home Guard Town Fighting Series* (1943), an eight-part training film designed to show the Home Guard how to clear a town that was occupied by the enemy. Baker was delighted with the opportunity as the 80-minute series was shot silent, with the commentary, sound effects and music added later. As the film was 'all action', with the story told in 'moving pictures', it 'was a golden opportunity' – 'what more could a first-time director want?'[26] Although 'it was supposed to look real ... we staged every bit of it' and he had six weeks to shoot the film: 'It was a pretty good schedule. A pretty ambitious project ... But it was a good project for me and gave me some visibility, and it's funny that my first film as a director should be a feature, so to speak. It really helped.'[27]

Prior to this film he had read books on the subject of directing, 'mostly from Russia and by or about Pudovkin and Eisenstein',[28] and he gained a knowledge of montage and the way editing could affect the meaning of a film. Baker, however, was more interested in the way emotional intensity, and audience involvement, could be developed in action films such as westerns. Hence, 'D.W. Griffith was the man for me'.[29] The 'best single piece of advice about film direction I ever got', however, came not from these luminaries, but from Ray Pitt, executive producer at AKS, who told him to always 'cover yourself with a cutaway'.[30] This meshed with Hitchcock's dictum that when in trouble, 'cut to a laughing Chinaman' – or – 'look for a story which has good sub-plots offering parallel action'.[31]

The *Home Guard Town Fighting Series* was filmed in Birmingham over four weeks. Following this film he was assigned to another instructional film, *According to Our Records*, which stressed the importance of accurate records. At this time, 1943, Eric Ambler was appointed to the unit as a writer and he, subsequently, became the head of AKS. Towards the end of the war the two men began discussing what they were going to do after hostilities ceased and Baker told him that he had no intention of going back to Gainsborough as a second assistant director.[32] Ambler then revealed that he was planning to write a script based on J. Sheridan Le Fanu's Gothic novel, *Uncle Silas* for Filippo Del Guidice at Two Cities Films, and he invited Baker to direct it.

After the war, before Hollywood

Baker directed six more informational films after *According to Our Records*, including *Read All About It!* (1945), which was written by journalist Jack House. This film challenged the notion that because it is in the papers it must be true and it was a 'modest success'.[33] This film may also have assisted Baker with his depiction of a fictional newspaper operation in his third feature film, *Paper Orchid* (1948). Baker left the AKS and joined Ambler at Denham Studios, which had been acquired by the Rank Organisation from Alexander Korda in the late 1930s, to prepare for *Uncle Silas*. Production was scheduled for November 1946 but it was postponed when Denham's coal-based heating was removed during a period of severe weather conditions and the new system, based on oil, had not yet been installed.[34] *Uncle Silas* was made the following year, but not by Baker as Charles Frank directed the film. Baker did, however, make a film from a Le Fanu novel – *The Vampire Lovers* in 1970.

Because of the delay with *Uncle Silas*, executives at Two Cities suggested to Ambler that he should write an original screenplay. He came up with Baker's first film, *The October Man* (1946). Ambler also produced the film, and although Baker considered Ambler a better novelist than screenwriter[35] *The October Man* had a first-rate script. The shoot, however, was not an entirely happy experience for Baker as the planned twelve-week schedule extended to seventeen weeks. He blamed much of the delay on the battle between the sound recording department and the camera department, and he was especially frustrated by the laborious lighting processes followed by Erwin Hillier and his 'cantankerous' camera operator Bob Thompson. Baker did not get on with either man.[36] Baker's relationship with Ambler was also damaged by the delays and by the tenth week the producer–writer had lost confidence in his director. After the completion of the film, which was generally well received by the British critics, Baker's option to direct another film for Two Cities was not picked up.

Baker was not worried, at this stage, by the studio's action as he was happy with *The October Man* as a 'modest but sound start as a director and I would never do anything else. To me, it was a job for life.'[37] There were, however, no immediate prospects to work as a director and Baker did what he always did when there were lulls in his career: he tried to create work for himself. He was never happy just waiting for opportunities to arise, and during this lull he tried, unsuccessfully, to write a thriller. Producer Paul Soskin approached Baker late in 1947 to make a film for Two Cities based on Esther McCracken's play *No Medals*, which had been playing in the West End since 1944. The problem was the script, written by two people without any experience as scriptwriters: McCracken and Soskin. A more experienced scriptwriter, Val Valentine, was brought in to write additional material but the problem of the film's poor dramatic structure was never satisfactorily resolved.

No Medals reunited Baker with Erwin Hillier, his cinematographer on *The October Man*, although he did have a more agreeable camera operator, Eric Besche, this time. The film's title was changed to *The Weaker Sex*, which suggested a comedy based on the 'battle of the sexes'. Instead, it was sentimental homage to the women and men fighting the war on the home front. Although Esther McCracken's play was very popular during its West End run in 1944, 'playing to full houses for over 700 performances',[38] Baker argued that the film's lack of success was due primarily to the fact that audiences 'did not want to be reminded of those [war] problems; they were having enough trouble coping with the peace. It was a neat and tidy job, but it did nothing to enhance the prestige of anyone concerned'.[39]

Most newspaper critics shared this view and their response was only luke-warm. The reviewer for the *Evening News* (23 September 1948) argued that 'I doubt if this is a tactful time to remind us of the hopes and heroisms of June 1944'. Others criticised the film for trying to update the play with post-war material. The *Daily Mail* (24 September 1948) complained, for example, that VE Day, where the play concluded, was a more appropriate point to end the film than the 'endless and certainly anti-climactic series of post-war sequences'. The *Sunday Graphic* (26 September 1948) agreed, as did Hubert Griffith in the *Sunday Express* (26 September 1948), who thought the post-war scenes were 'perfunctory and conventional'. *The Times* (27 September 1948), on the other hand, was more concerned as to whether the film was a 'mirror' of the period, and the reviewer concluded:

> Well, yes and no. No, in so far that the realism after which it strives, the realism of the middle-class semi-detached house on the south coast, paradoxically, fails it just when it is being most precise in its details – the gas stove, the daily help, the queues, the rations, and all the rest of it – and that at the heart of the whole chronicle dwell weakness and sentimentality, but yes, in that occasionally it says simply and forthrightly what so many people think.

The film's sentimentality was also a problem for the *News Chronicle* (26 September 1948), but not for the *News of the World* (26 September 1948), who disagreed with all those who found fault with the film: 'I see that according to my fellow critics "The Weaker Sex" ... is riddled with faults. Therefore I ask your indulgence for being incapable of detailing these grave weaknesses. I must have missed them because I was enjoying myself so much'. One of the problems for the film, however, was that it was released at the same time as *The Winslow Boy* – a few critics, such as in the *Daily Worker* (25 September 1948) and the *Sunday Times* (26 September 1948), dismissed Baker's film as 'sugary fiction', and not up to the standard of *The Winslow Boy*.

Paper Orchid, Baker's next film, was filmed at Nettlefold Studios at Walton-on-Thames, named after Archibald Nettlefold, who purchased it in 1926. Originally, this small studio was developed by British film pioneer Cecil Hepworth, and after his bankruptcy in 1923 it became the base for many independent productions over the next thirty years. *Paper Orchid*, a low-budget film with a seven-week shooting schedule, was produced by Ganesh Productions with financial support from Columbia Studios. Scripted by Val Guest, it was based on a novel by Arthur La

Bern, who also wrote *It Always Rains on Sundays*. The film, with a Fleet Street setting, had dual plotlines combining the machinations of two newspaper companies with a murder mystery. Despite a good cast – which included Hugh Williams, Hy Hazell, Andrew Cruickshank, Walter Hudd, and Sidney James as the love-stricken crime reporter – the film never received a widespread general release in Britain.

After two commercially unsuccessful films, Baker in late 1948 was becoming concerned: 'Gradually I was beginning to worry. Spring came, but everything was dead, as far as I was concerned. I had directed three pictures, but I was travelling on a descending curve. Looking back, I remember it as an agonisingly long and depressing time.'[40] Things, however, soon changed. Baker accepted an invitation from close friend Kay Walsh to lunch at Elstree Studio, where she was working on Alfred Hitchcock's *Stage Fright*. He found himself sitting with Hitchcock and most of the cast, including Marlene Dietrich, and during the luncheon he received a phone call from Jay Lewis that changed his career. It was an offer to direct *Morning Departure* (1950), the film that 'rescued' him and took him to the United States and Twentieth Century-Fox.[41]

Morning Departure was based on Kenneth Woollard's play and the script was written by William Fairchild, who also wrote *Passage Home*, Baker's first film for Rank after his return from Hollywood. Baker was eager to direct *Morning Departure*: 'This was one of those rare occasions when I read a script and knew with absolute certainty that the film would be a big hit'.[42] However, the production was not all plain sailing and there was the distinct possibility at one stage that he would be replaced as director. After it was completed, there was another possibility that the film would be shelved for some time. Fortunately, for Baker's career, none of these possibilities eventuated. Nevertheless, when the *HMS Truculent* collided with a large freighter in the Thames, causing the deaths of 64 sailors, there was speculation that this was an inappropriate time to release *Morning Departure*. After the Admiralty endorsed the censor's decision to release the film, it opened strongly and the *Truculent* disaster became, in one sense, an integral part of the film's promotion, as it was mentioned in most reviews. It is also addressed in the film's foreword:

> This film was completed before the tragic loss of *HMS Truculent*, and earnest consideration has been given as to the desirability of presenting it so soon after this grievous disaster. The producers have decided to offer the film in the spirit in which it was made, as a tribute to the officers and men of H.M. submarines, and to the Royal Navy ...

After completing location shooting in Portland on the submarine the

HMS Tiptoe and the mother ship the *HMS Maidstone*, Baker returned to Denham for principal photography. Lewis, however, told him he was 'appalled by how bad it [the footage] was'[43] and that from now on he would have to be on the set all of the time to make sure that nothing further went wrong. Over the next few weeks Baker had to suffer the indignity of Lewis's constant interference, while trying to keep the production running smoothly and not give the producer the slightest excuse to fire him. He soon realised that Lewis wanted to take over as director but, fortunately, Baker found that he had an ally amongst the film's financial backers, the British Film Finance Company, and it was decided that Lewis should be removed from the set and sent off to Dover with a second unit to film the salvage operations.[44] Baker never knew who made this decision but it saved his career. Without Lewis's constant interference the filming at Denham went smoothly.

The premiere of *Morning Departure* at the Gaumont Haymarket was a resounding success and during the evening Baker received word from his agent that Twentieth Century-Fox were interested in acquiring his services. In the meantime Eric Ambler, 'after a period of estrangement',[45] contacted Baker and offered him *Highly Dangerous* (1950), which was loosely based on Ambler's novel *Dark Frontier*. Baker, initially, was hesitant owing to the possibility of joining the Hollywood studio but, as there was no firm offer as yet, he accepted Ambler's semi-comic Cold War espionage thriller starring Margaret Lockwood and Hollywood actor Dane Clark.

Hollywood and Twentieth Century-Fox

Baker and art director Alex Vetchinsky travelled to Trieste to shoot plates for back projection for *Highly Dangerous* and, after flying to Paris for the premiere of *Morning Departure*, he received news of a firm offer from Twentieth Century-Fox. Baker completed *Highly Dangerous*, but he has never seen since it was completed in 1950: he does not have positive feeling about the film as he felt he never had a real grip on the film's mixture of comedy and drama. Also, the prospect of joining Twentieth Century-Fox upset his usual approach, which he describes as a kind of 'tunnel vision', where he allows nothing to disturb his concentration during production.[46]

Baker's excitement at working in Hollywood was heightened when he saw the studio: 'I was staggered by my first view of the 20th Century-Fox studios'.[47] His exhilaration was enhanced by the fact that Sam Fuller and Herman Mankowitz occupied offices next to him. This joy was soon shattered by the arrival of Jay Lewis, who told Baker that he had a long meeting with the head of production at Twentieth Century Fox, Darryl Zanuck, and informed him that he [Lewis] was creatively responsible for *Morning Departure*.[48] As Baker had not yet met Zanuck, he was fearful that this lie would damage his standing with Zanuck. This was confirmed when he met Zanuck's son-in-law André Hakim on the lot – when Hakim asked about the situation with Lewis, Baker gave him the facts: 'Whether I was able to dispel any doubts André may have had, I know not'.[49]

After Baker had been at the studio a couple of weeks, Sol Siegel, a senior producer at Fox, gave him Ranald MacDougall's script for a remake of *Berkeley Square*,[50] which was based on John Balderston's 1926 play. It had been filmed in 1933 with Leslie Howard and Heather Angel. Because Twentieth Century-Fox wanted to use funds that were frozen in Britain, it was decided to make the film in London, so after seven weeks in the United States Baker returned home. Tyrone Power, who had just completed a six-month run in the West End in *Mister Roberts*, was cast as Peter Standish, a depressed nuclear physicist living in an old house on Berkeley Square. After Peter finds the diary and papers of an ancestor he decides that he would prefer living in the eighteenth century, and a lightning bolt conveniently transports him back in time. He soon discovers that his romanticised perception of the period was misplaced and he struggles with family problems and a strong resistance to his ideas. To make matters worse he falls in love with Helen Pettigrew (Ann Blyth), the sister of his fiancée Kate Pettigrew (Beatrice Campbell) and this accentuates his torment. After the authorities destroy his experiments and try to incarcerate him in a mental asylum, Standish returns to the twentieth century via another lightning bolt.

For a romantic fantasy this is a peculiar film with a relentlessly bleak view of human nature and British society – both in the eighteenth and twentieth centuries. Helen Pettigrew, for example, dies of a 'broken heart' after Standish returns to the twentieth century. The ending tries to soften this aspect by arranging for Peter to meet Martha (Ann Blyth), the sister of his best friend Roger Forsyth (Michael Rennie), at Helen's grave. Martha, of course, is remarkably similar to Helen. Although Twentieth Century-Fox were keen to cast Jean Simmons as Helen/Martha, she was under personal contract to Howard Hughes, who would not release her. Other actresses interviewed included Audrey Hepburn, who was rejected by Baker, a decision he later regretted as 'she had exactly the right ethereal quality for the role.'[51] Eventually Zanuck's choice, untried Irish actress Constance Smith, was cast and after six weeks shooting she was replaced by Ann Blyth, who was on loan from Universal International. The studio issued a press release claiming that Smith was ill with pneumonia, but the real reason was her unsatisfactory performance. Re-shooting Smith's scenes with Blyth imposed a heavy cost on the production. Contemporary scenes in the film were shot in black and white and colour was used for the period sequences.

The film received only lukewarm notices from newspaper critics and was, Baker claimed, a 'modest hit but nothing special'.[52] It was released in 1951 as *I'll Never Forget You* in the United States and Australia and *The House on the Square* in Britain. Baker considered the film dated – like 'flogging a dead horse'.[53] On his return from London, Baker was introduced to Gary Merrill and his wife Bette Davis at the New York premiere of Twentieth Century Fox's biblical epic *David and Bathsheba*. Merrill was soon to star in one of Baker's Hollywood films, *Night Without Sleep* (1952), and Davis was to play a crucial role in 1967 when Baker replaced Alvin Rakoff on *The Anniversary* after shooting had commenced.

Baker's next film, *Don't Bother to Knock* (1952), was a difficult production and the director's skirmishes and problems with Constance Smith during *I'll Never Forget You* were only a minor prelude to working with Marilyn Monroe. Baker, who has been careful in interviews not to contribute to what he calls the 'Marilyn Monroe Industry',[54] that is, those people who continue to exploit her even after her death, admitted that he 'adored her':[55] 'I don't think she really liked me. Well, it was very unfortunate in a way. She could never trust anybody except the people who were going to do her harm. She was awfully good at that. She always picked the wrong ones.'[56] Although he felt she was not a great actress, and did not possess a great face or figure,[57] she had an 'animal magnetism' that provoked people to always want to touch her: 'I found myself doing it – putting my arm around her'.[58]

When the head of Twentieth Century-Fox, Joseph Schenk, decided that Marilyn Monroe should be cast as Nell, a mentally disturbed babysitter who threatens the life of a young girl, the film's executive producer Julian Blaustein and producer William Bloom opposed the decision.[59] Zanuck, however, endorsed Schenk's choice. Baker also opposed the decision and, although he knew far less about Monroe's background than the executives, his knowledge of her performances in *The Asphalt Jungle* and *All About Eve* made him consider this 'a grotesque piece of casting. But Zanuck had spoken'.[60] Baker was worried how the audience would accept Monroe as a seemingly plain, unstable woman although this was compensated, to some degree, by his awareness 'that Marilyn's own background had been similar to Nell's – if anything worse'.[61] However, he felt it was really a part for someone like

Jane Wyman, who won an Oscar for her part as a deaf-mute girl who is raped in *Johnny Belinda* (1948).

Zanuck had little time for Monroe and he considered *Don't Bother to Knock* of little importance.[62] Hence he wanted the film made as cheaply as possible and the film's budget was limited to $600,000.[63] The expert script by Daniel Taradash, who did not like the finished film,[64] the first-class cinematography by Lucien Ballard, and Richard Widmark's performance as the self-centred pilot Jed Towers, made it one of Baker's most memorable films. The casting of Marilyn Monroe in a dramatic role ensured that it would be one of his best-known films, matched only by the revival of interest in *A Night to Remember* following the release of James Cameron's blockbuster, *Titanic*, in 1997.[65]

Ballard, who at one time was married to Merle Oberon, was helpful to Baker in dealing with Monroe. The actress's poor punctuality, self-doubts and undue reliance on her personal drama coach Natasha Lytess created problems for Baker as her behaviour alienated not only the production team but also experienced cast members such as Elisha Cook Jr and Jim Backus. They watched as Monroe referred not to the director but to Lytess between scenes. Widmark expressed the frustration of the crew and cast between scenes at her behaviour ('Come on, will ya for Christ's sake!'[66]). Her inability to provide, and take, cues from the other actors meant that Baker had to dispense with master shots involving Monroe and the other actors. Instead he worked intensively with her in close-ups or medium close-up. This forced him to alter his usual approach:

> My method was, and still is, to present – with the actors – a complete mechanical layout of each scene as it came along, so as to enable the crew to get to work. Everyone then knows what the requirements are for the whole scene and what covering angles are going to be. Once the crew have finished their arrangements I take the actors through two or three rehearsals, during which the minor details are ironed out and the final polish is applied and the actors are led naturally into the first take.[67]

He had to modify this system and put the film together in a 'piecemeal' fashion where her performance was constructed from 'single lines and reactions from several takes'[68] Eventually, after Monroe delivered a line of dialogue with a German accent (Lytess was German), Baker barred the drama coach from the set. Monroe complained about this decision to Zanuck but he supported the director. Baker, however, was irritated by the whole episode: 'Oh, there was a terrible fuss. ... it was just an intolerable situation. It was just damned silly'.[69] Monroe finally accepted the decision.

Zanuck showed little interest in the final cut of the film except, as Baker points out, to devise 'its stupid title'.[70] The film surprised the studio head as it was a critical and commercial success, consolidated the career of Widmark, and provided a good introduction for Anne Bancroft, whom Twentieth Century-Fox then placed under long-term contract. It was also an important role for Monroe: she had been around various studios since her brief role in the 1947 film *Scudda Hoo! Scudda Hay!*, but after a long succession of dumb blondes and secondary romantic roles, *Don't Bother to Knock* offered her not only a lead role but also a dramatic part. Now, with the success of this film, even Zanuck had to take her seriously[71] and he soon cast her in one of her best roles, as the duplicitous wife in *Niagara* (1953).

Two weeks after completing *Don't Bother to Knock*, Baker was back at the studio filming *Night Without Sleep*, starring Gary Merrill, Linda Darnell and Hildegarde Kneff. This little-known film noir was co-scripted by Elick Moll and Frank Partos. This connection with Partos is particularly interesting as he also wrote (with an uncredited Nathanael West) one of the earliest Hollywood film noirs, *Stranger on the Third Floor* (1940), and there are similarities between both films. *Stranger on the Third Floor*, with its expressionistic dream sequence, dramatises a reporter's nightmare after his testimony incriminates an innocent man. *Night Without Sleep* also involves a nightmare, as a burnt-out composer wanders New York after emerging from an alcoholic stupor – not realising that he killed his wife the night before.

After viewing the rough cut of *Night Without Sleep* Julian Blaustein asked Baker to direct *White Witch Doctor*. He was sent to the Belgian Congo for four months to shoot background footage, after assurances from Blaustein that he would not be replaced as director when he returned from Africa. Having completed the arduous task of assembling the footage, he was replaced by veteran director Henry Hathaway owing, possibly, to the instructions of the film's female star, Susan Hayward. Baker was unconcerned about losing the film and, although he was fascinated by the location and had filmed a large amount of material, he was worried that the silly script would not do justice to its source material, an autobiographical novel by Louise A. Stinetorf. His fears that it would be just another Hollywood 'Jungle Jim' picture were confirmed.[72]

In Léopoldville he received the news from Hollywood that *Don't Bother to Knock* was a box-office hit with good reviews, and when he returned to the studio they took up the third option on his contract. *Inferno* (1953), Baker's final film for Twentieth Century-Fox, was one of his best, although it is rarely screened on television today. It was filmed in Apple

Valley on the edge of the Mojave Desert in the 3D process, also known as stereoscopy. This required two cameras three inches apart, which the production team bolted on to a large plate and then placed at right angles to each other on top of a dolly. Viewing the film required a pair of spectacles with polar lenses to match the projectors and this limited its release in 3D as many theatres did not have the appropriate equipment.

In the case of *Inferno*[73] this was a pity, as unlike most 3D films, it did not rely on the usual contrivances such as objects hurling towards the camera. Instead it contained one of the best performances in any of Baker's films, by Robert Ryan, plus a strong script by Frances Cockrell and luminous photography by Lucien Ballard, who photographed all of Baker's Hollywood films. The film with its desert setting was visually stunning. It also represented a formal and narrative challenge to the director to keep the audience interested in the musings and survival of a self-centred millionaire, with a broken leg, who has been abandoned in the desert by his wife and her lover, with little food and water, only six bullets in his revolver and no hope of help. *Inferno* gave Baker another opportunity to revisit, and rework, his most constant theme: the regeneration of a flawed, or emotionally vulnerable, protagonist.

Baker was excited by this challenge as it represented a return to 'pure film' with much of the story told through a combination of imagery and (Ryan's) voice-over – without great slabs of dialogue. This took him back to this first film for the AKS and the *Home Guard Town Fighting Series*, and *Inferno* offered a similar challenge: 'I had always had an ambition to make a picture in which the leading character spends long periods alone on the screen, where the interest would be in what he does, rather than what he says. A silent movie, a return to the most effective presentation that a film can offer.'[74]

Zanuck was impressed by a rough cut of the film although he ordered Baker to re-shoot the final act, insisting that the film's low-key ending be reworked. In the rough cut the lover (William Lundigan) abandons the wife (Rhonda Fleming) and heads off towards Mexico leaving the husband (Robert Ryan) to collect her by the side of the road and take her back to town (and a divorce). In the release version the husband, no longer interested in revenge, comes across the lover in a miner's shack and is forced to defend himself. In the ensuing fight the lover is killed when a lamp is knocked over, setting fire to the shack so that the roof falls on him. The husband picks up his wife the next morning and takes her back to town. The fight was included, at Zanuck's insistence, so as to exploit the 3D process. Baker kept such scenes in the rest of the film to a minimum.[75]

Inferno was only screened in 3D in New York, Los Angeles and

Chicago in the United States, and in London in Britain. Baker's tenure at Twentieth Century-Fox had come to an end, and although he had an offer from a minor studio to make a western[76] he was happy to return to Britain, where he wanted his son to be educated. Baker had some reservations about the studio system as it operated in the early 1950s, where control over the director was imposed by each department, but, overall, he was pleased with his three years with Twentieth Century-Fox, which he described as a 'wonderful experience'.[77] Hollywood was, he concluded, 'and probably still is, the best place on earth to make a film. Anything and anyone required can be supplied. It has the largest western audience. The outlook is international and not parochial'.[78]

The Rank years

The danger for Baker in returning to Britain after working at a major Hollywood studio was the 'always lingering question: "why did he come back?"'[79] Rank offered him a script by William Fairchild, based on Richard Armstrong's novel *Passage Home*, as they were keen to utilise the new process projection technique at Pinewood known as blue-backing or the travelling matte. This technique allowed the foreground to be separated from the background, thus providing a moving matte behind which the desired background could be inserted later.[80] This system was superior to the current method, back projection, and *Passage Home* (1954), with most of its scenes on a (studio) cattle boat, was an ideal film for this new process.

Although he was disappointed in the eventual result *Passage Home* was the quintessential 1940s and 1950s Baker film – classical in style and melodramatic/generic in its dramatic structure. It is not as epic as *A Night to Remember*, not as visually impressive as *The October Man*, and not as stoic as *Morning Departure*, but it conveys a quiet, pervasive sense of despair in its storyline, involving melancholy and sexual repression. The film's basic plot of a martinet captain (Peter Finch) with a troublesome crew and a beautiful young woman (Diane Cilento) on a cargo ship carrying, appropriately, dangerous bulls, from South America to Britain in the 1930s, is the stuff of simple melodrama.[81] Yet, like so many of Baker's film, it is much more than this.

Baker was less impressed by his next film, *Jacqueline* (1956), based on Catherine Cookson's novel *A Grand Man*: 'It was a monstrous farrago, and I played the innocent all the way through. I really didn't catch up with what was going on until the whole picture was all over and done with ... I sort of inherited the film in a way.'[82]

The film, according to Baker, was going to be directed by Brian Desmond Hurst who, he felt, would have been 'much better because he was Irish, for one thing and I'm not! And what we had, in the end, was what was meant to be a kind of Protestant story, a story about Protestant people; but, of course, it was entirely played by Catholics! And there is a difference, you know!'[83]

One of the major problems was obtaining a decent performance from Jacqueline Ryan as the young girl, who 'seemed frightened to death, not only of being in front of the camera, but terrified of everything and everybody around her'.[84] The critics, on the other hand, applauded Ryan's performance. The headline in the *Daily Mirror*'s review (8 June 1956), for example, said: 'It's Jackie's Film!' and followed by claiming that Jacqueline Ryan 'gives the performance of the week'. This was echoed by the *Evening Standard* (7 June 1956), whose reviewer claimed that the best reason for seeing this film was Jacqueline Ryan: 'A 12 year old moppet with the sad, sweet face of a newborn lamb, she can pluck the heart strings like a veteran harpist. And the whole film has been contrived with almost Dickensian thoroughness to keep us all soaked throughout in a warm shower of sentimental tears.'

Similarly, *The Times* (11 June 1956), argues that Ryan gives to her character 'a streak of honest vulgarity', while Dilys Powell, in the *Sunday Times* (10 June 1956), praised Ryan for an 'engaging performance'. This was also the view of the *News of the World* (10 June 1956) and Frank Jackson in *Reynolds News* (10 June 1956), who led his review with 'Jackie's The Cutest Kind of Colleen'. There were, however, a few dissenting voices, such as C.A. Lejeune in the *Observer* (10 June 1956): 'With reluctance, for I am sure that this is a kind film, I must say it fills me with distaste. I found the child's manner pert and uningratiating ... I was embarrassed by the sentiment and impatient with the comedy ... "Jacqueline", to my mind, is a nice, dull film.' Isabel Quigley in the *Spectator* (15 June 1956) also found the film 'mildly embarrassing, chiefly on account of a grossly miscast little girl', and only Cyril Cusack dancing a jig whilst snubbing his wife on Coronation night, as he turns from brow-beaten husband into a free spirit, 'redeems *Jacqueline* from the lower depths of banality'. Despite a strong promotional campaign and widespread press coverage the film never came into profit, and Baker, who was entitled to small share of the takings, did not receive any money.[85]

Tiger in the Smoke (1956) brought Baker together with producer Leslie Parkyn, Lewis's co-producer on *Morning Departure*, and he was delighted to direct a film that was based on a novel by one of his favourite writers, Margery Allingham. Without a screen credit or additional money, he was forced to complete the script when Anthony Pelissier left the production to direct a television spectacular with Eartha Kitt.

Baker, to create a constant sense of unease, shot the whole film with the camera on a baby crane so that it would be constantly moving. While he was successful in generating a pervasive sense of evil in the first half, it dissipates after the appearance of Jack Havoc in the cellar. Baker blames this on the casting of Tony Wright as the psychotic villain. Wright, who was imposed on the film by John Davis, weakened the film's polarised dramatic structure. As *Tiger in the Smoke* was an elemental melodrama based on the confrontation between pure and polar concepts of darkness and light, salvation and damnation, Havoc had to be the 'personification of evil'.[86] Wright, with his blonde hair and youthful appearance, lacked the requisite aura of menace and dominance that Jack Hawkins or Stanley Baker would have brought to the role.[87]

Baker's next film, *The One That Got Away* (1957), caused a mild controversy in Britain as it was based on the escape attempts of German pilot Oberleutnant Franz Von Werra, captured by the British when he crash-lands in an English field in September 1940. Considering that the Second World War was little more than a decade before this was a courageous film as it refused to caricature the German as evil. His daring is even more attractive due to the charismatic Hardy Krüger as Von Werra. Initially John Davis wanted Dirk Bogarde for the role and Baker resisted it as he thought the German should be presented as tough, cunning and arrogant, 'not a bit like our own dear Dirk',[88] he sarcastically notes. He was aware that Bogarde was planning to leave Rank as soon as he could and, anyway, he was too smart to accept a part for which he was so unsuited.[89] Veteran German actor O.W. Fischer, who was filming at Pinewood at that time, was also suggested but Baker thought he was too old. Baker was keen to cast an unknown and in Hamburg he found Hardy Krüger. After tests were shot in London John Davis agreed and the film made Krüger an international star.[90]

Much of *The One That Got Away* was filmed on location including an actual setting, Grizedale Hall in the Lake District, that had been used as a POW camp for German officers during the Second World War.[91] The Canadian scenes, including Von Werra's crossing of the St Lawrence River into the United States, were filmed in Sweden due to a prohibition from the Bank of England on using American dollars. When the filming fell behind schedule Baker was summoned to Earl St John's house near Pinewood, where he was told that there was concern that the film was presenting Von Werra as a hero. St John also complained about a lack of action. Although Baker reassured the executive that these rumours were not true, he later learned that the unit expected that he would be replaced as director.⁹² This did not happen and the film was both a commercial and critical success. He did receive a share of the profits from this film.

The second half of the 1950s was a great period for Baker as he followed this with his most prestigious film, *A Night to Remember* (1958). While Baker was considering a film adaptation of Walter Lord's book, after purchasing a copy from his favourite bookshop, the Piccadilly Bookshop,⁹³ William MacQuitty's wife was recommending it to her husband. MacQuitty arranged a meeting with Lord and they became life-long friends.

MacQuitty, who was born in Belfast in 1905, was present when the *Titanic* was launched on 30 May 1911 and it had made a deep impression on him:

> The spectacle of her huge hull rising above the slipway at the Harland & Wolff shipyard as the work of the shipbuilders progressed had provided my childhood with one of the most vividly remembered sights. The *Titanic* was, as all Belfast and the rest of the world knew, going to be the largest, best-designed and most beautiful ship ever to sail the high seas.⁹⁴

Yet, the 'news of her tragic fate twelve days later shocked the world. The inheritance of Victorian certainty was shattered and something had changed forever'.⁹⁵

MacQuitty had just completed *The Black Tent* for Rank, which he described as a 'Western desert romance',⁹⁶ which was filmed in colour and Vista-Vision on location in Libya. When he took his idea for another version of the *Titanic* story, to be filmed in black and white with double the budget of *The Black Tent*, to John Davis he received a hostile reaction from the managing director: '"It's just another shipwreck", he insisted, "on which you want to spend half a million"'. MacQuitty replied that it was far more than 'another shipwreck. It's the end of an era'.⁹⁷ Davis, keen to produce large-scale films suitable for an international market, relented and when he asked MacQuitty whom he wanted as director, the producer suggested Roy Baker:

> DAVIS: But he's eight weeks overdue on *The One That Got Away*.
> MACQUITTY: He'll be on time with this one, provided no one interferes.⁹⁸

MacQuitty explained later that he wanted Baker because 'he was a brilliant artist with a great sense of period'.⁹⁹ Both men agreed that the film would start with the formal launch of the ship, even though they had to fabricate this sequence as the *Titanic* was launched without ceremony and there was no footage of the ship sliding down the slipway. It was also decided that there would be no reference to White Star Chairman J. Bruce Ismay, who is only referred to in the film as the

'Chairman'. Nevertheless, sensitivity from the Ismay family still disrupted the production.

Filming extended from 15 October 1957 to 4 March 1958 and, as the Rank studio tank was not large enough to allow long shots of the lifeboats and the passengers in the water, location filming took place at Ruislip Lido, a reservoir near Pinewood Studios, from 15 to 23 October. The major shipping companies refused to cooperate, as MacQuitty discovered after planning the first shots showing the lifeboats filled with passengers being lowered down the side of the *Titanic* into the sea. As these shots needed to be filmed at night from a ship with the same colours as the *Titanic*, MacQuitty sought permission from the Shaw Savill Company because its davits were the same as the *Titanic*:

> We were promised the use of one of their ships during a weekend when it was in the Port of London at Royal Dock between voyages to South Africa. Meanwhile I bought lifeboats identical to those of the *Titanic* from the *Franconia*, which was being broken up. These were on their way from Scotland by road and shooting was due to begin on a Friday. On Thursday a very embarrassed Shaw Savill port captain telephoned me to say that the line's chairman had decided against the film. Permission to use one of the ships had therefore been withdrawn. Later I heard that the chairman was a friend of the Ismay family. This sensitivity could be accounted for by the fact that the Ismays were closely linked to the *Titanic* story through their interests in the White Star Line. The ship itself had been the fulfilment of the vision of J. Bruce Ismay as managing director of White Star. Subsequently, having survived the disaster, he came in for public criticism for what was seen as his erratic behaviour during the emergency of the sinking.[100]

The other major shipping companies also refused to cooperate and so the desperate producer contacted Thomas Ward, the Clyde shipbreakers. He then flew to Helensburgh where they were breaking up an old steamship, the *RMS Asturias*. MacQuitty found that the port side had already been demolished but the starboard side was intact, so by fixing a mirror on the camera, and ensuring that all lettering was written backwards, filming took place after Glasgow art students painted the white ship black.[101] Stunt men were then paid a pound a foot for the eighty-foot drop into the icy waters of the Clyde. However, when MacQuitty discovered that the property department had supplied the stunt men with heavy cork lifejackets he quickly substituted kapok, as the jackets would have otherwise broken the men's necks as they hit the water.[102]

Both Baker and MacQuitty agreed that the film should be told chronologically and its budget was set at just under half a million pounds.[103]

Baker suggested that Eric Ambler should write the script and MacQuitty, aware of his reputation as a novelist and the fact that Ambler also wrote the script for *The Cruel Sea*, readily agreed. Both men also felt that the film did not need stars as, in effect, the ship was the star. What they wanted was 'actors who could represent real people'[104] – with the exception of Kenneth More, whom they wanted for the crucial role of Second Officer Charles Herbert Lightoller. More, after *Genevieve* (1954), *Doctor in the House* (1954) and *Reach for the Sky* (1956), was now a star in Britain and both men believed he would not accept the part as Lightoller is only on screen for a relatively short period of time – MacQuitty estimated 20 minutes. Nevertheless, Baker was dispatched to Bermuda, where More was filming *The Admirable Crichton*, and he accepted the role.[105]

Prior to its general release, the film was screened for the Rank executives at their viewing theatre in Wardour Street. When the lights came on everybody waited for John Davis's reaction and he declared that *A Night to Remember* was the 'best film we have ever made'.[106] The film's premiere at the Odeon, Leicester Square, was equally successful and the British press was almost unanimous in its praise. Baker and MacQuitty believed, at this time, that the world was their oyster: 'We were still glowing with the tributes when Roy Baker said to me, "The door is wide open. We don't even have to push".'[107]

MacQuitty also received a letter from John Davis praising the 'untiring effort which you have put into this gigantic production and the great organizing work you put into helping the director with his work'. Two days later he was informed that Davis had decided not to renew his contract.[108]

Baker was to make two more films for Rank but *A Night to Remember* was, in the context of his standing in the British film industry, the high point in his career. He still had, however, one more film on his Rank contract and to maximise his chances of acquiring a good story he accepted Rank's offer to become a producer/director for three films over the next three years. Although Baker did not want to actually produce his films – Jack Hanbury basically performed this task on his next two films[109] – he did want control over the content. Earl St John offered him *The Singer Not the Song*. The company thought that this emotionally excessive melodrama, involving an Irish priest, a young girl and a Mexican bandit, would appeal to him – with Dirk Bogarde, whom Rank was desperate to keep at the studio, as the bandit.

Baker was not interested: 'There was not one single element in this story which appealed to me' and after discussing it with St John, Rank agreed to put this project aside. Baker even contemplated leaving film directing at this stage: 'what I really wanted was to take over the studio'[110] and replace Earl St John as head of production at Pinewood. With his status, seemingly, high at Rank, Baker invited John Davis to dinner at his house at Aston Clinton in Buckinghamshire. During the meal, which had to be shifted to a local restaurant, Davis made some vague references in this regard:

> Suddenly I knew I was not well enough prepared. I hadn't worked out a plan of action to put forward. The moment passed and we ordered our food. Typically John had caught me on the hop before we had time to settle into a conversation. I shall never know whether I missed a great opportunity or a disastrous failure. I am sure of one thing: if my next picture had been another smash hit, this 'ambition' would have come up again.[111]

To come up with a 'smash hit', and avoid *The Singer Not the Song*, he spent the next fifteen months preparing projects that never eventuated.[112] If they had, his career in the 1960s and 1970s might have been different. His plans included two plays and a book that were made into films – but not by him. *The Grass is Greener*, a play written by Margaret and Hugh Williams, was filmed in London by Stanley Donen with Cary Grant, Deborah Kerr, Robert Mitchum and Jean Simmons. *The Long and the Short and the Tall*, which Earl St John asked Baker to see at the Royal Court Theatre, was rejected by the studio and Leslie Norman directed the 1961 film, which starred Laurence Harvey, Richard Harris and Richard Todd.

The third project, a film version of Alan Sillitoe's *Saturday Night and Sunday Morning*, excited Baker. At this time, 1958, 'change was in the air', a situation that Baker had been aware of since the completion of *Passage Home* and *Jacqueline* in the middle of the 1950s:

> Both of these films were generally satisfactory by the standards of the time but the truth was, they could have been made before the war ... By now, in the middle of 1956, change was in the air. I wasn't fully conscious of it at the time, but I could feel that there were fresh breezes blowing. People speak of the Swinging Sixties, but it was all beginning to happen as early as 1954, when Kingsley Amis published *Lucky Jim*.[113]

After inviting Sillitoe to his house to discuss the possibility of a film, Baker saw the opportunity as an 'absolute winner'.[114] Samuel Goldwyn Jr, a long-time friend, recalled the importance of this meeting, not only for Baker's career but also for Rank and the British film industry:

> I can remember a meeting with Roy and Alan Sillitoe, even before his novel *Saturday Night and Sunday Morning* was published. Roy had read the galleys and desperately wanted to make it. He saw that British audiences were hungering for a new kind of picture and this could be it.

Roy was disappointed not only about this lost opportunity for himself, but that the times were changing and the so-called structure of the industry would not keep up with them. Rank failed to create an industry.[115]

Baker recommended the project to St John, and the Rank Organisation bought the rights. However, when J. Arthur Rank read the novel he asked that the rights be returned to the author without Sillitoe having to return the money. Rank decreed that the book was unsuitable for his company, which 'made films for the family audience'.[116] Baker, unaware that J. Arthur Rank personally objected to the novel,[117] prepared proposals for all three projects. On 2 December 1958, all three projects were rejected by the Rank production committee: *The Grass is Greener* was deemed immoral, *The Long and the Short and the Tall* had 'so many swear words', and *Saturday Night and Sunday Morning* was considered 'sordid and "common"'.[118]

When Baker had nothing to show for the past fifteen months, and no immediate prospects, John Davis resurrected *The Singer Not the Song* (1960). Davis, at a lunch to discuss the film with Baker, stressed the importance of obtaining Bogarde as he only had one film left on his contract with Rank. Baker was sent to Hollywood, where Bogarde was filming *Song Without End*, to persuade him to accept the role as the bandit and, after listening to Baker's pitch, Bogarde asked the question that was to plague the whole production: who would play the priest? At this stage the director did not know but was keen to cast Richard Burton. Burton, however, wanted the part of the bandit, not the priest. Paul Newman, Harry Belafonte, Anthony Perkins and John Cassavetes were also mentioned, but Earl St John decided on John Mills, a choice Bogarde vehemently opposed. He told Baker that: 'I promise you, if Johnny plays the priest I will make life unbearable for everyone concerned'.[119]

Unfortunately Bogarde lived up to his word and *The Singer Not the Song* was an unhappy production. Baker, still upset by his behaviour years later, said that as 'far as I am concerned he [Bogarde] was not a nice man' and the actor behaved outrageously, upsetting everybody working on the film.[120] Baker never knew what upset the actor so much and why he bitterly opposed the casting of John Mills. However, Bogarde, in 1990, provided a clue when he reflected on the film:

> It is about a young Mexican bandit who, with his gang, holds a small Mexican town to ransom. Then a young Canadian priest on his first mission comes in to try and disarm the situation; the bandit falls in love with him and that was basically the story. It was such a terrible script and they put John Mills in as the priest when it should have been someone like Paul Newman, as he was in those days. I should have been in blue jeans and a beat-up old jacket, driving an old Chevy, and there I was in

black leather and riding a white horse – I did the whole thing for camp and nobody had any idea what was happening! Mylène Demongeot played the girl who fell in love with the priest and who then kind of fell for me – you know, a beserk three-hander.[121]

This interpretation of the story is not entirely correct as the girl did not fall in love with the bandit. Nevertheless it shows that Bogarde, at least, interpreted the film as a gay love story. It should be noted that Baker did not offer this interpretation, preferring instead to focus on the infatuation of the girl for the priest.[122] He responded by saying that 'It wasn't a good book, it was the old phoney story of a little girl falling in love with a priest and it's been done so many times ... as far as I am concerned it just gives me the horrors'.[123] One of Baker's casting suggestions for the priest, Paul Schofield, suggests that his conception of the film was different from Bogarde's fantasy of two physically attractive male actors, Bogarde (in 'blue jeans and a beat-up old jacket, driving an old Chevy') and Paul Newman, involved in a 'beserk three-hander' with Mylene Demongeot.

Baker believed that *The Singer Not the Song* wrecked a promising career: 'My self-confidence was severely dented and it took me four years to get myself back on an even keel. I have never to this day fully regained the professional status I had at that time'.[124] The film was more popular in Europe, especially in France and Germany, than it was in Britain, and after 23 years it finally came into profit. When it was shown at a Baker retrospective at Dinard in 1993 he refused to introduce the film ('I loathe it and couldn't bear to see it again'), although the audience enjoyed it.[125]

Baker was more comfortable with *Flame in the Streets* (1961), based on Ted Willis's play *Hot Summer Night*. Although the film was superficially different from his earlier films, with its plot seemingly concerned with an inter-racial romance, it was another melodrama. However, it was a domestic, or family, melodrama that contained a substantial amount of emotional excess, especially from Brenda de Banzie as the mother of a young woman involved with a West Indian teacher. Her reaction to this relationship invests the film with an almost Gothic repulsion against sexual cohabitation between black and white. As the film progresses, however, the social problem aspects are assimilated into a more profound examination of the deep-seated problems within her own marriage.

Independent production and television

Unfortunately *Flame in the Streets* was not a commercial success, and when Rank withdrew from film production in February 1961 Baker's career as a feature film director was in jeopardy. This was compounded by the commercial failure of his next two films. This was the first time, with the exception of *Paper Orchid*, that Baker did not have the institutional support of a film studio. The first of these films, *The Valiant* (1962), an Anglo-Italian production shot in Italy, was a melodrama set in the Second World War concerning the desperate attempt by the commander of a British battleship (John Mills) stationed in Alexandria Harbour to ascertain whether two captured Italian frogmen have attached time-bombs to the hull of his ship.

It was poorly received in Britain and newspaper sub-editors tried to outdo each other with their headlines: 'That Sinking Feeling' in the *Sunday Telegraph* (7 January 1962), 'Ice Cold (on the Bridge) in Alex' in the *Evening News* (4 January 1962), 'Doubts Under the Surface' in the *Daily Telegraph* (6 January 1962) and 'CAPTAIN JOHN MILLS, R.N., MADE ME WANT TO ABANDON SHIP' in the *Sunday Express* (7 January 1962). While Leonard Mosley in the *Daily Express* (6 January 1972) was annoyed that the film did not stick to the facts, others, such as Margaret Hinxman in the *Daily Herald* (6 January 1962) and Penelope Gilliatt in the *Observer* (7 January 1962) considered the film old-fashioned, with Gilliatt ridiculing the film's 'stiff-upper lip': 'the captain played by John Mills goes far beyond any revue parody of the British war picture'.

Baker's next film, *Two Left Feet* (1962), a comedy based on the novel *In My Solitude* by David Stuart Leslie, was produced by Leslie Gilliatt and co-scripted by John Hopkins and Baker. The film tried to attract a young audience and Baker, when casting the film, issued a directive that everybody should be under 21 years of age.[126] With one exception, the cast was under 21 and it included Michael Crawford, Nyree Dawn Porter, Julia Foster and David Hemmings. After a positive sneak preview Baker's hopes that the film would be a success were high. These expectations were dashed because of difficulties in obtaining a release: the circuit bookers were reluctant to exhibit the film as it had no stars. This was compounded by the fact that the film attracted an X certificate and there was a policy of not releasing X certificate films during school holidays. This delayed its release until it was virtually abandoned on a poorly promoted double bill.[127]

Many reviews of the film noted that it had been left on the shelf for two years. Cecil Wilson in the *Daily Mail* (11 May 1965) was concerned that this would adversely affect the film's commercial potential:

Pity the poor producer of a trend-setting film which is held up so long that it eventually reaches the screen in a semblance of a trend follower.

This one, for example, blazed the trail of the artisan-adolescent Lucky Jim, the light-hearted, anti-hero blundering through a back-street jungle of steamy caffs, brassy dance halls and muddled moral values.

Yet after two years on the stocks it finds itself trailing behind a row of later, and mostly inferior, films which have over-taken it in the same cinema queue.

While others were less sympathetic, most conceded that the delay hurt the film at the box-office. John Coleman in the *New Statesmen* (5 May 1965) did not think that the film was 'all that good' but that the delay was a 'pity'. Nina Hibbin in the *Daily Worker* (15 May 1965) also noted the delay, and that whilst the film 'seems very trivial [there are] some attractive things in it and it has a general air of sympathetic interest in youth'. David Robinson in the *Financial Times* (14 May 1965) also had mixed feelings, and Leonard Mosley (13 May 1965) reiterated Baker's view that it would have been 'hailed as an example of the British "new wave" if it had been seen then [1963]. But something happened to it on the way to the cinema and others got in first'.

With the decline of the medium-budget genre film in the late 1950s and early 1960s, and Rank's demise as a prolific film company, Baker's prospects were not good. In 'the face of the social realism of the British New Wave and the low budget exploitation fare provided by, among others, Hammer horror and the *Carry On* series in the late 1950s and early 1960s', Peter Hutchings argues, the '"well-made" films of Baker and others begin to look rather old-fashioned.'[128] While other British directors closely associated with this type of film, such as John Guillermin and J. Lee Thompson, left Britain and established new careers in Hollywood, Baker went into British television, where he worked on a full-time basis from 1963 to 1967. He began dabbling in this medium in 1961 when he directed two episodes in the *Zero One* series, starring Nigel Patrick. Producers Robert S. Baker and Monty Berman offered him *The Saint* and he directed four episodes in 1963, three in 1964, nine in 1966, and two in 1968. During this period he also directed episodes of *The Human Jungle*, *Gideon's Way*, *The Avengers* and *The Baron*. In this five-year period Baker estimated that he directed 41 one-hour episodes in seven different series.[129]

Hammer – the pre-horror films

1967 was another turning point in Baker's career. An offer from Anthony Nelson Pitt at Hammer to direct the third Quatermass film,

Quatermass and the Pit (1967), brought him back to feature film production. Baker continued to direct episodes of *The Champions, Randall and Hopkirk (Deceased), Department S, Journey to the Unknown, The Persuaders, Jason King* and *The Protectors* while making feature films in the period from 1968 to 1972. He also decided to change his professional name to Roy Ward Baker, a decision he later regretted. It was motivated by the fact that there was a Roy Baker working as a sound editor at Hammer. Worried about the confusion with regard to the distribution of mail and telephone messages, a problem that he had experienced while working on *The Saint*, he suggested that the sound editor add an initial to his name. He refused. This confusion was compounded when the sound man moved into the same tax district and Inland Revenue accused Baker of concealing a second income.[130] Baker decided to add his mother's maiden name. This created a new problem with some believing that Roy Ward Baker was a new director: 'Thirty years later', Baker laments, 'I still find critics who know me well as a Hammer director and are unaware of all the films I made prior to 1962'.[131]

Quatermass and the Pit was screened on BBC television as a six-part serial in the period from December 1958 and January 1959 with André Morell as Professor Quatermass. Hammer bought the film rights from author Nigel Kneale in April 1961 but the project was shelved after Columbia Studio, Hammer's American partner at that time, expressed no interest. In 1964 Hammer invited Nigel Kneale to develop a new script but relations between Hammer and Columbia deteriorated and the project was put on hold until July 1966, when *Quatermass and the Pit* was included in a roster of films to be co-produced by Hammer and Seven Arts, with distribution in the United States by Twentieth Century-Fox.[132]

Val Guest directed the first two Quatermass films, *The Quatermass Experiment* (1955) and *Quatermass 11* (1957), but when he was not available for *Quatermass and the Pit* Anthony Nelson Keys offered it to Baker. He was delighted when the production was shifted from ABPC's Elstree Studios to the more spacious MGM Borehamwood Studios, as its back lot was ideal for the street sequences. The budget was set at £275,000, which was reasonably lavish by Hammer's standards, and filming began on 27 February 1967.

Nigel Kneale was happy with Baker's film and he especially liked the casting of Andrew Keir as Quatermass. Kneale disliked the earlier films, particularly *The Quatermass Experiment*:

[P]artly because I didn't like Brian Donlevy ... I met him and he seemed a very stupid man ... he was pretty ineffective ... The Quatermass I had was a rather worried and bothered man who'd brought something into the world without intending to. Donlevy didn't think about what he was doing. He did his usual thing – he was strong in authority, he knew how to do that, he knew how to shout at people. But it ended there.[133]

His only reservations concerning Baker's film were the quality of the special effects, and that the 'screaming girl' (Christine Finn) in the BBC teleplay 'was better than Hammer's screaming girl' (Barbara Shelley) in the 1967 film.[134]

The only sour note, which came years after the film's release, was Andrew Keir's criticism of the director at the Fourth Festival of Fantastic Films in Manchester in September 1993: 'The director – Roy Ward Baker – didn't want me for the role. He wanted Kenneth More ... and it was a very unhappy shoot, I have to tell you that. I'm putting it on record. Normally, I enjoy going to work every day. But for seven and a half weeks, it was sheer hell.' Keir also felt that

> some of the scenes were uneven, that's down to Roy Ward Baker. Because when you're directing you have to carry all of the actors' emotions in your head. You have to have your actors lean on you. By that I mean – you help them. I think there's one performance that didn't match what was happening on screen ... Barbara Shelley. That's because she wasn't helped. The director should have taken her through that, talked her through it.[135]

Keir's views were a surprise to Barbara Shelley as she claimed that *Quatermass and the Pit* 'was a film I enjoyed very much, directed by Roy Ward Baker, one of my favourite directors'.[136] Earlier, in a 1974 interview in *Bizarre Magazine*, Baker claimed that he was mad about Barbara Shelley – 'mad in the sense of love. We used to waltz about the set together, a great love affair. It puzzles me about her. She should be much bigger than she is, but I don't think she really cares whether she is a star or not. She can act, God, she can act!'[137]

Quatermass and the Pit was released on 19 November 1967, with another Hammer production, *Circus of Fear*, as the support feature. Twentieth Century-Fox re-edited Hammer's trailer, changed the film's name to *Five Million Miles to Earth*, and released it in the United States in March 1968. It was a commercial success and Baker followed it with two more films for Hammer: *The Anniversary* (1967) and *Moon Zero Two* (1969).

In 1965 *The Nanny* – starring Bette Davis, directed by Seth Holt and produced by Jimmy Sangster for Hammer – was a substantial hit on both sides of the Atlantic. It made *Kinematograph Weekly*'s list of top money-makers for 1965.[138] The production of the film was not, for

Sangster, a happy period due to the behaviour of Bette Davis. When it was completed, and Davis left London for the United States, Sangster's wife Monica vowed that if her husband ever made another movie with the American actress she would leave the country. By early 1966 Twentieth Century-Fox, who distributed Hammer's films in the United States at that time, had received $2,250,000 from *The Nanny* and were keen for another film starring Davis. Thus Hammer executive Anthony Hinds asked Sangster to see a play called *The Anniversary* written by Bill McIlwraith. Sangster subsequently wrote a script and Davis was cast in the lead role, played by Mona Washbourne on stage, as the bitter matriarch of the Taggart family. On the day Davis landed in London, Monica Sangster packed her bags and went to live in their house in the South of France until the film was completed.[139]

As Seth Holt was unavailable, Daniel Petrie was contacted but Sangster was unable to meet all of Petrie's demands. Television director Alvin Rakoff was approached but, as Davis had contractual right to veto the director, she had to be persuaded to accept Rakoff. She reluctantly agreed after Sangster told her that another director would be found if she changed her mind. Filming commenced on 3 May 1967 at ABPC studios and there was friction from the start. Sheila Hancock, who played Karen Taggart, was angry after Davis announced that she would have preferred Jill Bennett in the part (Bennett had appeared in *The Nanny* with Davis). Hancock, together with other cast members who had appeared in the play, such as Jack Hedley and James Cossin, resented the adulation expected, and received, by Davis.[140] By the end of the first week, Sangster later recalled, 'we were three days behind and all was doom and gloom. Bette hated everyone and everyone hated her. Most of all she hated Alvin'.[141]

Davis summoned Sangster to her dressing room after filming finished on 8 May and he knew what her opening line would be: 'I've starred in sixty-three movies ...' She told him that she objected to the 'television techniques' used by Rakoff, who blocked and marked his actor's moves in advance, and, she argued, if he continued working on the film her nerves would not stand it and she would be a 'basket case within a week'.[142] Davis refused to appear the following day and Rakoff filmed around her. On 10 May Davis still refused to appear and production stopped. Hammer's co-production partner Seven Arts paid Rakoff in full and hired Baker, who had known Davis since his period in Hollywood in the early 1950s. But, as Sangster points out,

> Roy's nobody's fool. He knew we'd already shot a week and he didn't want any of Alvin's material going into the final cut. Who knows, there could have been a credit dispute. So he told us he didn't like the way the

staircase came down into the centre of the main room, he'd prefer it come down at an angle. Result, we had to rebuild the set and everything shot to date had to be thrown out.[143]

Production of *The Anniversary* resumed on 15 May although it was still a troubled production as other cast members, who were fond of Rakoff, 'took his leaving badly. They were all professional enough not to let it show in their performance, but the atmosphere on the set was wicked'.[144] While the camera operator nearly quit when he heard that Roy was taking over, the focus puller left after claiming that Baker was rude to him. Baker did his best in difficult circumstances although, Sangster wrote, he 'managed to get up everybody's nose in the process'.[145] Sangster concluded that the film 'wasn't nearly as good as it could have been. We really needed Seth Holt on that movie. As Bette Davis had said, he [Holt] was a "mountain of evil" and would have made a great job of bringing Mrs. Taggart to life'.[146]

Filming of *The Anniversary* concluded on 12 July and it began its commercially successful circuit release on 18 February 1968, supported by the low-budget science fiction thriller *The Night Caller*. When the film was released in the United States on 7 February to mixed reviews, Alvin Rakoff described it as a 'mess of a film built around Davis' foolish, overbaked posturing and camera-hoggings'.[147]

Davis received nearly £72,000 for her role as the vicious matriarch who gathers her family each year to celebrate the anniversary of her marriage to her late husband. Taggart uses the opportunity to humiliate and control her hapless sons. While Henry (James Cossin) has a penchant for stealing, and wearing, women's underwear, Terry (Jack Hedley) and Karen (Sheila Hancock) plan to leave the family business and emigrate to Canada. Taggart's youngest son Tom (Christian Roberts) makes the mistake of bringing his pregnant fiancée, Shirley (Elaine Taylor) to the 'party'. After Henry is surprised stealing women's clothing, he dumps them in Terry's car, providing Mrs Taggart with an opportunity to blackmail Terry and force him to abandon his plan to leave Britain. Karen, however, has other ideas and nearly succeeds in wresting control away from her mother-in-law. She fails and the film ends on a bleak note with Mrs Taggart telling the portrait of her dead husband: 'It's been a lovely day Dad. Till next year'.

The critics were less concerned with the film and more with Bette Davis. Ernest Betts set the tone with the heading 'Bitch of the Year' in *The People* (14 January 1968) and despite the fact that 'Bette Davis carries it all off in the grand manner', he was not impressed with the film: 'if this is a specimen of black comedy, give me one that's whiter than white'. Ann Pacey's review in the *Sun* (1 January 1968), 'Enter

Bette Davis as a one-eyed monster', criticised 'Roy Baker's direction [as it] never really allows you to believe that you are watching anything other than a photographed play'. The *Daily Telegraph* (12 January 1968) review also emphasised the theatricality of the film and that 'it may in fact have been a fundamental error to cast Miss Davis at all. The character herself is enough of an oddity without any additional Davis flourishes. Mona Washbourne played it "straight" on the London stage and thus achieved a degree of casual menace which grew into something monstrous. Miss Davis is monstrous to begin with: and the result is fewer surprises'. Felix Barker in the *Evening News* (11 January 1968), 'BETTE, the one-eyed monster', was not impressed and found the film 'unpleasant'; Margaret Hinxman in the *Sunday Telegraph* (14 January 1968) maintained that, for 'all the good, considerate work put in by director Roy Baker, the film, as a sensible entity, is ruined simply by having her as its pivotal personality' and that the rest of the cast 'appears to be acting in a different, more sober film'.

David Robinson, in the *Financial Times* (12 January 1968), concluded that the film 'remains a rather solid mass of stage talk and stage business' and with the casting of Bette Davis, 'instead of Mona Washbourne, you are likely to find yourself with something different. Hammer's film version predictably turns McIlwraith's matriarchal farce into a much more extravagant horror comic'. On the other hand, Penelope Mortimer, under the heading 'Triumphant Gorgonism' in the *Observer* (14 January 1968) liked the film ('this is triumphantly a Bette Davis picture, and as such takes its modest place in history'), as did Nina Hibbin in the *Morning Star* (13 January 1968), 'What a wicked old Mum', and she argues that the film 'succeeds in being both insanely funny and very sad', a view shared by Clive Hirschhorn in the *Sunday Express* (14 January 1968).

'The most topical and up-to the-minute film ever made' was how producer Michael Carreras described *Moon Zero Two*, Baker's next film. The promotional material from Warner-Pathé described it as an 'exciting adventure in space' and claimed that it 'parallels the Western in some ways, replete with gun fights, miners prospecting for valuable ores and a barroom brawl'. By assimilating some of the conventions from two popular 1950s genres, the western and science-fiction, and adding a layer of topicality with the upcoming moon landing, Hammer hoped to cover all bases. They failed badly. The most successful British science-fiction films during the 1950s and 1960s were the three Quatermass films, plus *X the Unknown* (1956) and Joseph Losey's *The Damned* (1961). Most were comparable to their American counterpart by combining elements of horror with a paranoid invasion narrative.[148]

Moon Zero Two lacked the cultural subtext of these films. It began as a story outline prepared by Gavin Lyall, Frank Hardman and Martin Davison in the early months of 1967 and Hammer, keen to capitalise on NASA's imminent moon landing by the Apollo mission, budgeted the film at £500,000. They took the idea to Twentieth Century-Fox, who rejected the project,[149] but then Warner Bros/Seven Arts agreed to supply the finance.

Principal photography took place between 31 March and 10 June 1969 based on Michael Carreras' script.[150] Carreras had great plans for *Moon Zero Two* and, anticipating its success, started to prepare a sequel and a television series. Unfortunately the film was a commercial and critical failure. Right from the start there were problems in showing people moving about on the moon in a realistic fashion and Baker even visited Stanley Kubrick, who was completing *2001: A Space Odyssey* (1968) at the MGM British studio, for advice. While Kubrick spent three years making his film, Baker had less than three months and a much smaller budget. And it showed. The film's main weakness, however, was the script and, as Baker complained, 'so much time was spent on solving the production problems that not enough attention was paid to the characters or the story'.[151]

The film's plot follows the conventions of the B-Western closely. The Moon of 2021 is a mining colony that closely resembles a Western frontier town where American Bill Kemp (James Olson) operates a battered ferry ship (similar to a stagecoach) with his Russian partner Karminski (Ori Levy). Their basic business is salvaging damaged satellites. Clementine Taplin[152] (Catherina Von Schell) asks Kemp to find her brother Wally, a prospector, who has gone missing on the far side of the moon. Meanwhile the film's villain, J.J. Hubbard (Warren Mitchell), is interested in a huge asteroid, 6,000 tons of gemstone sapphire, which is about to make its closest approach to the moon since 1968. After discovering Wally's body, Clementine and Kemp are attacked by Hubbard's men, who want the dead man's site as a landing spot for the asteroid. After they escape Kemp becomes embroiled in a barroom brawl with Hubbard's bodyguard Harry (Bernard Bresslaw) back at the Lazy 'B' Saloon. Kemp and Karminski, assisted by Clementine, outwit Hubbard and send him to his death. The film concludes with Clementine inheriting her brother's claim.

This story outline could easily have been filmed as a Tim Holt or Johnny Mack Brown western in the late 1940s. The single joke soon wears thin and there is little surprise in the film's use of familiar generic convention – a bar-fight in zero gravity, which may have appeared funny on paper, is ludicrous when presented in slow-motion. Similarly, the shoot-out with laser guns and a poker game do not work – either as a form of parody or in their own right.[153] The film's best moment is the brief excerpt from John Ford's *Stagecoach* (1939), which is shown as an in-flight movie. Although Baker had a poor opinion of the film[154] and accepted some of the blame, the poor script and small budget for such an ambitious film were primary reasons for its failure.

The critics were not impressed. Ian Christie in the *Daily Express* (14 October 1969) set the overall tone with his headline: 'Infantile – even for small children'. The *Times* (16 October 1969) described the dialogue as 'witless', Ann Pacey in the *Sun* (14 October 1969) called the film 'silly', Cecil Wilson in the *Daily Mail* (14 October 1969) thought it was a 'whole load of nonsense', Penelope Mortimer in the *Observer* (19 October 1969) argued that it was as 'silly a piece of pseudo-science fiction as you could hope to find', Derek Malcolm in the *Guardian* (17 October 1969) thought it was 'dreadfully made' and that he would 'take Burt Kennedy any day', the *Sunday Mirror* (19 October 1969) concluded that the 'film falls flat on its astronaut', while Alexander Walker in the *Evening Standard* (16 October 1969) argued that while the 'basic idea is quite amusing' the film was weighed down by its 'heavy-handed facetiousness'. The reviewer in the *Daily Sketch* (15 October 1969) noted that the movie 'proves a pet theory of mine ... that the moon is as boring as a holiday camp' and only Felix Barker in the *Evening News* (16 October 1969) gave it a positive review: 'By keeping just this side of extravaganza, and never losing its sly humour, it makes a very engaging comedy'.

In between *The Anniversary* and *Moon Zero Two* Baker directed two made-for-television films, *private i* (1968), which was screened on American television as *The Spy Killer*, and *Foreign Exchange* (1968). Both films were based on the first two novels written by Jimmy Sangster. Initially, Sangster hoped that his script would be made into a feature film for theatrical release after Gulf and Western agreed to finance the project – providing a reasonable star was cast in the lead role. Initially Rod Steiger was interested but refused the lead role when a substantial part for his wife, Claire Bloom, could not be developed. American producer Harold Cohen then persuaded Sangster to allow his novels to be made as television films as part of ABC's *Movie of the Week*, a new concept on American television in the late 1960s. This involved a 90–minute film for American television with additional footage so that it could also be released as a 100–minute theatrical film outside of the United States. The budget, however, was tight: $400,000 per film to cover everything – overheads, contingencies, completion guarantees, producer's fees and all other direct costs.[155]

Sangster hired Baker to direct both films and Baker was credited as 'Roy Baker', not 'Roy Ward Baker'. Sangster wanted Trevor Howard as the 'slightly down-at-the-heel private investigator'[156] and Laurence Olivier as the duplicitous head of the secret service. The plan was to film all of Olivier's scenes on one set, his office, except for one day at a rural location. Therefore, costs could be kept to a minimum as Olivier's total commitment would not extend beyond five days. As this was affordable, Sangster was excited, especially after he received the news that Olivier was looking to 'do something on American TV and this seemed a good opportunity'.[157] Sangster went ahead and booked space at Pinewood Studios and scheduled the films to be made concurrently:

> And by that I didn't mean back to back. Scenes in the lead's shabby office for both movies to be shot in sequence, same with the scenes in his apartment, same with scenes in Olivier's office. The two scripts were printed on different color paper and the clapper boy had to check with the continuity girl before each shot to make sure he was using the right clapper board. No good marking a shot for *Private I* if it was meant for *Foreign Exchange*.[158]

Sangster was upset when he received word from the American network that they did not want Trevor Howard or Laurence Olivier as they were not big enough names on American television. As substitutes they sent Robert Horton and Sebastian Cabot. Horton was a minor actor in westerns and action films in the 1950s (such as *Return of the Texan*, 1952 and *Apache War Smoke*, 1952) before television 'stardom' as Flint McCullough in the long-running (1957–62) television western *Wagon Train*. However, even though his status in *Wagon Train* increased after Ward Bond's death, he failed to make much of an impression in his next series, *A Man Called Shenandoah* (1965–66). On the other hand, Cabot appeared in British films in the 1930s and 1940s, including a number of the *Old Mother Riley* films. His career, however, did not blossom until he left Britain for the United States, where he had supporting roles prior to his most prominent role as the English butler in *Family Affair*, which screened on television from 1966 to 1971. The imposition of Horton and Cabot angered Sangster who argued that Horton, in particular, was not appropriate to play the hard-boiled private detective: 'I'd written seedy, he was going to play suave'.[159] Horton even brought his own stylish wardrobe, so Sangster gave in.

Although Baker was disappointed that *private i/The Spy Killer* was not able to fully realise his desire to assimilate the conventions of the hard-boiled private eye with the 1960s Cold War espionage melodrama, the film was, within the limitations imposed by its limited budget and the censorship restrictions of American television, a worthy addition to the 1960s cycle of cynical spy films.[160] The opening scenes are, however, more in keeping with Dashiell Hammett's hard-boiled story *The Maltese Falcon*, which was filmed three times by Warner Brothers in the 1930s and early 1940s. Private detective John Smith (Robert Horton), who works out of a low-rent, back street office in Soho, is employed by a glamorous female client, Danielle Dunning (Barbara Shelley), to follow her husband. The iconic aspects are reinforced by the inclusion of Eleanor Summerfield[161] as Smith's secretary Mrs Roberts, a character not unlike Effie, Spade's secretary in *The Maltese Falcon*.

The relationship between Danielle and Smith is an edgy one owing to the fact that she was once married to Smith. She also claims that her husband's affair is with a man. However, she does not object on moral grounds and merely wants evidence of her husband's infidelity for a lucrative divorce settlement. Smith begins his surveillance of Dunning dressed in a trench coat but the hard-boiled conventions are soon assimilated into the downbeat world of espionage and politics. The film, on the other hand, retains the broad narrative structure of the genre as Danielle's request is shown to be merely a pretext for a convoluted plot involving government agencies and foreign spies.

Smith, consistent with the genre, is a flawed hero who is plagued by nightmares. He is not just a private detective but also a retired professional assassin who was once employed by the British Government under the supervision of Max (Sebastian Cabot). Now Max and an Albanian agent, Igor, both seek a notebook compiled by Dunning's husband of the names of the western agents operating in China. The storyline, which consists of a series of betrayals, concludes with the revelation that the agents were Russian and the British Government actually wanted the notebook to fall into the hands of the Chinese so as to accentuate tension between these two countries. Smith, who refuses to betray the Russian agents, is ultimately considered expendable by the British Government.

Hammer – the horror films

By late 1969 Baker had directed three films for Hammer but not, as yet, a horror film. This changed when he was offered *The Vampire Lovers* (1970), a reworking of Sheridan Le Fanu's novella *Carmilla*, which was serialised in the London magazine, *The Dark Blue*, between December 1871 and March 1872. Drawing upon vampire mythology and folklore, the novella was an erotic Victorian tale. *The Vampire Lovers* originated with producer, and former actor, Harry Fine in 1969. Fine had just completed the troubled production of *The Rise and Rise of Michael Rimmer* for David Frost and Warner Bros, and he was preparing another film for Frost when, after perusing the Dublin Gate Theatre Book, he came across stills of a play the Earl of Longford had adapted from Le Fanu's novella. Fine estimated that the play had been staged in 1933 or 1934.[162]

He obtained a copy of Le Fanu's story and passed it on to Tudor Gates. Gates, who had been an assistant theatre manager to Fine in the mid-1950s, had been working as a scriptwriter for some years. He contributed to various British television productions produced by Fine, and others, and although he had co-written *Barbarella* (1968) for Roger Vadim, he was not aware of Vadim's 1960 version of Le Fanu's *Carmilla, et mourir de plasir*.[163] Gates was excited by the opportunity to 'update' the story by foregrounding the lesbian activities of the female vampire Mircalla as well as introducing a 'startling amount of female nudity':

> [I]t was definitely my idea. I went to see a number of Hammer Films. While I enjoyed them, the one thing that struck me was that they were terribly outdated, at least for the modern cinema-going public. That was the time over here when the floodgates of censorship opened. I felt that the thing to do was to bring Hammer Films up to the seventies. So I deliberately threw in the nudes and the lesbians and all the rest of it. I believe it was the first time they'd done that.[164]

As Fine was also working on other productions he brought in Michael Style, who had produced only one film, the sexploitation film *Monique* (1969). In November 1969 Fantale Films, Fine's film company,[165] submitted a story outline to James Carreras at Hammer. Carreras loved the film's title and quickly set up a co-production deal with American International Productions (AIP), who supplied the $400,000 budget. He gave them two months to write the screenplay and complete the preproduction details, and filming began at Elstree on 19 January 1970.

Fine endorsed Hammer's choice of director, Roy Ward Baker, and the two producers were happy with his work.[166] Baker, on the other hand, felt that he was 'at odds with them' for most of the film[167] and that the two producers were disappointed that he did not include more nudity and give greater emphasis to the more sensational aspects in the script ('Well, I wasn't going to do that').[168] This film, he points out, 'was full of traps for the unwary'[169] and it was a 'bit of a battle'.[170] In retrospect he felt that he was 'slightly conned' by Fine and Style as they seduced him into the project, because of his interest in Le Fanu, when all they really wanted to do was make a sensational exploitation picture. 'Strictly speaking, this was not generally the Hammer style. Looking at my previous record, this was not my style either'.[71]

Ingrid Pitt, on the other hand, has a different interpretation of Hammer's attitude to nudity and the eagerness of Fine and Styles to fully exploit the liberalisation of censorship at that time. She felt that while James Carreras was supportive of the film's nudity, Fine and Style were a 'bit po-faced' about it. When a scene involving full frontal nudity on her part was coming up she met Fine and Style, 'looking very dejected, walking in the opposite direction. As I drew near I stopped and ripped open my dressing gown with all the *brio* of an experienced flasher on Hampstead Heath'.[72]

Although the British X Certificate's minimum age had just been raised from 16 to 18, John Trevelyan, the secretary of the British Board of Film Censors, worried about specific scenes in Tudor Gates's script, especially one involving a breast with puncture marks made by Mircalla's teeth. He was also concerned that another scene showed one of Mircalla's victims having a 'dream orgasm ending in a scream'.[73] Trevelyan sent a confidential note to James Carreras asking him to use his 'personal influence' with the producers to keep the film within 'reasonable bounds'.[74] Both scenes, however, appeared in the film.

The casting of Ingrid Pitt as Mircalla in *Vampire Lovers*, with her distinctive husky voice and Polish accent, was crucial to the film's success. Initially Shirley Eaton was suggested for Mircalla but James Carreras rejected her as being too old at thirty-two years of age.[75] – However, Pitt may have been as old as Eaton although there is considerable confusion as to the date of birth of the Polish actress. One version claims she was born in 1943 on a train taking prisoners to a concentration camp, while another records her date of birth as 1937.[76] Pitt had a colourful background. She was caught up as a young child in the Holocaust, raised in Poland, and trained as an actress in East Berlin, where she joined the Bertolt Brecht Berliner Ensemble in 1959, allegedly swimming across the river Spree at night in 1962. She eventually arrived in Los Angeles, joining the Pasadena Playhouse before moving to Spain in 1964 where she started appearing in films, including a small part in *Doctor Zhivago* (1965). A lead role in the low-budget melodrama *The Omegans* (1968), filmed in the Philippines, was followed by appearances in American television programmes and a supporting part in the Clint Eastwood war film, *Where Eagles Dare* (1968). After this she languished in London, sometimes working as a waitress to support herself and her young daughter.[77]

There are different versions as to how she came to be cast as Carmilla/Mircalla in *The Vampire Lovers*. Harry Fine claims that he recommended Pitt, 'after she arrived at our office one day, rather mysteriously, almost like Carmilla arrives at Castle Karnstein'.[178] Pitt, on the other hand, said that she won the part when she met James Carreras at a party: 'I was so frantic to get work, I thought I'd do anything. I worked so hard on Jimmy Carreras to get work that he finally said, "What do you want? Blood?" And I said, "Yes! Yes!"'.[179] To appease AIP, who were concerned about the casting of a relative unknown in the lead role, Hammer agreed to provide a strong supporting cast, which included George Cole, Kate O'Mara, Dawn Addams, Madeline Smith, Pippa Steele, Douglas Wilmer and Jon Finch. To reassure AIP even further Peter Cushing was offered a cameo role just before shooting began. Cushing was then introduced to the press with Pitt at the Savoy Hotel six days before filming of the interiors began at ABPC's Elstree studios.

Location shooting took place at the Moor Park Golf Course in Hertfordshire where the clubhouse, which was a mansion used by Henry VIII, doubled as the manor house. The film came in on time and on budget and it was a commercial success in Britain and the United States, making Ingrid Pitt a cult figure and minor star. It was not only one of Hammer's best horror films, it was also one of Baker's best and most commercially successful films. Anticipating that *The Vampire Lovers* would be a box-office success, James Carreras set up a script conference for a follow-up film, *Lust for a Vampire*, only two days after Baker's film had finished production. Terence Fisher was scheduled to direct but a road accident forced him to leave the film and Jimmy Sangster took over the direction. *The Vampire Lovers* went into general release on 4 October 1970 and *Lust for a Vampire*, with Danish actress/model Yutte Stensgaard as Mircalla, premiered a few months later. Although *Lust for a Vampire* did reasonably well in Britain, it failed to generate much business in the United States. In the last of the so-called Fantale/Hammer trilogy, *Twins of Evil*, released in October 1971, Mircalla is relegated to a minor role.

The virtues of *The Vampire Lovers*, its poetic imagery and pervasive melancholy, are missing from Baker's next film, *Scars of Dracula* (1970). This is one of the weakest of the seven Hammer films starring Christopher Lee as Dracula.[180] In preparing for the film Baker read Bram Stoker's novel and he hoped that he could insert 'elements of magic and the supernatural'.[181] He was also interested in recreating the moment in Bram Stoker's book when Jonathan Harker looks out of his window, high up in a tower in Dracula's castle, and sees the vampire climbing up the wall: 'That's the one where Dracula crawls down the wall. Well, he had to do it, but there were problems. It meant that a new set had to be built. Hammer didn't want to do it because of the expense, but I stuck to my guns and insisted upon it. I argued that we would be using the set for other scenes and they grudgingly agreed to it.'[182]

Other than a lacklustre script, most of Baker's problems were due to the film's small budget, which is reflected in the special effects. Hammer, who were rarely extravagant in this regard, were not in a position to spend a lot of money on *Scars of Dracula*. Having lost a series of American partners in the 1960s, the last being AIP with *The Vampire Lovers*, the studio was entering its final phase. In 1969 James Carreras offered EMI a 75 per cent interest in Hammer and when this failed he sought new partners, such as the Tigon Group, to take over the company. *Scars of Dracula* was the first film in a new deal with Anglo–EMI, although Rank would also, briefly, resume co-production deals with Hammer and they financed the follow-up film, *Twins of Evil*. Nevertheless, the trade press proudly proclaimed that Baker's film and its co-feature *The Horror of Frankenstein* were the first Hammer films to be made with entirely British finance. The budgets, however, were meagre and much less than the relatively luxurious days when Hollywood companies such as Twentieth Century-Fox and Warner Bros/Seven Arts invested in Hammer's films.

In November 1969 EMI, who had assumed control of the ABPC Elstree Studios, agreed to finance two Hammer films: *Horror of Frankenstein* and *Scars of Dracula*. The budget for each film was set at £200,000 and this necessitated a very tight shooting schedule, even by Hammer's standards. Veteran Hammer producer Aida Young was assigned to the film and she believed this signalled an end of an era: 'It was really the beginning of the end for Hammer. And everybody knew it. We went about it as if it were any other film – but I remember at the time we were all rather despondent at the terrible schedule we were given.'[183] Young also recalled that the 'script wasn't very good. I think at that stage I had decided no more Draculas. I did it because I wanted to work and I loved working at Hammer as a producer'.[184] Baker also confirmed that the budget was small: 'I knew things were very tight. The producer, Aida Young was a thoroughly businesslike person, and a bit of slave driver. She forced the picture through at a tremendous pace, with no hanging about. God help us if we hadn't come in on time.'[185]

Aida Young's reluctance to make another Dracula film for Hammer was shared by Christopher Lee, and in a letter written in early 1970 to Gloria Lillibridge, for *The Christopher Lee Club Journal*, he outlined his misgivings: 'However, we come to the old familiar scene now Hammer Films, and another Dracula. Think of it! Another Dracula!. This is titled THE SCARS OF DRACULA, another subtle and intelligent title.'[186]

Although Lee was relatively happy with the script, as he had more screen time ('it's considerably better than the last one'), he wondered why there was no mention of his resuscitation at the beginning of the film as this had been the practice in all of his previous Dracula films for Hammer. Lee believed that Hammer was preparing to continue the series without him if he demanded the same money he received for his last film. If they put in another actor, he pointed out, they would not need to explain away what happened to him at the end of *Taste the Blood of Dracula*. He was not, however, distressed at the prospect of not appearing as Dracula for Hammer: 'I'm hoping for the day when I'll be able to say "I don't want to do your film for two reasons – I can't do it because I'm doing another film at the same time and secondly I don't want to do your film because I don't want to do anymore pictures for you of this kind."'[187] Lee did not want to abandon the genre but was hoping for a better class of film:

> [W]hen I shall be making these sort of films as well as they ought to be made and making them for the right amount of money, as prestige productions, like ROSEMARY'S BABY, for instance, and making them really well, with good scripts, good directors and good casts.
> When you work in the bush leagues for these people, none of these things, except very rarely, seem to come together.[188]

However, as there were no offers at that time, he reluctantly accepted the role. But the signs were not good:

> Apart from anything else, I've reached the end of my resourcefulness with this character. If you play a character four or five times like I have, you really don't know what more to do with it. Again, one is always limited by the script and what one's asked to do and say and how one's expected to look, but I honestly don't know what more to do with this character. There are no more faces I can make and no more expressions I can make and very few other 'things' I can do with the character. The result is always going to have a sameness about it which I think is disastrous for an actor and rather boring for the audience. There it is, I may have to do it, but I hope and pray, as I have for the last two pictures, that it will be the last time.[189]

Scars of Dracula was released in October 1970 with *The Horror of Frankenstein*, another misguided Hammer attempt to update one of its horror staples that had turned into a laboured parody. Both films did reasonably well in Britain grossing nearly £56,000 in London.[190] However, when Hammer offered *Scars of Dracula* to Warner Bros for an American release the Hollywood company passed and the film was picked up by a small distributor, Continental Films, who did not have sufficient money to adequately promote the film in the USA. *Scars of*

Dracula was the last attempt by Hammer to rework the Gothic world of Stoker's novel with a mid-European setting. The next two Dracula films, *Dracula A.D. 1972* (1972) and *The Satanic Rites of Dracula* (1974), are set in the 1970s while Hammer's final Dracula film, *The Legend of the Seven Golden Vampires* (1974), is set in China.

Roy Baker started directing *The Avengers* in 1965 with Brian Clemens writing and producing many episodes. After production of the series ended in 1969 Clemens wanted to resume his career in feature films, which began in 1956. In 1970 Baker, while having lunch with Clemens and others in the Elstree restaurant, discussed different variations on stock horror characters such as Frankenstein, Dracula and the Mummy. Suddenly Clemens 'sat up and quietly said: "I've got it. Dr. Jekyll drinks the magic potion and ... he turns into a woman!"'.[191] The table roared with laughter but Clemens was not deterred and wrote his idea down on the back of an envelope and took it to James Carreras:

> Jekyll changes from a powerful man – into a slim, beautiful, full-breasted woman! And yet he retains his male mind. And his male drives. And his male strength ... [Jekyll] uses Sister Hyde as the perfect disguise – roams the streets like Jack the Ripper – seeking out his victims ... and they are easy to find, because why should they fear a woman like themselves? ... murdering them and pillaging their bodies for experiments.[192]

Carreras quickly approved the project, to be called *Dr Jekyll and Sister Hyde* (1971) and Clemens brought in his partner from *The Avengers*, Albert Fennell, to co-produce the film. Hammer considered Jimmy Sangster, Peter Sasdy, Alan Gibson and Gordon Hessler before offering the film to Baker in December 1970. Baker was delighted: 'When I was given the script it cheered me up no end: once again I had a good one. It was ambitious, too. It demanded atmosphere and good performances. There were hints of the female characteristics in the male and vice versa and other subtleties to explore. Or to explore with subtlety.'[193]

The casting of the two lead roles was crucial to the film's success as the two actors had to play the male and female side of one character. In 1969 Hammer, who were in dispute with Christopher Lee, decided to replace him with Ralph Bates for *Taste the Blood of Dracula* (1969). However, when Hammer's American partner, Warner Bros/Seven Arts, found out that Lee would not be in the film they objected and Anthony Hinds's script was hurriedly rewritten to include him. This necessarily affected the status of Bates' role as Lord Courtley, a depraved aristocrat whose body, after his brutal death, mutates into Lee's Count Dracula. Bates followed this film with the lead role as Victor Frankenstein in *The Horror of Frankenstein*.[194] When Cushing's wife fell gravely ill just prior to the filming of *Lust For a Vampire* Bates took over his role.

Kate O'Mara, the French Governess Mme Perrodot who offers herself to Mircalla in The Vampire Lovers, was Clemens and Fennell's first choice as Sister Hyde but James Carreras insisted on Jamaican-born model and actress Martine Beswick,[195] who had taken the lead role in their 1966 production of Slave Girls.[196] This film, directed by Michael Carreras, followed Beswick's supporting role in Raquel Welch's One Million Years B.C. (1966), the most commercially successful film ever made by Hammer. Earlier, Beswick had appeared in small roles in three James Bond films with the most prominent being the fighting gypsy in From Russia With Love (1963).

Baker was pleased that Beswick was cast as the dominant Sister Hyde as he felt that 'with some attention to their hair and slight adjustment of their heels of their shoes she and Ralph looked like identical twins. It was miraculous and was the key element in making the plot believable'.[197] The financial returns from the film, however, were not strong and the double bill of Dr Jekyll and Sister Hyde and Blood From the Mummy's Tomb grossed only £2,376 in its opening week at London's New Victoria. This did not improve all that much when the film went into general release.[198] On the other hand, Hammer's version of the popular television show On the Buses, which was filmed at Elstree at the same time as Dr Jekyll and Sister Hyde, and cost only £97,000 to produce, was a substantial hit, grossing £1.4 million in its first six weeks in Britain and Australia.[199] By the early 1970s the signs for the traditional Hammer horror film were not good.

Amicus

Milton Subotsky, an American writer/producer who emigrated to Britain in 1959, initially found things tough in London, producing only three films in his first five years. His first British Film, City of the Dead (1960), starred Christopher Lee in a Salem witchcraft tale and it was distinguished only by the fact that it killed off its heroine (Venetia Stevenson) early in the story, a device recalling Hitchcock's Psycho. Subotsky followed with Richard Lester's first feature film It's Trad, Dad! in 1961. In 1964 Subotsky and his New York-based partner Max Rosenberg produced Dr Terror's House of Horrors, the first of a series of horror portmanteau films that became associated with Amicus, their new company name.[200] The omnibus format was not new in the cinema, as there were early examples in Germany with Hoffman Erzaehlungen (1911, 1916 and 1923). In Britain it was associated with Ealing's prestigious horror film Dead of Night (1945).

There are two types of portmanteau films:[201] one where the stories are not connected other than originating from a single author such as Somerset Maugham in films such as *Quartet* (1948), *Trio* (1950) and *Encore* (1951); or a television series such as *Douglas Fairbanks Presents*, which led to a number of omnibus films in the early 1950s.[202] In the second type of portmanteau film the episodes are connected by a link-narrative, the form that Amicus utilised in *Dr Terror's House of Horrors* (1964), directed by Freddie Francis, where the stories were linked by Peter Cushing's Dr Schreck. Schreck, as Death, predicts a disastrous future for five people in a railway carriage. Amicus replicated this format in 1967 with *Torture Garden*, based on four stories by Robert Bloch, with Burgess Meredith as Dr Diabolo providing the link between each story. Robert Bloch wrote the four tales for the next Amicus omnibus film, *The House That Dripped Blood* (1970), and Ingrid Pitt starred in one episode, 'The Cloak', as the vampire Carla.

The Amicus approach to the genre was noticeably different to the Hammer style. It was less respectful of the genre's conventions and mildly self-reflexive; atmosphere and suspense were not, generally, key elements in these films. Each episode also contained a 'surprise' final twist, which was invariably sadistic and perverse. Subotsky edited his films very tightly – a skill he developed in 1949 when he edited a package of western feature films to a running time of 26 minutes so that they could fit a half-hour television schedule.[203] He was drawn to the portmanteau format:

> So you don't bore an audience. It's very hard to find a story that can sustain interest for ninety minutes. In the segment films you can tell four or five stories and each story only runs the length of time it should – its natural length. You can make a very fast-moving variety show of different kinds of horror stories and audiences seem to like it. I like it.[204]

In developing this format Subotsky acknowledged his debt to *Dead of Night*: 'Actually DEAD OF NIGHT is what we pattern our anthology films on. DR. TERROR'S HOUSE OF HORRORS and all the multi-story films we've done were patterned after DEAD OF NIGHT.'[205]

Asylum is one of best, if not the best, examples of the Amicus style and Baker regarded it as one of his favourite films.[206] What distinguishes it from other Amicus omnibus films is the fact that the framing story is integrated into the four episodes. The filming, Baker recalls, went as 'smooth as silk'[207] and he employed a different colour style for each episode:

> I treated the sequences in different styles ... we had one sequence where we aimed for a pastel, glamorized, long focal length lens type of effect.

This was the Charlotte Rampling and Britt Ekland sequence, and we thought it suited the story. In one sequence ['The Weird Tailor'] we strived for a bleached, almost black and white effect, not so much in the photography, but in the composition of the sets and costumes, and in another we aimed for cheap, gaudy colors, because the characters were rather cheap and nasty, and we kept the cameras constantly on the move.[208]

Asylum won the Grand Prix for Best Picture Award at the Paris Convention du Cinéma Fantastique.

Baker's next film, *And Now the Screaming Starts!* (1973), was a traditional single-plot film and quite different in style from his portmanteau films. It was closer to the Hammer style dispensing with the 'jokey', knowing tone of the Amicus films. Nevertheless, Subotsky maintained his usual working method of intense script development followed by an equally intense editing period. In between he left Baker alone, a situation the director appreciated:

I'm left very much to my own devices during filming. Milton is hardly ever seen on the set. He comes in usually about half past twelve to say he's seen the rushes, and he lets me know if they're okay or if he has a query on some technical point, and then he disappears and I don't see him again. I see very little of him when we're shooting.

He likes the writing and discussing of the script. We discussed AND NOW THE SCREAMING STARTS! at very great length while we were shooting ASYLUM. As a matter of fact, we actually rewrote it from top to bottom, although he went off to do all of the actual work. After he casts the picture and puts it on the floor, he leaves the rest to me, and he really won't take a serious interest in it again until we start cutting. He enjoys that part of it.[209]

Baker was less impressed with Subotsky's partner, Max Rosenberg, and blamed him for changing the film's title from *Fengriffen*, the title of screenwriter David Case's novel, or the alternative title *Bride of Fengriffen*, to the crass *And Now the Screaming Starts!* He felt that although *Fengriffen* was 'not much of a title [it] was a lot better than the one wished on us'.[210] However, he was wrong on this point as Subotsky chose *And Now the Screaming Starts* – Rosenberg's only contribution was to provide the punctuation. Subotsky rejected the more Gothic sounding *Fengriffen*, and *Bride of Fengriffen*, as they were not 'strong' enough and 'wouldn't get the audience'.[211] Instead, he preferred 'I Have No Mouth and I Must Scream' but this was the title of a story by Harlan Ellison, and when Ellison refused permission to use it, Subotsky choose *And Now the Screaming Starts!* Aware of the need to attract international audiences, he argued that *And Now the Screaming Starts!* 'translates well into other languages'.[212] Although the film cost more than the average Amicus film – due to its period setting, which meant additional costs for costumes, wigs and hairdressers – Subotsky was pleased with Baker's efforts and while Freddie Francis remained his favourite director for the omnibus films, the producer claimed that Baker had greater expertise in working with actors.[213]

Baker's third film for Amicus, *The Vault of Horror* (1973), was another attempt by Amicus to capture the style of the 1950s horror comics of Al Feldstein and William Gaines. An earlier attempt, *Tales From the Crypt* (1972), resulted in their most financially successful movie. The five stories in this film are linked by a hooded crypt keeper (Ralph Richardson), who offers each person a vision of their future, which turns out to be a reprise of their past mistakes, before the film's 'twist' ending – their descent into hell.

The Vault of Horror,[214] was also based on the stories of Feldstein and Gaines and follows the same formula with five stories, each with a 'shock' ending. Finally, the participants learn that they are trapped in a cemetery where they are condemned to relive their experiences every night. Subotsky thought that this film, their sixth portmanteau film, was 'very different from our other horror films. It's not gory or gruesome – well, only in tiny parts. It's very inventive and it's funny. It's full of laughs and self-parody, kind of tongue-in-cheek.'[215] This tone is evident in the first episode, 'Midnight Mess', involving a man (Daniel Massey) who murders his sister (Anna Massey) for the inheritance only to find himself in a restaurant populated by vampires. The episode ends with him strung upside down with a silver tap jutting from his neck to provide blood for the patrons. The final image of Massey's body hanging upside down feeding blood to the vampires was censored in the United States and replaced with a still-frame.

Other episodes in the film were equally perfunctory, each with a 'twist' ending. In 'The Neat Job' Critchit (Terry-Thomas) frustrates his wife Eleanor (Glynis Johns) to the point where she kills him and keeps his organs in neatly labelled jars; 'This Trick'll Kill You' shows the revenge on a magician (Curt Jürgens) by an Indian rope-climber after he kills her; 'Bargain in Death' involves Maitland (Michael Craig), a man who faked his own death so as to defraud his insurance company. He is, firstly, double crossed by the 'friend' (Edward Judd) who promised to dig him up from his grave and then, in a final twist, his head is punctured by a grave digger trying to sell the body to medical students; 'Drawn and Quartered', the final episode, borrows from the basic premise of Oscar Wilde's *Dorian Gray* as a vengeful painter (Tom Baker) uses his paintings to achieve retribution on his agent and two 'friends' who have conspired to cheat him of money and recognition. However, when turpentine accidentally spills on to his self-portrait, the artist is killed by a truck.

Each episode is brief and the emphasis is less on the thinly drawn characters than the events and the predictable twist. Subotsky, however, defended his formula: 'If you are telling five stories plus a framework story in 90 minutes you can do all sorts of things and not bore an audience for very long if one of the stories isn't good'.[216] He was proud of the fact that he was able to cut the original running time of *The Vault of Horror* from two hours to 87 minutes: we 'cut it as tightly as we possibly can, and nothing stops for a second'.[217]

Hammer, Hong Kong and *The Legend of the Seven Golden Vampires*

On 31 January 1973 Sir James Carreras resigned from Hammer and his son Michael, who had left the company in January 1971, assumed full control. Sir James's last production was *The Satanic Rites of Dracula* and it was also Christopher Lee's seventh, and last, appearance as Dracula. Production on this film ended on 3 January 1973,[218] although it was not released for another twelve months. Hammer, in early 1973, was in dire financial straits and desperately needed new sources of finance as money from the Hollywood studios was no longer available. Also the prospects of British companies filling the gap were not good as EMI, Hammer's most recent partner, told Michael Carreras that it was not going to provide ongoing finance.[219]

As martial arts films in general, and Bruce Lee in particular, were popular at that time, Hammer showed interest in developing another kind of exploitation film – especially as it appeared that the company could obtain access to the most prolific producer of martial arts films. Hammer scriptwriter and producer Don Houghton had, through his father-in-law, a connection with Run Run Shaw, the head of a successful film company based in Hong Kong. This combination of factors resulted in Baker's strangest film, *The Legend of the Seven Golden Vampires*.

While Baker thought that the idea of combining two exploitation film genres, kung fu and vampire, was a good idea, he was not overly enthusiastic about directing such a film.[220] He arrived in Hong Kong in late 1973 and his gloom worsened when he surveyed the production facilities at the Shaw Studios. Films were shot silent, with dialogue dubbed later in many languages, and the stages were 'enormous tin sheds with no sound proofing at all'.[221] He was also concerned about the prospects for location filming as there was little open space in Hong

Kong, and Don Houghton's script called for a caravan crossing of a desert.[222] The only option 'was a spot on a hill right by the border of China proper'.[223] There were also communication difficulties between the English and the local crew, particularly with regard to sound recording, and there were accusations that the English crew refused to 'co-operate civilly with their Chinese co-workers'.[224]

The production techniques of the Hong Kong studio differed from Baker's normal approach and this led to friction. For example, the film's co-producer Vee King Shaw, argued that a local crew should choreograph, and film, the martial arts sequences. Baker, on the other hand, believing that it was his overall responsibility to 'make a Hammer film for distribution in the English-speaking markets',[225] insisted on directing these sequences himself. Principal photography began on 22 October 1973, and after viewing a rough cut of the first kung fu scene on 31 October Run Run Shaw demanded that all action sequences be filmed by one of his studio directors. Henceforth the martial arts sequences were choreographed by Liu Chia-Liang and a second unit was formed under the direction of Chang Cheh, a Shaw Brothers director.[226] This decision produced a noticeable inconsistency in the film's style and the attempt to merge Baker's classical set-ups and 'realist' presentation with the anti-classical, anti-realist martial arts techniques favoured by the Shaw Studios produced a jarring effect. This is readily apparent, for example, in the scenes involving the undead. Chang Cheh also filmed additional martial arts scenes for a 110-minute 'Far East' version.[227]

The plot, which is reasonably coherent, begins in 1804 when the body of Dracula's Chinese disciple Kah (Chan Shen) is taken over by the Count (John Forbes-Robertson). A century later Professor Van Helsing (Peter Cushing), lecturing at China's Chung King University, argues that there is a correlation between the activities of Dracula and the local legend of the seven golden vampires where, each year, during the seventh moon, seven vampires in golden masks violate a remote village. On one occasion an old farmer kills one of the vampires and seizes the medallion containing its life force, and the farmer's grandson, Hsi Ching (David Chiang, who was the Shaw Brothers' answer to their rival Bruce Lee), gives the medallion to Van Helsing. He asks him to join with his siblings in their fight against Dracula who has kidnapped women from the Szechwan village of Ping Kwei.

Van Helsing's expedition to Ping Kwei includes Hsi Ching's five brothers and sister Mai Kwai (Shih Szu) and Van Helsing's son Leyland (Robin Stewart). It is financed by an independent young Scandinavian woman Vanessa Buren (Julie Ege). During the journey Hsi Ching falls in love with Vanessa Buren and Mai Kwai forms a romantic relationship with Leyland. At the climactic battle at Ping Kwei Buren is bitten by a vampire and Hsi Ching is forced to kill her and himself. Mai Kwai is carried off by the last vampire whereupon she is rescued by Van Helsing after he confronts, and destroys, Dracula.

The film necessitated changes to Hammer's vampire mythology so as to include Eastern as well as Christian iconography. It also touched upon a transgressive critique of colonialism, a theme that was not unknown in Hammer films.[228] I.Q. Hunter, for example, notes that Hammer often used the exotic to criticise Western attitudes.[229] This is achieved through the use of a familiar plot, based on the same premise as John Sturges's *The Magnificent Seven* (1960) which, in turn, was a remake of Akira Kurosawa's *The Seven Samurai* (1954). In *The Legend of the Seven Golden Vampires*, Van Helsing comes to the rescue of beleaguered Chinese farmers plagued by the annual violation of their village. In this case, however, the source of all their troubles is Count Dracula, a figure of Western colonialism, rendered literal in the film's opening scene when Dracula merges his body with his Chinese disciple Kah. Yet the cultural implications of the film are, ultimately, ambiguous. While the Chinese farmers are seemingly dependent on the assistance of a Western figure, Professor Van Helsing, the source of the violation, Dracula, can be interpreted in different ways, as I.Q. Hunter argues: 'Dracula is both the worst of Western Culture, going East to gratify his desire for sexual and sadistic fantasy, and that recurrent figure of Western fantasy and nightmare, the man of power who goes native, blending his identity with the Other.'[230] Yet, as Hunter points out, whilst Van Helsing is a more acceptable face of Western influence, the frail Peter Cushing does little to help – until the final moments when he kills Dracula by driving a stake through his heart. Hsi Ching, Mai Kwai and her brothers kill the seven vampires. Ultimately, the film presents the East sympathetically, as a land threatened by Dracula's 'freelance colonialist abroad in Mainland China'.[231]

Ideologically, *The Legend of the Seven Golden Vampires* is one of the more complex Hammer films. As a Hammer horror film, however, it is fatally weakened by Lee's decision that he would not play Dracula again for the studio after *The Satanic Rites of Dracula*. Without him, Dracula's appearance is reduced to a few scenes at the start and finish and Lee's replacement, John Forbes-Robertson, who appeared as the 'Man in Black' in *The Vampire Lovers*, was a poor substitute. His heavily rouged appearance gives the role a camp demeanour and the film misses the sad fury that characterised Lee's contribution to the role.

The Legend of the Seven Golden Vampires has its admirers but it is only

A CAREER OVERVIEW 61

a bizarre footnote in the career of Roy Ward Baker. Although Tom Johnson and Deborah Del Vecchio suggest that the film did 'fantastic business' in Britain and the Far East,[232] there is little evidence that the film did anything to revitalise Hammer's fortunes.[233] Warner Bros declined to distribute the film in the United States and the American rights were eventually sold to Dynamite Entertainment, who re-edited the film into an incoherent mess. This version, which was released in 1979 as *The Seven Brothers Meet Dracula*, opens with a sequence of action scenes taken from various parts of the film – including the vampires rising from their graves, which occurs near the end of the Hammer version. The desire to show as much nudity and violence as possible, unencumbered by plot coherence or meaningful dialogue, leads to the vampire raid on Ping Kwei, where the female villagers are ravaged, being repeated three times throughout the film.[234]

Television: *Minder, Sherlock Holmes* and a rebellious Hayley Mills

Baker was 'shell-shocked after the Hong Kong farrago'.[235] Earlier he had British television to fall back upon in lean times. For example, he continued to direct programmes such as *The Champions, Randall and Hopkirk (Deceased), Department S, Journey to the Unknown, The Persuaders, Jason King* and *The Protectors* between 1967 and 1972. However, he completed principal photography for *The Legend of the Seven Golden Vampires* on 11 December 1973 with no prospects. He did not direct a film or television series for the next four years, until producer Robert S. Baker invited him back for two episodes of *The Return of the Saint*. During the period, which he describes as 'four years in the desert',[236] he was restless and eager to work so he wrote scripts, prepared outlines of television series and 'bombarded everyone I knew with them. I found no takers'.[237] He was also involved in the preparation of audio-visual presentations for companies, although this did not turn out as well as he had hoped.[238] *Danger UXB* and a working trip to Poland in 1979 to direct five episodes of *Sherlock Holmes and Doctor Watson*, starring Geoffrey Whitehead and Donald Pickering, for veteran American television producer Sheldon Reynolds, preceded the *Minder* series, where he directed thirteen episodes between 1979 and 1988. Baker also directed the final (double) episode, 'An Officer and a Car Salesman', which was screened in Britain on 26 December 1988. In 1979, between filming episodes of *Minder*, Baker travelled to Kenya for the television adaptation of Elspeth Huxley's 'fictionalised autobiography', *The Flame Trees of Thika*. This was screened as seven one-hour episodes on British television in 1981.

After a disagreement with one of the main actors, David Robb, on the first day of filming Baker found that he had, for the first time in his career, a 'rebellious cast', which included Hayley Mills.[239]

Baker followed this with his final feature film, *The Monster Club* (1980), another portmanteau film produced by Milton Subotsky. *The Monster Club*, the weakest of his four films for Subotsky, was less of a horror film than a comedy spoof that was based on three stories by R. Chetwynd-Hayes. The episodes were linked by the less than humorous dialogue between Vincent Price and John Carradine at a disco populated by vampires. Music in the club was supplied by UB40. The film did not receive a theatrical release in the United States and it virtually ended Milton Subotsky's career as a film producer.

A much better film, although it was produced for television, was *The Masks of Death* (1984). The sound editor on the film was Roy Baker, the man who provoked Baker into changing his name in 1967. The story was written by Anthony Hinds, who had worked with Baker at Hammer on *Scars of Dracula* (as John Elder). This was not Hinds' first involvement with the famous detective as he co-produced, with Michael Carreras, *The Hound of the Baskervilles* in 1958 with Peter Cushing as Sherlock Holmes.

In 1968 Cushing reprised the role of Holmes and *The Masks of Death* was his third appearance as the detective. Great care was taken by Hinds (as John Elder), Roy Baker and scriptwriter N.J. Crisp to remain faithful to the style, atmosphere and characterisations created by Conan Doyle, although the film was not based on one of his stories. It was also fitting that John Mills, as Watson, should appear in Baker's last film as Mills was his leading man in his first feature film, *The October Man*, and five subsequent films – *Morning Departure*, *The Singer Not the Song*, *Flame in the Streets*, *The Valiant* and *The Masks of Death*.

The film begins in 1926, with Holmes and Watson in retirement at Baker Street, as Watson tells a young woman, Miss Derwent (Susan Penhaligon), how Holmes prevented a great catastrophe just prior to the Great War. This provides the motivation for a flashback to 1914. When a mutilated body, with a face of a man 'who had witnessed some unintelligible terrible evil', is found in the Thames, Inspector Alec MacDonald of Scotland Yard (Gordon Jackson) seeks Holmes' assistance. His investigation is paralleled by an accompanying plot involving the attempts of the Home Secretary (Ray Milland) to prevent war with Germany. He introduces this strand when he brings a German diplomat, Graf Udo Von Felseck (Anton Diffring), to see Holmes.

The German invites Holmes and Watson to visit him at Purbridge Manor in Buckinghamshire where the detective meets the woman,

Irene Adler (Anne Baxter), he loved a quarter of a century before. Embittered by her rejection of him, he tells her 'I am not a wholehearted admirer of womankind. Women are never to be entirely trusted. Not the best.' At Purbridge Manor Holmes also realises that Von Felseck has created a trail of false clues to lure him to his death, a deduction confirmed by Adler. Returning to London, the film concludes when Holmes and Watson destroy a German plot to feed poison gas into British homes. *The Masks of Death* is a nostalgic, elegiac film with two elderly characters, Holmes and Watson, and two elderly actors, Cushing and Mills, performing one last heroic action. Baker's unobtrusive, professional direction of the conventional story seamlessly integrates veteran actors such as Anne Baxter, Ray Milland and Anton Diffring into this fine film.

Baker continued to direct British television series such as *The Irish RM* and *Fairly Secret Army* and his last television programme, an episode of *The Good Guys* starring Nigel Havers and Keith Barron, was screened in 1993 when he was 76 years old.

Notes

1 Baker, *The Director's Cut*, p. 5.
2 Wheeler Winston Dixon, 'Twilight of the Empire: The Films of Roy Ward Baker. An Interview', *Classic Images*, Volume 234, December 1994, p. 15.
3 Baker, *The Director's Cut*, p. 8.
4 *Ibid.*, p. 10.
5 *Ibid.*, p. 14.
6 *Ibid.*
7 *Ibid.*, p. 15.
8 *Ibid.*, p. 17.
9 *Ibid.*
10 *Ibid.*, p. 20.
11 Karloff came to the studio to make *The Man Who Changed His Mind* (1936).
12 Baker, *The Director's Cut*, p. 21.
13 *Ibid.*, p. 19.
14 The film was released as *Lady Jane* in 1985, directed by Trevor Nunn with Helena Bonham Carter as Lady Jane Grey.
15 Baker, *The Director's Cut*, p. 155.
16 *Ibid.*, p. 23.
17 *Ibid.*, p. 28.
18 *Ibid.*, p. 31.
19 Author's interview with Roy Ward Baker, September 2000.
20 Baker, *The Director's Cut*, p. 32.
21 Jeffrey Richards, *A Night to Remember: The Definitive Titanic Film*, London: I. B. Tauris, 2003, p. 38.
22 *Ibid.*
23 *Ibid.*, pp. 37–8.

24 Baker's own term to describe his period prior to 15 February 1940, when he joined the army.
25 See Baker, *A Director's Cut*, p. 114.
26 Ibid., p. 38.
27 Dixon, 'Twilight of the Empire', p. 16.
28 Baker, *A Director's Cut*, p. 38.
29 Ibid., p. 39.
30 Ibid., p. 38.
31 Ibid.
32 Author's interview with Roy Ward Baker, September 2000.
33 Dixon, 'Twilight of the Empire', p. 16.
34 Baker, *A Director's Cut*, pp. 42–3.
35 Author's interview with Roy Ward Baker, September 2000.
36 Baker, *A Director's Cut*, p. 43.
37 Ibid., p. 45.
38 Ibid.
39 Ibid., p. 46.
40 Ibid., p. 47.
41 Author's interview with Roy Ward Baker, September 2000.
42 Ibid.
43 Baker, *A Director's Cut*, p. 48.
44 Author's interview with Roy Ward Baker, September 2000.
45 Baker, *A Director's Cut*, p. 51.
46 Ibid., pp. 54–5.
47 Ibid., p. 55.
48 Ibid., p. 57.
49 Ibid.
50 Carol Reed was the studio's first choice as director.
51 Baker, *A Director's Cut*, p. 59.
52 Dixon, 'Twilight of the Empire', p. 18.
53 Author's interview with Roy Ward Baker, September 2000.
54 Ibid.
55 Baker, *A Director's Cut*, p. 64.
56 Dixon, 'Twilight of the Empire', p. 18.
57 Author's interview with Roy Ward Baker, September 2000.
58 Ibid.
59 Ibid.
60 Baker, *A Director's Cut*, p. 65.
61 Ibid., p. 66.
62 Author's interview with Roy Ward Baker, September 2000.
63 Ibid.
64 Ibid.
65 The cover of Baker's autobiography includes photos of Monroe and a still from *A Night to Remember*.
66 Dixon, 'Twilight of the Empire', p. 34.
67 Baker, *A Director's Cut*, pp. 48–9.
68 Ibid., pp. 69–70.
69 Dixon, 'Twilight of the Empire', p. 34.
70 Baker, *A Director's Cut*, p. 73.
71 Ibid.
72 Author's interview with Roy Ward Baker, September 2000.
73 Zanuck again imposed the title on Baker's film. The film was based on a story called *Waterhole*.

74 Baker, *A Director's Cut*, p. 82.
75 Author's interview with Roy Ward Baker, September 2000.
76 *Ibid.*
77 Baker, *A Director's Cut*, p. 86.
78 *Ibid.*
79 Author's interview with Roy Ward Baker, September 2000.
80 Ward Baker, *A Director's Cut*, p. 87.
81 Baker felt that the film would have worked better if it had been set in 1885, rather than the 1930s, on a sailing ship. Author's interview with Roy Ward Baker, September 2000.
82 Wheeler Winston Dixon, 'Twilight of the Empire', Part II, *Classic Images*, Volume 235, January 1995, p. 26.
83 *Ibid.*
84 Baker, *A Director's Cut*, p. 91.
85 *Ibid.*, p. 91.
86 Author's interview with Roy Ward Baker, September 2000.
87 *Ibid.*
88 Baker, *A Director's Cut*, p. 96.
89 Author's interview with Roy Ward Baker, September 2000.
90 *Ibid.*
91 *Ibid.*
92 Baker, *A Director's Cut*, p. 98.
93 Author's interview with Roy Ward Baker, September 2000.
94 William MacQuitty, *Titanic Memories: The Making of A Night to Remember*, London: National Maritime Museum, 2000, p. 8.
95 *Ibid.*
96 *Ibid.*, p. 9.
97 *Ibid.*
98 *Ibid.*, p. 10.
99 *Ibid.*, p. 11.
100 *Ibid.*, p. 13.
101 *Ibid.*, p. 14.
102 *Ibid.*
103 *Ibid.*, p. 31.
104 *Ibid.*, p. 15.
105 Baker, *A Director's Cut*, p. 95.
106 MacQuitty, *Titanic Memories*, p. 24.
107 *Ibid.*, p. 25.
108 *Ibid.*
109 Author's interview with Roy Ward Baker, September 2000.
110 *Ibid.*
111 Baker, *A Director's Cut*, p. 109.
112 Author's interview with Roy Ward Baker, September 2000.
113 Baker, *A Director's Cut*, p. 91.
114 Author's interview with Roy Ward Baker, September, 2000.
115 Samuel Goldwyn Jr, 'Afterword', in Baker, *A Director's Cut*, pp. 164–5.
116 Baker, *A Director's Cut*, p. 109.
117 Baker did not know of J. Arthur Rank's objections for another forty years. Author's interview with Roy Ward Baker, September 2000.
118 See Baker, *A Director's Cut*, p. 110.
119 *Ibid.*
120 Author's interview with Roy Ward Baker, September 2000.
121 Brian McFarlane, *An Autobiography of British Cinema. By the Actors and*

Filmmakers who Made it, London: Methuen, 1997, p. 70.
122 Author's interview with Roy Ward Baker, September 2000.
123 McFarlane, *An Autobiography of British Cinema*, p. 52.
124 Baker, *A Director's Cut*, p. 113.
125 *Ibid.*
126 *Ibid.*, p. 117.
127 *Ibid.*
128 Peter Hutchings, 'Authorship and British Cinema', p. 187.
129 Baker, *A Director's Cut*, p. 123.
130 See Marcus Hearn and Alan Barnes, *The Hammer Story*, London: Titan Books, 1997, p. 129. See also Baker, *A Director's Cut*, pp. 122–5.
131 Baker, *A Director's Cut*, p. 125.
132 Hearn and Barnes, *The Hammer Story*, p. 117.
133 Marcus Hearn, 'Rocket Man', *Hammer Horror*, Number 7, September 1997, p. 18.
134 *Ibid.*, p. 20.
135 'Andrew Keir Interviewed by Stephen Laws', *Little Shoppe of Horrors*, Number 12, April 1994, p. 108.
136 'Barbara Shelley', *Little Shoppe of Horrors*, Number 12, April 1994, p. 102.
137 Cited in an editor's note, in 'Andrew Keir', p. 108.
138 Hearn and Barnes, *The Hammer Story*, p. 93.
139 See Jimmy Sangster, *Do You Want It Good or Tuesday? From Hammer Films to Hollywood! A Life in the Movies*, Baltimore: Midnight Marquee Press, 1997, p. 96.
140 Hearn and Barnes, *The Hammer Story*, p. 119.
141 Sangster, *Do You Want It Good or Tuesday?*, p. 99.
142 Hearn and Barnes, *The Hammer Story*, p. 119.
143 Sangster, *Do You Want It Good or Tuesday?*, p. 101.
144 *Ibid.*
145 *Ibid.*
146 *Ibid.*
147 Hearn and Barnes, *The Hammer Story*, p. 119.
148 See I.Q. Hunter (ed.), *British Science Fiction Cinema*, London: Routledge, 1999.
149 Hearn and Barnes, *The Hammer Story*, p. 128.
150 Michael Carreras was the son of James Carreras, co-founder of Hammer. *Moon Zero Two* shares some of the self-reflexive, and facile, tendencies of other films scripted and produced by Carreras – such as *Prehistoric Women* (1968).
151 Baker, *A Director's Cut*, p. 129.
152 Clementine is the heroine in John Ford's western *My Darling Clementine* (1946).
153 For a more comprehensive, and less critical, view see Hunter, *British Science Fiction Cinema*.
154 Author's interview with Roy Ward Baker, September 2000.
155 Sangster, *Do You Want It Good or Tuesday?*, pp. 103–10.
156 *Ibid.*, p. 110.
157 *Ibid.*
158 *Ibid.*
159 *Ibid.*, p. 111.
160 Such as *The Spy Who Came In from the Cold* (1965) and *The Ipcress File* (1965).
161 Summerfield was Alastair Sim's secretary in the parody of the hard-boiled conventions in *Laughter in Paradise* (1951).
162 'Harry Fine Interviewed by Richard Klemensen', *Little Shoppe of Horrors*, Number 4, May 1984, p. 39.
163 'Tudor Gates Interviewed by Bruce G. Hallenbeck'. *Little Shoppe of Horrors*. Number 4, May 1984, p. 43.
164 'Tudor Gates', p. 43.

165 Comprising Harry Fine, Michael Style and Tudor Gates.
166 'Harry Fine', p. 39.
167 Author's interview with Roy Ward Baker, September, 2000.
168 *Ibid.*
169 Baker, *A Director's Cut*, p. 129.
170 Author's interview with Roy Ward Baker, September, 2000.
171 Baker, *A Director's Cut*, p. 130.
172 Hearn and Barnes, *The Hammer Story*, p. 137.
173 *Ibid.*
174 *Ibid.*
175 *Ibid.*, p. 136.
176 Pitt's date of birth has been variously recorded as 1937, 1943 and 1945.
177 See 'Ingrid Pitt by Greg Turnbull', *Little Shoppe of Horrors*, Number 4, May 1984, pp. 62–3.
178 'Harry Fine', p. 39.
179 'Ingrid Pitt', pp. 65–6.
180 Bruce Hallenbeck, on the other hand, argues that the film is deliberately crude and is, in effect, *Varney the Vampire*, 'the old penny dreadful novel from 1847, all dressed up with fangs bared. It's that, and it's a bit of HORROR OF DRACULA/ DRACULA PRINCE OF DARKNESS and a lot of the old Universal monster movies'. See Bruce G. Hallenbeck, 'Scars of Dracula', *Little Shoppe of Horrors*, Number 13, November 1996, p. 113.
181 Author's interview with Roy Ward Baker, September 2000.
182 'Roy Ward Baker Interviewed by John Stoker', *Little Shoppe of Horrors*, Number 13, November 1996, p. 116.
183 Quoted in Hallenbeck, 'Scars of Dracula', p. 110.
184 Quoted in Aida Young, 'Three's a Crowd: SCARS OF DRACULA', *Little Shoppe of Horrors*, Number 13, November 1996, p. 115.
185 Quoted in Hallenbeck, 'Scars of Dracula', p. 111.
186 Quoted in *Ibid.*, p. 108.
187 *Ibid.*
188 *Ibid.*
189 *Ibid.*, p. 109.
190 Hearn and Barnes, *The Hammer Story*, p. 139.
191 Baker, *A Director's Cut*, p. 134.
192 Quoted in Hearn and Barnes, *The Hammer Story*, p. 148.
193 Baker, *A Director's Cut*, p. 134.
194 Publicity photos were released showing Peter Cushing handing over his most famous role to Bates.
195 Also known as Martine Beswicke.
196 Also known as *Prehistoric Women*, the film was not released until 1968.
197 Baker, *A Director's Cut*, p. 135.
198 See Hearn and Barnes, *The Hammer Story*, p. 149.
199 See *ibid.*, p. 150.
200 Milton Subotsky chose 'Amicus' because it means 'friendly'. See Chris Knight, 'The Amicus Empire', *Cinefasntastique*, Volume 2, Number 4, summer 1973, p. 7.
201 See Peter Hutchings, 'The Amicus House of Horror', in Steve Chibnall and Julian Petley (eds), *British Horror Cinema*, London: Routledge, 2002, p. 135.
202 In 1953, for example, Terence Fisher directed two episodes – 'The Surgeon' and 'Take a Number' – and Charles Sanders one – 'The Scream' – which were combined and released as a feature film, *Three's a Company*.
203 See Knight, 'The Amicus Empire', pp. 5–7.
204 *Ibid.*, p. 9.

205 Ibid.
206 Author's interview with Roy Ward Baker, September, 2000.
207 Baker, A Director's Cut, p. 137.
208 Chris Knight, 'And Now the Screaming Starts!', Cinefantastique, Volume 2, Number 4, summer 1973, p. 6.
209 Ibid.
210 Baker, A Director's Cut, p. 137.
211 See Knight, 'The Amicus Empire', p. 16.
212 Ibid.
213 Ibid., p. 15.
214 To capitalise on the success of Tales From the Crypt, Baker's film was reissued as Tales From the Crypt Part II. Also, some sources cite, incorrectly, Baker's original title as Vault of Horror instead of The Vault of Horror.
215 See Knight, 'The Amicus Empire', p. 17.
216 Ibid., p. 16.
217 Ibid., p. 17.
218 The Satanic Rites of Dracula was not a major financial success, especially after Warner Bros decided against releasing the film in the United States.
219 Hearn and Barnes, The Hammer Story, p. 134.
220 Author's interview with Roy Ward Baker, September, 2000.
221 Baker, A Director's Cut, p. 139.
222 Author's interview with Roy Ward Baker, September, 2000.
223 Baker, A Director's Cut, p. 139.
224 Hearn and Barnes, The Hammer Story, p. 165.
225 Baker, A Director's Cut, p. 140.
226 Hearn and Barnes, The Hammer Story, p. 165.
227 Ibid.
228 See, for example, The Mummy (1959), where there is an extended debate between Peter Cushing and an Egyptian nationalist concerning the moral authority of the British to plunder Egyptian artefacts.
229 See The Abominable Snowman (1957), The Plague of the Zombies (1966), and The Reptile (1966). I.Q. Hunter, 'The Legend of the Seven Golden Vampires', Postcolonial Studies, Volume 3, Number 1, p. 86. See also David Pirie, A Heritage of Horror: The English Gothic Cinema, London: Gordon Fraser, 1973, p. 124.
230 Hunter, 'The Legend of the Seven Golden Vampires', p. 85.
231 Ibid.
232 Tom Johnson and Deborah Del Vecchio, Hammer Films: An Exhaustive Filmography, Jefferson, NC: McFarland and Company, 1996, p. 372.
233 Marcus Hearn and Alan Barnes argue that The Legend of the Seven Golden Vampires, Shatter (1974), and To the Devil a Daughter (1976) were all 'expensive failures'. See Hearn and Barnes, The Hammer Story, p. 135.
234 Other changes included reducing Van Helsing's address to the students, and taking Kah's visit to Dracula's castle and inserting it into a less appropriate sequence later in the film.
235 Baker, A Director's Cut, p. 140.
236 Ibid., p. 141.
237 Ibid.
238 Author's interview with Roy Ward Baker, September 2000.
239 See Baker, A Director's Cut, p. 150.

'Realism' – *Flame in the Streets* and *A Night to Remember*

Realism is my forte[1]

After meeting with Alan Sillitoe late in 1958, Roy Baker recommended to the Rank Organisation that they buy the rights to Sillitoe's novel *Saturday Night and Sunday Morning*. They agreed. However, when the company's production committee met on 2 December they rejected his proposal, as the book was now considered 'sordid' and 'common'.[2] After he had spent the previous fifteen months developing a series of projects, without getting one off the ground, this rejection was a blow to Baker and left him with little alternative but to reconsider *The Singer Not the Song*.

Baker had been aware that 'change was in the air'[3] for some time, especially after the publication of Kingsley Amis's novel *Lucky Jim* in 1954 and the production of John Osborne's play *Look Back in Anger* in May 1956. He also realised that the top management at Rank was out of touch, as 'there was a reluctance to take risks, not only with money, but also with audience appeal. Anything remotely controversial was a non-starter'.[4] What would have happened to both Rank and Baker if the company had agreed to adapt Sillitoe's novel? It might have resulted in a compromised production such as *The Wild and the Willing* with only a superficial nod to the 'realism' of New Wave films such as *A Taste of Honey* (1961) or *The Loneliness of the Long Distance Runner* (1962). Or, it might have resulted in a film unlike any of the films Baker had directed at Rank or Twentieth Century-Fox.

Jeffrey Richards suggests that *Saturday Night and Sunday Morning* would have been a suitable project for Baker as, together with one of his other submissions, *The Long and the Short and the Tall*, both were 'in his favoured realist mode'.[5] Richards also includes *A Night to Remember* within this 'realist mode'. I am not so sure. The 'realism' of *A Night to Remember* and the 'realism' of Karel Reisz's *Saturday Night and Sunday*

Morning are not the same kind of 'realism'. Each is predicated upon a different set of cultural and moral assumptions which affect the structure of each film.

Many factors affect a feature film. One is the institutional context, and Reisz's film was produced by an independent company, Woodfall Films, eager to challenge the conservatism of the British film industry, especially the type of film that Rank was associated with in the 1940s and 1950s. Reisz came from a different film culture and different time from Baker. Baker gained his early education from masters of the classical cinema – such as Carol Reed, Alfred Hitchcock and Robert Stevenson – at Islington in the 1930s. This was refined by his experiences at AKS during the war and his early features for Two Cities/Rank and Twentieth Century-Fox. He was a product of the British and Hollywood studio system, a fact he freely acknowledges. From 1947 to 1961 he directed films for two major film organisations: Rank (and companies owned or associated with Rank such as Two Cities) and Twentieth Century-Fox.[6] While he was unhappy about the attitude of some of the departmental heads at Pinewood, he was content to be working within the studio system – both in Britain and the United States. He was pleased with his three years in the Hollywood system: 'I had done some good work and it certainly turned me into a professional instead of a gifted amateur'.[7]

Reisz, along with Lindsay Anderson and Tony Richardson, was a key figure in the Free Cinema movement that emerged in Britain the 1950s, a movement that came out of the Royal Court Theatre.[8] Reisz thought of *Saturday Night and Sunday Morning* as a part of this movement and an extension of his earlier film *We Are the Lambeth Boys* (1958). Unlike Baker, Reisz, Richardson and other proponents of Free Cinema did not have the desire to make big-budget films for the international market at Pinewood or Elstree.[9] *A Night to Remember*, on the other hand, was financed as part of Rank's policy, announced in 1956, of only producing films with 'international appeal': films that could be 'vigorously sold in foreign markets'.[10] Both men also differed in their conception of, or at least emphasis on, what constitutes a 'film director'. While Reisz, and other Free Cinema proponents, emphasised the aesthetic dimension,[11] Baker rejected any notion of 'personal style' or even that he had a personal style of filmmaking.[12] His attitude was that filmmaking was a collaborative effort with the director a part, a key part, of the team.[13]

Although he was denied the opportunity to adapt *Saturday Night and Sunday Morning*, he did direct a 'social problem' film: *Flame in the Streets* (1961). This film, together with his most prestigious film, *A Night to Remember*, provides an insight into Baker's form of 'realism'. Jeffrey

Richards considers the latter film a 'docu-drama' with its 'adopted ... style of sober realism from his previous films',[14] While he proposes a strict dichotomy between the 'realism' of Baker's version and the 'melodrama' of other versions of this story, I propose to show how the 'realism' of Baker's films was at the service of a more pervasive presentation of melodrama.

Peter Hutchings, in his essay on realism in the British cinema in the late 1950s and early 1960s, 'Beyond the New Wave', argues that 'in the case of the pre-1959 genre films of Baker, [Val] Guest, [John] Guillermin and [J. Lee] Thompson, there is an intermittent engagement with realist practices and themes, which predates and in many ways anticipates the realism of the New Wave films'.[15] Hutchings notes that 'just about every ambitious British film-maker', including Baker, Bryan Forbes, Guy Green, Guest, Guillermin and Lee Thompson, 'seized upon the possibilities offered by the new realism as an appropriate way of forwarding their own professional aspirations'.[16] Although he does not specify the exact nature of these 'realist practices and themes', and how they relate to the New Wave films, his essay suggests a more dialectical concept involving the interrelationship between realism and genre/melodrama. Instead of perpetuating the notion that 'realism' denotes a singular style, such as Richards's view of *A Night to Remember* as 'documentary authenticity',[17] it is more accurate to view realism in such films as multiple and heterogeneous, and the 'realist' practices in *A Night to Remember* and *Flame in the Streets* as another way of rendering life as morally legible.

If, as Linda Williams argues, the film invites us to 'feel sympathy for the virtues of beset victims, if the narrative trajectory is ultimately concerned with a retrieval and staging of virtue through adversity and suffering, then the operative mode is melodrama'.[18] Melodrama, however, does not just reside in simple, or theatrical, representations of these goals. As Peter Brooks shows in his study of the melodramatic imagination of the fiction of Henry James, melodrama can be found in works 'thought to represent the height of subtlety and psychological realism'.[19] As in *A Night to Remember* and *Flame in the Streets*, but not *Saturday Night and Sunday Morning*.[20]

Saturday Night and Sunday Morning (1960)

After J. Arthur Rank returned the rights of *Saturday Night and Sunday Morning* to Sillitoe, they were purchased by producer Joseph Janni. However, when he was unable to obtain financial backing, Woodfall

Films acquired them and Reisz was selected to direct. Prior to this Reisz had been involved in the Free Cinema screenings at the National Film Theatre. One of the last films to be shown was Reisz's *We Are the Lambeth Boys* which recorded the visit of a young cricket team to a public school. The idea of the film, he explains, was to 'give screen time to people and events that had not been seen on the screen ... I felt it was worthwhile to have a five-minute sequence of the boys horsing around in the yard, knocking a cricket ball around in the nets. I thought it was interesting. We wanted to start from observation of the contemporary world.'[21]

Narrative causality is not an important aspect of this film. It is also, relatively, unimportant in *Saturday Night and Sunday Morning*, a film that Alan Lovell describes as 'almost an anti-style' because the camera 'does only enough work to tell the story as simply and directly as possible. Because of this, the audience is encouraged to make judgments for itself'.[22]

The film begins with the camera sweeping across the production line at the Raleigh Bike factory in Nottingham and picks out Arthur Seaton (Albert Finney) working at his lathe. Seaton's voice-over:

> Nine hundred and fifty four, nine hundred and fifty bloody five, another few more and that's the lot for Friday [a factory supervisor hands him an envelope]. Fourteen pounds, three and tuppence for a thousand of these a day. No wonder I've always got a bad back, though I'll soon be done. I'll have a fag in a bit. No use working every minute God sends. I could get through in half of the time if I worked like a bull. Though they'd only slash my wages so they can get stuffed! Don't let the bastards grind you down, that's one thing I've learned ... I'd like to see anybody try to grind me down, that'd be the day! What I'm out for is a good time. All the rest is propaganda.

Seaton is interested only in his own pleasure. He does not change as he shows little affection or interest in the welfare of his fellow workers, family or girlfriends. While Seaton's father is mesmerised by television, his son takes sadistic delight in drinking a sailor under the table at the pub, placing a dead rat on the bench of a female worker and firing a pellet into the broad backside of his nemesis, the local gossip Mrs Bull (Edna Morris). While selfishly pursuing Brenda (Rachel Roberts), the wife of a fellow worker, Jack (Bryan Pringle), he also chases after Doreen (Shirley Anne Field), a local girl.

Arthur derives as much pleasure from deceiving Jack as he does from sex with Jack's wife. He tells his friend Bert (Norman Rossington) that it 'serves him [Jack] right for being so slow'. When Brenda informs Seaton that she is pregnant, his immediate response is that it will ruin his fun that night ('What a wonderful Friday night!'). Later, when she realises that Arthur is losing interest in her, Brenda tells him:

BRENDA: You know the trouble with you. You don't know the difference between right and wrong. I don't think you ever will
ARTHUR: Maybe I won't. But I don't want anyone to teach me either!
BRENDA: You'll learn one day
ARTHUR: We'll see.

Finally, after a beating from Jack's brothers, Arthur leaves Brenda to concentrate on Doreen, who is less carefree with her sexual favours. The film closes on an indeterminate note, with Arthur and Doreen on a hill overlooking the city planning their future. Arthur realises that his options in life are limited and that he is about to become one of the 'fish' who gets caught in the end because they can't 'keep their chops off the bait'. But he also retains his contempt for the working class who are 'dead from the neck up', content with a television set and a packet of fags. His final act of defiance takes the form of a symbolic gesture as he throws a stone at a neat, sterile house, with a bathroom – the type of house that he may soon be living in. Unlike Sillitoe's novel, Arthur is never presented as a victim in the film.[23] When he warns Doreen that this won't be the last stone he throws, his regeneration is not presented as a likely outcome. Nor does the narrative structure of the film ever assume that it should be.

Flame in the Streets (1961)

By 1961 even Rank, as John Hill notes, 'had jumped on the social problem/ realism bandwagon with productions of its own like *Flame in the Streets* (1961) and *The Wild and the Willing* (1962).'[24] Yet, as Peter Hutchings argues, film realism is an elusive concept as it dates and 'inevitably gives itself up to its own deconstruction and reinterpretation'.[25] A more useful concept is verisimilitude, or regimes of verisimilitude – various systems and forms of plausibility, motivation and belief. Verisimilitude means 'probable', 'plausible' or 'likely' and it 'entails notions of propriety, of what is appropriate and therefore probable'.[26] Steve Neale, drawing upon concepts developed by Tzvetan Todorov, distinguishes between two types of verisimilitude: generic verisimilitude and cultural verisimilitude. Neither equates in any direct sense with 'reality' or 'truth'. Cultural verisimilitude, as Todorov argues, is a discourse based on what the public believes to be true.[27]

Realism, or realism as an ideology, can 'partly be defined by its refusal to recognize the reality of its own generic status, or to acknowledge its own adherence to a type of generic verisimilitude'.[28] There are, for example, less obvious references in Reisz's film to any system of generic verisimilitude, while *Flame in the Streets* and *A Night to Remember* draw upon familiar character types and dramatic devices such as pathos and suspense.

The claim of the New Wave films to 'realism' stems, initially at least, from their subject matter, the Midlands and north of England locations and their focus on the working class. These films were not populated by a sentimentalised working class but aggressively anti-establishment figures. There was also a more explicit presentation of sex and other topics that had been heavily censored in the past.[29] To this list Robert Murphy adds 'psychologically rounded characters'.[30]

Flame in the Streets shares some of these characteristics. The film's 'shocking' subject matter (inter-racial sex and marriage), together with its focus on working-class people and trade-union policies, would, seemingly, qualify it as a New Wave film. Although Robert Murphy includes an extended analysis in his chapter on the British realist tradition in *Sixties British Cinema*,[31] it seems to have been ignored and rarely, if ever, is seen as part of this cycle.[32] Perhaps the film's meloramatic context discouraged its inclusion.

The film, scripted by veteran television and film writer Ted Willis,[33] had its genesis in Willis's 1958 stage play *Hot Summer Night*.[34] The British critics immediately categorised it as a social problem movie. Isabel Quigley, for example, began her 30 June 1961 review in *The Spectator* by outlining the characteristics of this genre:

> The British sociological film, which first appeared as we now know it in the war and then seemed amazingly fresh, bright and pointed, is now firmly – in fact immovably – established: recipe plain-to-stodgy, final taste perfectly predictable; progressive but 'sensible' and all points of view given an airing. First and foremost, it has a Problem (intolerance, colour, crime) and the people are there to illustrate it ... The family will live in a mean, small street and the interiors will look carefully right, halfheartedly comic relief being provided by older members ... It is advertised as searing, thought-provoking, blisteringly out-spoken, but its impact is mild ...
>
> Roy Baker's *Flame in the Streets* ('A' Certificate) runs so true to type that you can tell from the word go what will happen ...
>
> The action takes place on Guy Fawkes night against a background of rockets and incipient riot. The background will be familiar to everyone, if not from life at least from documentary views of it ... With the obvious visual comparison between the outward and inward flames and fireworks Roy Baker does well ... In fact it has a good deal to recommend

it – seriousness, spirit, an observant eye: if only it wasn't just like its predecessors, so painstakingly explicit, so flatfooted.

Eve Perrick also emphasised the film's 'sociological' basis of 'projecting a problem' in her review for the *Daily Mail* (22 June 1961) while others, such as Felix Barker in the *Evening News* 22 June 1961), under the heading 'Would You Let Your Daughter Marry a Negro?' and Thomas Wiseman in the *Sunday Express* ('It's Mr. Mills versus the anticolour brigade', 25 June 1961), emphasised its 'controversial' subject matter. Similarly, Paul Dehn in the *Daily Herald* (23 June 1961) took this aspect even further with the heading 'This terrifying and ferocious film'. Dehn notes that words 'like "nigger", "black bastard" and "whore" repeatedly jolt one like an uppercut. A mother ... confesses that the thought of her daughter ... in bed with a Negro makes her want to vomit'. Dehn also praised Baker's contribution ('for once' Roy Baker directed a film 'worthy of his high talent'), as did Alexander Walker in the *Evening Standard* (22 June 1961), although he also criticised the film's 'muzzy sentiment'. Walker praised Peter Lincoln's forceful rebuff of Jacko Palmer's (John Mills) attempt to dissuade him from marrying Kathie on the grounds that 'even Negroes resent mixed marriages ... Come the pitiless reply: "Yes, we have had good teachers"'. Walker claimed that it was a 'pity that all of the film is not so resolutely unsentimental'.

While Walker believed the film's pathos weakened the film, the *Times* reviewer (23 June 1961) was uncomfortable with its action sequences. He or she concluded that the film was 'a competent piece of sensational journalism, with all of the fatal ambiguity of its kind. It says all the right things, and makes all the right gestures, but at the same time its determination to extract the maximum excitement from a full-scale race riot near the end does undeniably undermine any serious intention it may have and cast the gravest doubts on its maker's sincerity of purpose.' In other words, both Walker and the *Times* reviewer caught a whiff of melodrama in the form of pathos and action.

Both devices, pathos and action, are used in the film to establish the 'victims': a necessary attribute of melodrama. In terms of the film's racial drama, which is only one part of *Flame in the Streets*, Jim Pines argues that the 'representation of blacks as "victims" or "social problems" limits the possibility of developing black characterisations beyond the narrow parameters of this dual stereotype'.[35] Alexander Walker put it another way when he complained: 'And why, oh why, do we never see a bad coloured person. Even the Jamaican slum landlord gets only a gentle beard-singeing from *Flame in the Streets*'.

In the manner of the 'well-made' classical film, it begins with a symbol which resonates throughout the film. This has a 'primacy effect'[36] in immediately foregrounding the film's dominant theme. After the credits, and the date (5 November), the camera cuts to a close-up of the head of a straw Negro doll. This doll, a clear symbol of persecution and oppression, is used throughout the film and, especially, near the end when it is placed on a Guy Fawkes bonfire. At the start of the film its head merely flops helplessly forward, foreshadowing the film's theme of racial persecution, as two young boys prop it up outside the gates of a Notting Hill Gate furniture factory.

Inside the factory West Indian workers are harmoniously singing 'Whose Living'.[37] A young blonde woman from administration brings papers into this predominantly black male working area and a West Indian worker exchanges a knowing look with her. The light-hearted banter amongst the men continues until it is interrupted by Les (Michael Wynne), the film's villain,[38] and his two white mates who resent the fact that there is a black man (Gomez) in charge. An older generation of white workers in the factory, led by Harry Mitchell (Meredith Edwards) are also opposed to this situation. Mitchell warns another worker that 'one of these days, mate, you'll wake up and find the spades have taken over this place and you'll wonder how it all happened.' Mitchell's prediction is made in the men's toilet to an elderly tradesman standing in front of the urinals, a touch of visual 'realism'. Mitchell repeats his warning to the union secretary, Jacko Palmer (John Mills), that the men won't take orders from a spade. Jacko's refutes Mitchell's claims and resents the term 'spade' to describe Gomez: 'Spade, what kind of word is that?'

While Jacko is defending Gomez at work, his daughter Kathie (Sylvia Syms)[39] goes swimming in the local baths with Peter Lincoln, a Jamaican teacher. Here Mitchell's workplace fears are transformed into the sexual anxieties of black males co-habiting with white females. This is represented by the reaction of a white, middle-aged female attendant who, after watching Kathie and Peter together in the pool, remarks 'that's one thing I do draw the line at'. Prejudice in the film is shown to be both economic and sexual and the two strands come together in the treatment of Gomez and his white wife Judy (Ann Lynn). The problems they face anticipate the opposition Kathie and Peter will encounter.[40] Late in the film, as Kathie searches for Peter, the two women meet and Judy describes the difficulties in living with a black man in British society at that time: 'I just wished there was somewhere in this world where Gabe and me had the right to be happy'.

Interestingly, *Flame in the Streets* assimilates this social problem into a family melodrama involving Jacko and his wife Nell (Brenda de Banzie). Her anxiety for Kathie is embedded in her own domestic unhappiness as the film gradually shifts its focus from the racial drama to the lost dreams, and lack of fulfilment, of a unionist's wife. Nell has had to repress her material and sexual desires to keep a marriage together for her daughter's sake and she has chosen to live her life through Kathie. When she discovers that her daughter plans to marry a West Indian, she feels her sacrifice has been in vain and erupts in a tirade of racial and sexual paranoia. First she warns Kathie that they [West Indians] are 'not like us' as they 'live like animals'. Later, after Jacko has successfully defended Gomez at the union meeting and secured his promotion, Nell loses all control when Jacko fails to persuade Kathie to give up Peter:

> NELL: When I think of you and that black man sharing the same bed!
> KATHIE [*horrified*]: O' Mum!
> NELL: It's filthy! Disgusting! It makes my stomach turn over. I'm going to be sick!
> [KATHIE *starts to leave the room*]
> NELL: You can't wait can you? You're no better than the whores in High Street. You can't wait to be with him, that's the truth. All you want is one thing!
> [JACKO *is horrified at the nature of his wife's outburst*]
> JACKO: Nell!
> [KATHIE *runs down the stairs as her mother follows, screaming after her*]
> NELL: Go with him then, make your bed and lie on it, go to your nigger, go to your nigger!

The film condemns Nell's outburst by cutting from her abuse to the symbolic image of a straw Negro on the bonfire. She is not, however, reduced to a purely negative caricature. Earlier, when Jacko's father tries to alert his son to Nell's unhappiness, Jacko tells him that there are 'more important [union] things to be done'. Later, he is shocked by Nell's outburst and it forces him to reassess his marriage, particularly after his wife tells him that she planned to leave him many times over the years. Nell explains to Jacko that she felt she was only part of the fixtures:' When you [Jacko] came home, you came as a visitor' and 'you made love to me as if it was a quick drink'. 'I wanted', Nell tells him, 'the thought that you couldn't live without me'.

Nell's racial anxieties are not as easily resolved as the worker's economic fears. Jacko overcomes the objections to Gomez's appointment through a mixture of moral principle and economic pragmatism. He reassures his union members that the promotion is both the right thing to do in terms of equity and the right thing to do in term of their own self-interest. If they don't, he warns them, the blacks will form an alternative pool of cheap labour. Similarly, at the end of the film, he is able to convince Nell that he really loves her ('people like you need people like me'). However, he has less success overcoming Nell's anxieties and the final image in the film reflects this uncertainty. After Gomez suffers extensive burns following an attack by white youths at the bonfire, Jacko takes Kathie and Peter back to his house and goes upstairs to reassure Nell that he loves her. Together they walk downstairs to Kathie and Peter and the film concludes on a tentative note, a tableau, as both sides nervously face each other.

To its credit, the film does not present a contrived 'happy' ending with Nell and Kathie reunited. Instead, it reworks a staple device of nineteenth-century theatrical melodrama – the tableau – to document the nervousness (in 1961) to the prospect of marriage between black and white. In this regard it is useful, more than 40 years later, to consider Eve Perrick's response to the film in the *Daily Mail* (22 June 1961), when she claimed that she was on Nell's side 'in everything she said and did'. The film concludes with the camera pulling back to a completely static image of Nell and Jacko on the extreme left-hand side of the frame and Kathie and Peter on the extreme right with a lot of space between them. This melodramatic device, the tableau,[41] is used in the film to provide a 'realistic' ending in the context of 1961. It allows the possibility of a rapprochement between Nell and the Kathie while, visually, pointing to the distance yet to be covered.

A Night to Remember (1958)

Ernest Betts, in his 6 July 1958 (*People*) review of *A Night to Remember*, declared:

> Forget the dimensions of Jayne Mansfield for a moment and consider the anatomy of a smash-hit ... This tremendous picture tells you what movie success is made of ... Take it from me, this story of panic at midnight aboard a mighty ship will panic the box-office. Why do I say this?
> 1. Because it's real – every scene hits you with a deadly and exciting realism.
> 2. Because it's brilliantly acted and directed. Kenneth More stars effectively, but he can't out-star the ship. She's a ship with a ready-made Oscar.
> 3. Because it's big in every way – in emotion, conflict, drama, suspense, action and spectacle. It takes you aboard to the heart of the disaster.

Derek Hill, in the *Tribune* (11 July 1958), was less impressed and his review was titled 'The Titanic won't keep British films off the rocks'. Hill argued that the film was less 'historical realism' and more 'film realism':

> Any film with Roy Baker's name on the directorial credit is guaranteed to be a craftmanlike job. The sheer competence of *A Night to Remember* is perhaps the most striking thing about it ... Yet for all of its accomplishments, *A Night to Remember* is not a success. The reason for its failure seems to me to lie in the great gulf between the years of research that have gone into ensuring that every incident and detail are completely authentic and the conventional approach to the subject.
>
> What is the point of checking on the authenticity of instances of cowardice and heroism if the situations are then written and shot as if they were screen fiction ... it was the job of the director and scriptwriter Eric Ambler to make these moments ring true. If ever a film needed realistic treatment, it was *A Night to Remember*. Instead it was given the most smooth of Pinewood polishes.

It is the difference, and assumptions, between these two reactions that will occupy the rest of this chapter. Most British newspaper reviews agreed with Betts: Dilys Powell in the *Sunday Times* (6 July 1958) argued that it was a 'very good film' and, aside from 'one or two embarrassing moments' near the start, 'Roy Baker's direction makes the final scenes only too real. As a feat of reconstruction this is a brilliant film'; C.A. Lejeune in the *Observer* (6 July 1958) praised the film and the fact that 'Roy Baker handles his huge work of direction like a veteran, and I doubt if Eric Ambler has ever written a more nicely calculated screenplay. As a clean-cut, unbiased, dramatic presentation of a momentous fact in history, the British film seldom did a better job than this'. David Robinson in the *Financial Times* (7 July 1958), on the other hand, responded to the film's distinctive style, which he thought was a 'kind of impressionist staged documentary, making its effect through a fragmentary collection of reconstructed incidents'.

Less impressed was Hollis Alpert in the *Saturday Review* (10 December 1958), who wondered why the British were so interested in another version of the story ('Not the *Titanic* again!') while Philip Oakes in the *Sunday Despatch* (6 July 1958) declared his dislike for 'prestige films' such as *A Night to Remember* and rated the film 'worthy, well-meant and dull'. William Whitebait in the *New Statesman* (12 July 1958) was not impressed with the film's realism, and while he conceded that the 'whole action, with the people responsible and the ships concerned, has been depicted with fair accuracy', the film 'falls short of the realism such a film demands'.

The 'London Film Critic' of the *Manchester Guardian* (5 July 1958) reiterated the prevailing ethos at this time as regards 'realism' and 'melodrama' when she or he argued that the film 'does not reduce itself to melodrama: it covers a multitude of factual aspects of the disaster and, to some extent at least, it individualises a great many of the 3,000 or so people who were on board. It does not melodramatise or unduly sentimentalise but allows the drama to develop, as it were, of its own true and considerable impetus'.

Derek Hill's review, unlike many others, does not confuse the 'years of research that have gone into ensuring that every incident and detail are completely authentic' with 'realism'. 'Reality', for most critics, was vaguely related to the film's 'documentary' style, which, in turn, was somehow associated with the film's 'plainness' and lack of 'star treatment' (*Manchester Guardian*). Hill, on the other hand, detected the classical style in his criticism of the film for having 'the most smooth of Pinewood polishes'.

Jeffrey Richards reiterates many of the assumptions of the reviewers, especially the *Manchester Guardian*, in his comparative study of *A Night to Remember* as the 'definitive *Titanic* film'.[42] He emphasises the film's 'sober realism' and 'documentary authenticity' as a way of differentiating it from other versions, which he classifies under the broad category as 'romantic melodramas'. Richards concludes that *A Night to Remember* is, like 'all films, ... a product of its times but in its innate integrity, documentary authenticity, emotional truthfulness and celebration of heroic stoicism it transcends its own period to become timeless and universal.'[43]

Richards, similar to the *Manchester Guardian* critic in 1958, juxtaposes 'realism' and 'melodrama'[44] as the basis for his comparison as if the meaning of these terms is unequivocally clear and singular. He even refers to Baker's film as a 'docu-drama' and a 'neo-realist classic'.[45] To justify this claim Richards refers to the 'code of conduct for documentaries laid down by [Alberto] Cavalcanti in 1948. Yet this 'code' is little more than a sweeping set of stylistic suggestions that do little to differentiate between the style of British documentaries and the aesthetic norms that David Bordwell has argued as central to the classical Hollywood feature film.[46] Cavalcanti's advice included such broad suggestions as '[do] not forget when you are filming, each take is part of a sequence and each sequence is part of the whole: the most beautiful take, taken out of place, is worse than the most banal', '[do] not invent camera angles when they are not necessary: gratuitous angles are distracting, and destroy emotion' and '[do] not be confused in your argument: a truthful subject should be told with clarity and simplicity'.

Although Richards, and the *Manchester Guardian* critic, do not specify what constitutes a 'melodrama', there is a clear indication that it is seen as a different, and inferior, mode. Richards notes, for example, in his comparison of the British reaction to Baker's film and the response to 1953 Hollywood film *Titanic*: 'What runs through the reviews is a demand for factual authenticity, a distaste for melodrama and in some cases an undisguised hostility towards Hollywood for tampering with the facts of the tragedy that was felt to be common property of the audience'.[47] This, in turn, is consistent with the way Roger Manvell assumed a hierarchy involving realism and melodrama in his 1947 essay, which argued that there was a distinct shift in the British film industry in the period from 1942 to 1945 as 'real war subjects', as 'distinct from ... melodramas', took over.[48]

Manvell, Richards and the *Manchester Guardian* critic perceive film melodrama as an elementary, contrived, excessive mode of cinema. There is some basis to this perception as the mode developed during the late eighteenth century in France before spreading to Germany, Britain, America and other areas in the early years of the nineteenth century. This simple mode was defined by its clear demarcation between good and evil and the eventual triumph of virtue. It was also characterised by its three main characters – hero, heroine and villain – and an excessive, expressive hyperbolic aesthetic involving a clear emotional 'rhythm' between high and low points in the drama as pathos, action, coincidence, sudden reversals, and other devices were employed to retrieve innocence and virtue.[49] These conventions, popularised by the 10-20-30 cent theatres in the United States and Drury Lane in Britain in the 1890s and early 1900s, were readily assimilated into the cinema in the sensational melodramas of the nickelodeon boom in the early twentieth century.[50]

Another, subtler, form of melodrama that appealed to middle-class audiences also developed in the latter half of the nineteenth century. It was known by various names, such as the 'well-made melodrama'[51] or the 'modified melodrama'.[52] This form of melodrama incorporated 'well-made' aesthetic values and techniques, such as compositional unity and causal coherence, elements that also characterised the classical feature film after 1917.[53]

This awareness of both the significance of melodrama and its mutation into more sophisticated forms accompanied its critical rehabilitation by literary and theatre critics in the 1960s.[54] Later, in 1974, Brooks's study of Balzac and James, two writers not commonly associated with the lowbrow excesses of nineteenth-century theatrical melodrama, clarified the aesthetic and cultural significance of melodrama as a 'peculiarly modern form'[55] that underpins much of popular culture.[56] Still later Steve Neale, Christine Gledhill, Linda Williams and others reiterated the significance of this mode in terms of the cinema and the fact that it was never a singular genre. Instead 'melodrama, in all its guises, was both a fundamental pro-genitor of nearly all of Hollywood's non-comic genres, and a fundamental source of many of its cross-generic features, devices and conventions' (Neale),[57] a 'genre-producing machine' (Gledhill),[58] and the 'dominant form of popular moving-picture narrative' which 'drives the production of a great variety of familiar film genres' (Williams).[59] Nor should it be perceived as the opposite of realism, as Richards and the *Manchester Guardian* critic assume. Melodrama frequently 'decks itself out in the latest trappings of realism in order to command recognition of the world it represents'[60] as it strives to gain the 'imprimatur of realism'.[61]

Baker's films are located within this mode – including *A Night to Remember*. The 'realism' of this film, and *Flame in the Streets*, differs from the 'realism' of *Saturday Night and Sunday Morning*. The moral legibility of Baker's films is the same as the emotional and moral registers of melodrama. However subtly rendered, it is the world of victims and pathos.

Pathos in *A Night to Remember*

Pathos is an integral aspect of *A Night to Remember*. In some ways, it is inevitable that this is the case as the basic story involves the deaths of 1490 people who did not deserve to die. The dramatic situation is essentially what Brooks calls a drama, or logic, of the 'excluded middle', the 'very logic of melodrama'.[62] The story is one of a fight for survival against enormous odds. This leaves very little space for moral relativity as it involves victims who are placed 'at the point of intersection of primal ethical forces ... [so] as to confer on the character's enactments a charge of meaning'.[63] It is, above all else, a story of bravery and victims – victims of the elements, victims of class prejudice, victims of national arrogance and hubris, and victims of fate. This last facet, victims of fate, is central to *A Night to Remember* as the film constantly reminds the audience that many people would have been saved if the *Californian*, which was within viewing distance of the stricken liner, had been able to comprehend its distress messages. Instead, it was left to the *Carpathia*, more than four hours away, to come to its rescue. But for 1490 people it was too late, a motif reiterated in different ways throughout the film.

Pathos, as Williams notes, 'involves us in assessing suffering in terms of our privileged knowledge of its nature and causes'.[64] We, the audience, know what is going to happen and this produces the 'elicitation of a powerful feeling of pity'.[65] This, pathos, according to Aristotle, is a 'sort of pain at an evident evil of a destructive or painful kind in the case of somebody who does not deserve it, the evil being one which we might imagine to happen to ourselves'.[66] It consists of two related parts – 'a kind of visceral physical sensation triggered by the perception of moral injustice against an undeserving victim' which 'touches on the sense in which pathos requires identification', thereby provoking a degree of self-pity.[67] This conception, argues Ben Singer, 'affirms the degree to which the power of pathos derives from a process of emotional identification or, perhaps more accurately, of association, whereby spectators superimpose their own life (melo) dramas onto the ones being represented in the narrative'.[68]

Mostly, as in *A Night to Remember*, it exploits the audience's powerlessness by provoking a 'sense of loss' and it often occurs when 'what one character knows is reconciled with what another knows, but "too late". In death scenes, for example, tears unite us not to the victim who dies but to the survivors who recognize the irreversibility of time'.[69] Even Derek Hill, who disliked *A Night to Remember*, admits that, on an emotional level, it had an effect: 'Curiously, some of the film's most moving moments – and from time to time it is genuinely moving – succeed, despite this weakness. The farewell of a wife and her three children to her husband is handled in an almost theatrical manner, yet it remains strangely touching.'

This is a reference to the film's most sentimental scene as Robert Lucas (John Merivale) attempts to persuade his wife and children to leave the ship knowing that he will, most likely, never see them again. Earlier in the night Lucas had sought Thomas Andrews (Michael Goodliffe), the ship's designer, for the truth concerning the ship's real situation. After reassuring Andrews that he 'is not the panicking kind', the designer tells Lucas that there is only an hour before the *Titanic* will sink. Lucas returns to his family but does not convey this information to his wife (Honor Blackman). Later he escorts them to the deck and tries to deflect the seriousness of the situation by casually telling his wife that cousin Henry will be angry as the *Titanic* will be two days late in reaching New York. However, this ruse fails and his wife realises the true situation and tells him that she is not going into the lifeboat. Robert replies that it 'is only a matter of form for you and the children to go first'. Reluctantly she agrees and Robert kisses his sleeping son on the forehead with the farewell 'Goodbye, my dear son' before handing him into the boat. Although Lucas never sees his family again, as he dies when the ship sinks, the film returns to this moment at the end by showing the (Lucas) family rocking horse floating in the water.

This is only one example of pathos in the film. After Captain Smith yells 'abandon ship', an elderly steward is shown comforting a little boy. Although he reassures the child that they will find his mother, the audience knows that mother and child will never be reunited. The film cuts back to the steward and the boy a number of times before the ship finally disappears under the water. On one occasion the steward warns panicking passengers to keep clear of the child. Significantly, the last image on the ship before it sinks is the steward with his coat wrapped around the little boy.

Similarly, the honeymooners, Mr and Mrs Clarke, who appear regularly throughout the film, decide to stay together and they die when a funnel falls on them as they flounder in the cold sea. Pathos is also the dominant emotion in the final scenes involving bandmaster Wallace Hartley and his decision to stay on the ship. When members of his band re-join him, and they play 'Nearer, My God to Thee', the film exploits the sentimental basis of this situation by showing the distressed reaction of the passengers in the boats. As the ship sinks, Hartley's music is heard on the soundtrack. The film's final images reiterate this sense of 'too late'. As the survivors return (on the *Carpathia*) to the place where the *Titanic* sank, they (and the audience) see a cello floating in the water (a reminder of the Hartley's heroic gesture), a baby's crib and the rocking horse that belonged to Robert Lucas and his family.

A Night to Remember: a social problem film?

Baker's film remained, within the limitations of a commercial feature film, faithful to its source, Walter Lord's best-selling book.[70] Lord's book included a reconstructed log of the main events of the ship's maiden voyage[71] and a complete passenger list divided by class with italics to indicate those who survived. Lord interviewed sixty-three survivors and studied the reports of the official enquiry. Ambler's script even reproduced verbatim some of the dialogue from Lord's book. This sense of 'authenticity' is reinforced by the film's low-key style and the stoic reaction of the passengers and crew to the disaster which, Richards argues, gives an 'overwhelmingly British feel to the film'.[72] This sense is complemented by the absence of any romantic relationships and the decision to simulate the narrative structure of Lord's book, and not just concentrate on two or three characters or stars. MacQuitty and Baker also stressed the film's attention to detail whereby Alex Vetchinsky, and his assistants at Pinewood, faithfully recreated aspects of the *Titanic*:

'Their scrupulous attention to detail brought the whole thing to life. The grand staircase was marvellous and the first-class dining-room was exactly like the original. During the scene of lunch at the captain's table we served the same food as on the fatal day.'[73]

Yet the film is neither a catalogue of events and facts nor a totally accurate record as it contains a number of 'mistakes' and alterations to the known facts. These 'mistakes' include relatively unimportant aspects – such as the painting that dominates the screen behind Thomas Andrews in the first-class smoking room: it should have been of Plymouth Harbour but instead it is 'The Approach to the New World'.[74] More significant 'mistakes' include the depiction of the way in which the ship finally sinks beneath the water. James Cameron, with the advantage of recent research, is correct in showing the *Titanic* breaking into two parts before sinking – not the sliding beneath the waves as in Baker's film. Also Violet Jessop, a survivor, complained that there were numerous 'mistakes' in the film, including the fact that she 'begged' costume designer Yvonne Caffin not to put women on board in 'beflowered, beplumed hats of the period as American women (and they were mostly Americans) would never wear street hats on board and look what met your eyes at the Captain's table! Everything except the kitchen stove on their heads!'[75]

A Night to Remember begins with a pre-credit sequence that also has no basis in reality – the film shows a wealthy woman launching the *Titanic*, flanked by Thomas Andrews and White Star chairman J. Bruce Ismay (referred throughout the film only as the 'Chairman'). This is followed by newsreel footage of a liner sliding down the slipway to the water. This was entirely fabricated, as the *Titanic* was launched without any formal ceremony and there was no footage of the launch.[76] Also, the middle-class accent of Kenneth More as Second Officer Charles Herbert 'Bertie' Lightoller was more in keeping with the fact that he was the most prominent character in the film and, hence, the film tried to satisfy the expectations of its target audience. As historian Richard Howells points out, 'Kenneth More's Lightoller ... speaks with "received pronunciation": that is to say, the text-book, middle-class English still associated with radio and television newsreaders ... The character of Lightoller, therefore, has been elevated in class terms, by the use of Kenneth More's middle-class accent'.[77]

A Night to Remember also contained a number of 'composite' characters – such as Murphy (the Irish leader) and the gambler Hoyle, while Sir Cosmo and Lady Duff are presented as Sir Richard and Lady Richard.[78] Other characters lose their American nationality in the film and are transformed into British passengers – including Robert Lucas, his wife and children, honeymooners Mr and Mrs Clarke and the gambler Jay Yates (played by the distinctive British actor Ralph Michael). When questioned as to why he changed Yates from an American to a British gambler who swims away to his death rather than climb into a crowded upturned boat, Roy Baker argued that 'it was a British film made by British artists for a British audience'.[79] Yet, as Richard Howells points out, the sinking of the *Titanic* was a 'truly Anglo-American event' as it 'was a British registered ship, built with American money, captained and sailed by a British crew, and patronized – certainly in first-class – most prominently by American passengers'.[80] While dramatic licence justifies Baker's decision to change the facts and foreground the British experience, it also reinforces the axiom that aesthetic and commercial considerations generally take precedence over historical 'authenticity'.

There is also doubt as to the tune played as the ship sinks. In *A Night to Remember* the 'Horbury' version of 'Nearer, My God, to Thee', written by the British minister John Bacchus Dykes in 1881, is used. Walter Lord's novel, on the other hand, cites the Anglican hymn 'Autumn'. Lord's choice was based on the memory of wireless operator Harold Bride. Jeffrey Richards, on the other hand, argues that no film has ever used the most likely version of 'Nearer, My God, to Thee', which was Sir Arthur Sullivan's 'Propior Deo'. Richards points out that as Wallace Hartley was a devout Methodist, this version was probably used – a thesis supported by his family who were so convinced of this fact that they carved the opening bars of 'Propior Deo' on a monument above Hartley's grave.[81]

In some ways this comparison between the known facts and the film is a pointless exercise as there are always going to be compromises, composite characters, national bias and omissions in adapting any major historical event to a commercial feature film. What is more revealing, and more interesting, is the film's point of view with regard to these 'facts'. Both William MacQuitty and Roy Baker claimed that the film 'had no political agenda'. Baker: 'We had no political agenda. All three [Baker, MacQuitty and Ambler] of us saw it as a chance to do something authentic. It was not a critique, it was a demonstration of class attitudes that everybody accepted at the time.'[82]

Nevertheless, the film contains a clear, if subtle, critique of not only the British class system but also the prevailing ethos which, in its arrogance, caused the deaths of many people. The film emphasises the privileges of class right from the start as representatives of each class begin their journey to board the *Titanic* – Sir Richard and his wife represent the first-class passengers; the honeymooners, the Clarkes, the second class; whilst a group of Irish emigrants, including Murphy, represent the steerage passengers. There is a regular pattern of class comparison throughout the film. In one of the most striking sequences, for example, the film cuts from the Irish emigrants vigorously singing 'We're Off to Philadelphia in the Morning' to a long tracking shot of Sir Richard and his wife walking through the first-class dining room. Later, as the *Titanic* begins to founder, women from first-class are shown boarding the lifeboats while the Irish desperately try to reach the upper deck. Along the way they encounter a number of physical barriers, including a locked door and a steward who tries to block their escape. Eventually they make it to the first-class dining room where Kate, one of Irish women, gasps in awe at the lavish surroundings.

Most of the steerage passengers are doomed. Yet, as the film shows, many of the first-class passengers appear unconcerned, as if the people in steerage were somehow 'different' and less human. This attitude is reinforced in a light-hearted moment soon after the iceberg hits the ship. The steerage passengers, unaware that the ship will soon sink, play an impromptu game of soccer with a large piece of the ice. Their game is watched by a wealthy English couple:

GENTLEMAN: Oh, well-played sir! [he is excited by the spectacle] I say, let's go down and join the fun!
WOMAN: But *they're* steerage passengers!

Later, as the situation becomes serious, displays of selfishness and irritation from the first-class passengers are more frequent. When a wealthy woman is ordered to assemble on the deck she tells everybody that this is 'tiresome' as 'everybody knows this ship cannot sink'. When news that the ship is sinking becomes widespread the first-class passengers are shown clamouring for their valuables at the purser's office. Later, when most of the women from first class are in lifeboats, and people are dying in the sea, a passenger suggests to Lady Richard (Harriette Johns) that their boat, which is less than half full, should return and pick up people in the water. She responds by refusing the request: 'we're crowded enough as it is. I am most unwell'. This is an important scene. Many more people, including the crew, would have survived if all, or even some, of the half-empty lifeboats had returned to rescue those in the sea – only one boat returned.

As Lady Richard and her husband Sir Richard (Patrick Waddington) are the real-life Sir Cosmo (and Lady) Duff,[83] and, in terms of the film, represent upper-class attitudes, this scene presents a critique of an inequitable social system. The working- and second-class passengers were, by far, the most vulnerable groups on board as most were unable to secure a berth in the lifeboats. While 60 per cent of first-class passengers survived, only 44 per cent second-class and 25 per cent of steerage lived through this disaster.[84]

Lady Richards's selfishness is mirrored by a complaint from another wealthy woman that a sailor is smoking ('People ought to control themselves') – this comment is made when people are dying in the water. The actions of the brash, unpretentious American woman Molly Brown (Tucker McGuire) provides a stark contrast to the pampered, self-indulgent behaviour of her British counterparts. Brown orders the women in her boat to assist in the rowing and later urges the sole sailor in the lifeboat, Quartermaster Hitchens, to go back and pick up people in the sea. Her boat was the only one to return.

The film is also critical of the behaviour of the 'Chairman' (Frank Lawton). Although his name is never disclosed, it is J. Bruce Ismay, Managing Director of the White Star Line. Rank, fearing a libel suit, decided that he should not be named in the film.[85] His selfish behaviour parallels the attitude of the first-class passengers. Symbolically, he represents the cause of the disaster – British hubris. Before the ship hits the iceberg, he is merely a blustering nuisance but afterwards he is an obstacle hindering the safety of the passengers. Lightoller, on more than one occasion, tells him to keep out of the way. One rebuke is so strong that a crewmember comments that there will be trouble when they reach New York. Finally, in direct violation of Captain Smith's orders that women and children must be given preference, Ismay sneaks aboard a lifeboat ahead of the women and children waiting to board. A close-up of an officer supervising the boats registers his disgust at Ismay's action.

Baker, in a 1994 interview, describes the Managing Director of the White Star Line as 'the villain of the piece'.[86] The reason so many people died, the film suggests, was the result of a nation that arrogantly believed it would overcome all obstacles –natural or man-made. This theme is introduced early in the film when a pompous passenger on a train carrying Lightoller and his wife to the ship, objects to Lightoller's joke concerning an advertisement for Vinolia Otto toilet soap for the use of first-class passengers on the *Titanic*. When Lightoller jokingly says 'the rest don't wash, of course', the man (Mr Bull, 'the typical Englishman'), interprets his comments as unpatriotic.

> MR BULL: My wife and I find your sneering remarks in bad taste. Let those who wish to belittle their country's achievements do so in private. Every Britisher is proud of the unsinkable *Titanic*

This is followed by Bull's comment that the 'newspapers say she [*Titanic*] is a veritable floating city, a symbol of progress, of man's final

'REALISM' 89

victory over nature and the elements'. This theme is reiterated late in the film when Lightoller, in a lifeboat, discusses the ramifications of the disaster with Colonel Archibald Gracie (James Dyrenforth):

> LIGHTOLLER: If we had been steaming a few knots slower, or if we sighted that berg a few seconds earlier, we might not even have struck. If we carried enough lifeboats for the size of the ship instead of just enough to meet the regulations, things would have been different again, wouldn't they?
> GRACIE: Maybe, but you have nothing to reproach yourself with. You've done all that any man could and more. You're not [pause], I was going to say, you're not God, Mr Lightoller.
> LIGHTOLLER: No seaman ever thinks he is. I have been at sea since I was a boy, I have been in sail, I've even been shipwrecked before. I know what the sea can do, but this is different.
> GRACIE: Because we hit an iceberg?
> LIGHTOLLER: No! Because we were so sure, because even though it's happened, it's still unbelievable. I don't think I'll ever feel sure again – about anything.

Lightoller's chastened reaction to the disaster, in effect, 'answers' the display of arrogance by John Bull at the start. The ramifications of Bull's attitude were profound, as ultimate responsibility for the enormous loss of life belongs to a society that was so sure of itself that it failed to protect its citizens with sufficient lifeboats. This was compounded by the refusal of the first-class passengers to return to assist people in the water. Although the *Titanic* met the Board of Trade requirement of sixteen lifeboats for a vessel over 10,000 tons, this was not nearly enough to carry its 2201 people to safety.

The film concludes with a printed epilogue, similar to other social problem films as well as the propaganda films produced during the Second World War.[87] These films reminded audiences that the 'problem' addressed in the film was not yet over, that the issue was not yet fully resolved. Similarly, *A Night to Remember* closes with the images of the cello, baby carriage and the rocking horse in the water, (and a lifeguard from the *Titanic*) as the epilogue explains: 'But this is not the end of the story – for their sacrifice was not in vain. Today there are lifeboats for all. Unceasing radio vigil and, in the North Atlantic, the international ice patrol guards the sea lanes making them safe for the peoples of the world.' This epilogue is, in effect, a substitute for melodrama's third act where, as Brooks explains, there is a 'full panoply of violent action which offers a highly physical "acting out" of virtue's liberation from the oppressive efforts of evil'.[88] Because the basic facts of the *Titanic* story were so well known, it was impossible for the film to conclude with a 'happy ending'. Instead, the film tries to show how the lives of those lost in the disaster are 'redeemed' by the fact that 'their sacrifice was not in vain. Today there are lifeboats for all'.

The story of the *Titanic* – 1958 and 1997

The *Titanic* hit a large iceberg at 11.40 pm on 14 April 1912. The ship sank at 2.20 am and the *Carpathia* arrived just after 4.00 am. 1490 people died out of the 2201 on board. It was the greatest maritime disaster in history and it 'sent a thrill of horror round the world'[89] as there were millionaires, celebrities, artists and journalists on a ship that was declared 'unsinkable'. There are five sound feature film versions. *Atlantic* (1929), directed by E.A. Dupont at Elstree; *Titanic* (1943), directed by Herbert Selpin in Germany; *Titanic* (1953), directed by Jean Negulesco in Hollywood; Baker's *A Night to Remember* and James Cameron's 1997 Hollywood version. There are also two made-for-television films: *S.O.S. Titanic* (1979) and *Titanic* (1996). I wish to briefly compare Baker's film with James Cameron's blockbuster.

Both *A Night to Remember* and James Cameron's 1997 version are melodramas, only different kinds of melodrama. Cameron's film, with its transparent desire to intensify the romance between Jack Dawson (Leonardo DiCaprio), an enterprising steerage passenger, and Rose De Witt Bukater (Kate Winslet), an independent-minded passenger from first class, belongs to the tradition of simple nineteenth-century melodrama: what McConachie calls 'traditional melodrama'[90] – with its stock characters, strong emotions and a rigid moral polarisation between the virtuous hero and heroine (Jack and Rose) and the upper-class villain Caledon ('Cal') Hockley. Although the promotional material *emphasised* the extent of the efforts of the filmmakers to ensure 'historical accuracy', the film merely updated melodramatic staples such as spectacle, suspense and romantic intrigue. This included not only the heavily promoted image of the lovers on the bow of the ship, but scenes such as Cal's servant chasing Jack around the ship with a revolver, Rose rescuing Jack by cutting through his handcuffs in the brig as the water is about to engulf them and the spectacle of the *Titanic* floundering in the sea.

A Night to Remember belongs to the tradition of the 'modified melodrama' with its 'well-made' qualities. Excess is minimised, motivation carefully established and stereotypes are less obvious. Importantly, the films were produced nearly forty years apart, in different film cultures, with different target audiences in mind (and, consequently, different values).[91] This difference between the two films is, largely, a matter of style and emphasis and the later film is shaped by the

'REALISM' 91

demands of Hollywood in this era of the blockbuster. Baker's film, on the other hand, reflects the distinctive qualities of the British cinema in the late 1950s, qualities that are characterised by 'good taste', restraint and reticence, or what Jeffrey Richards calls 'sober realism'.[92]

Notes

1 Roy Baker quoted in Richards, *A Night to Remember*, p. 46.
2 Baker, *The Director's Cut*, p. 110.
3 Author's interview with Roy Ward Baker, September 2000.
4 Baker, *The Director's Cut*, pp. 115–16.
5 Richards, *A Night to Remember*, p. 48.
6 *Paper Orchid* was produced by Ganesh, an independent company, which released the film through Columbia British.
7 Baker, *The Director's Cut*, p. 86.
8 See Erik Hedling, 'Lindsay Anderson and the Development of British Art Cinema', in Robert Murphy (ed.), *The British Cinema Book*, London: BFI Publishing, 2001, pp. 241–3.
9 McFarlane, *An Autobiography of British Cinema*, p. 476.
10 Richards, *A Night to Remember*, p. 29.
11 See McFarlane, *An Autobiography of British Cinema*, p. 476.
12 Author's interview with Roy Ward Baker, September 2000.
13 See Baker, *The Director's Cut*, p. 102.
14 Richards, *A Night to Remember*, p. 60.
15 Peter Hutchings, 'Beyond the New Wave: Realism in British Cinema, 1959–1963', in Murphy (ed.), *The British Cinema Book*, pp. 150–1.
16 *Ibid.*, p. 150.
17 See Richards, *A Night to Remember*, p. 114.
18 Williams, *Playing the Race Card*, p. 15.
19 *Ibid.*
20 It would be a mistake to exaggerate the stylistic differences between *Saturday Night and Sunday Morning* and *Flame in the Streets* (and also *A Night to Remember*). As Andrew Higson argues, it is 'important to recognise that part of the realist claim for [*Saturday Night and Sunday Morning* and *A Taste of Honey*] ... is that they are no different from the classical Hollywood film'. See Andrew Higson, 'Space, Place, Spectacle: Landscape and Townscape in the "Kitchen Sink" Film', in Andrew Higson (ed.), *Dissolving Views: Key Writings on British Cinema*, London: Cassell, 1996, pp. 135–6.
21 McFarlane, *An Autobiography of British Cinema*, p. 476.
22 Quoted in Murphy, *Sixties British Cinema*, p. 19.
23 See Reisz's interview in McFarlane, *An Autobiography of British Cinema*, p. 477.
24 John Hill, *Sex, Class and Realism: British Cinema, 1956–1963*, London: British Film Institute, 1986, p. 48.
25 Hutchings, 'Beyond the New Wave', p. 151.
26 See Steve Neale, *Genre and Hollywood*, London: Routledge, 2000, p. 32.
27 See Todorov in *ibid.*
28 See Steve Neale, 'Questions of Genre', *Screen*, Volume 31, Number 1, spring 1990, p. 48.
29 See Hutchings, 'Beyond the New Wave', pp. 146–7.
30 Murphy, *Sixties British Cinema*, p. 34.

31 Ibid., pp. 47–52.
32 This cycle, generally, includes *Room at the Top* (1959), *Look Back in Anger* (1959), *The Entertainer* (1960), *Saturday Night and Sunday Morning* (1960), *A Taste of Honey* (1961), *A Kind of Loving* (1962), *The Loneliness of the Long Distance Runner* (1962) and *This Sporting Life* (1963). Also, *Billy Liar* and *Darling* are sometimes included. See Hutchings, 'Beyond the New Wave', pp. 146–8.
33 Willis created, amongst other television series, the long running *Dixon of Dock Green*, starring Jack Warner.
34 See Murphy, *Sixties British Cinema*, pp. 48–9 for a comparison between the two productions.
35 Jim Pines, 'British Cinema and Black Representations', in Murphy (ed.), *The British Cinema Book*, p. 179.
36 David Bordwell borrows this term from Meir Sternberg to show how the classical cinema 'creates a fixed baseline against which later information is judged'. See Bordwell, Staiger and Thomson, *The Classical Hollywood Cinema*, p. 37.
37 This gives the opening sequence a contrived sense of 'film realism' as opposed, for example, to the opening scene in *Saturday Night and Sunday Morning*.
38 Les is a descendant from the post-war thug, a figure found in many British films of that period – most notably Dirk Bogarde's Tom Riley in *The Blue Lamp* (1950) and James Kerrney's Roy Walsh in *Cosh Boy* (1952).
39 It is a little disconcerting watching John Mills and Sylvia Syms play father and daughter. Three years before *Flame in the Street* Syms was a nurse in J. Lee Thompson's war drama *Ice Cold in Alex*, and during the film she seduces Captain Anson, played by John Mills.
40 This is reinforced by the physical similarities between Ann Lynn and Sylvia Syms. Both are young with similar hair colouring.
41 The tableau in nineteenth-century theatrical melodrama was a key non-verbal device to maximise the audience's emotional response and allow the audience to see 'meanings ... emotions and moral states rendered in clear visible signs'. See Brooks, *The Melodramatic Imagination*, p. 62. It was mostly used at the end of scenes and acts to present the characters' attitudes, which were compositionally arranged and frozen for a moment to give, like an illustrative painting, a visual summary of the emotional situation. See Brooks, *ibid.*, p. 48.
42 See Jeffrey Richards, *A Night to Remember: The Definitive Titanic Film*. Reviewed by Geoff Mayer in *Screening the Past*, issue 15. www.latrobe.edu.au/screeningthepast. Updated 2 July 2003.
43 Richards, *A Night to Remember*, p. 114.
44 This privileging of one style of film as 'real' and 'authentic' has ramifications beyond just *A Night to Remember* for, as Christine Gledhill argues, it derives from the 'drive to preserve cultural space and leadership for a middle-class intellectual elite [which] polarises melodrama and realism as critical values ... On the one hand, realism, in its association with restraint, underplaying, and the reasoning mind, is valued as masculine, relegating emotion and pathos as feminising'. See Gledhill, 'Rethinking Genre', p. 236.
45 Richards, *A Night to Remember*, p. 62.
46 See Bordwell, Staiger and Thomson, *The Classical Hollywood Cinema*, Part One.
47 Richards, *A Night to Remember*, pp. 96–7.
48 Quoted in *ibid.*, p. 75.
49 See Earl F. Bargainnier, 'Melodrama as Formula', *Journal of Popular Culture*, Volume 9, Number 3, 1975; Neale, *Genre and Hollywood*, pp. 196–7; and Ben Singer, *Melodrama and Modernity*, New York: Columbia University Press, 2001, pp. 44–58.
50 See Singer, *Melodrama and Modernity*, Chapter 6.

51 See Bruce A. McConachie, *Melodramatic Formations: American Theater and Society, 1820–1870*, Iowa City: University of Iowa Press, 1992, pp. 225–7.
52 See Frank Rahill, *The World of Melodrama*, Philadelphia: University of Pennsylvania Press, 1967, p. xv.
53 See Kristin Thompson, 'The Formulation of the Classical Narrative Style, 1909–1928', in Bordwell, Staiger and Thomson, *The Classical Hollywood Cinema*, Part Three.
54 See, for example, Eric Bentley, *The Life of the Drama*, New York: Athenaeum, 1964; Michael Booth, *English Melodrama*, London: Herbert Jenkins, 1965; David Grimsted, *Melodrama Unveiled: American Theater and Culture, 1800–1850*, Chicago: University of Chicago Press, 1968; and Robert Heilman, *Tragedy and Melodrama: Versions of Experience*, Seattle: University of Washington Press, 1968.
55 Brooks, *The Melodramatic Imagination*, p. 14.
56 Ibid., pp. 198–206.
57 Neale, *Genre and Hollywood*, p. 202.
58 Gledhill, 'Rethinking Genre', p. 227.
59 Williams, *Playing the Race Card*, p. 23.
60 Ibid.
61 See ibid.
62 See Brooks, *The Melodramatic Imagination*, p. 18.
63 Ibid., p. xiii.
64 Williams, 'Melodrama Revised', p. 49.
65 See Singer, *Melodrama and Modernity*, p. 44.
66 Ibid.
67 See ibid.
68 Ibid., p. 45.
69 Williams, *Playing the Race Card*, p. 32.
70 Walter Lord, *A Night to Remember*, London: Longmans, Green and Co, 1956.
71 Ibid., pp. 152–4.
72 Richards, *A Night to Remember*, p. 74.
73 Baker, *The Director's Cut*, p. 101.
74 Richards, *A Night to Remember*, p. 33.
75 Quoted in *ibid.*, pp. 33–4.
76 See *ibid.*, pp. 56–7.
77 See Richard Howells, 'Atlantic Crossings: Nation, Class and Identity in *Titanic* (1953) and *A Night to Remember* (1958)', *Historical Journal of Film, Radio and Television*, Volume 19, Number 4, 1999, p. 433.
78 Richards, *A Night to Remember*, p. 57.
79 Quoted in *ibid.*, p. 74.
80 See Howells, 'Atlantic Crossings', p. 421.
81 See Richards, *A Night to Remember*, pp. 120–1.
82 Quoted in *ibid.*, p. 71.
83 Ibid., p. 57.
84 Ibid., p. 8.
85 Ibid., p. 57.
86 Dixon, *Twilight of the Empire, Part II*, p. 28.
87 Propaganda films in the Second World War tried to reassure wartime audiences that the military disasters at Pearl Harbor, Wake Island and Bataan were only the part of the story, not the *end* of the story. See, for example, *Wake Island* (1942), *Flying Tigers* (1942) and *Bataan* (1943).
88 Brooks, *The Melodramatic Imagination*, p. 32.
89 Richards, *A Night to Remember*, p. 4.
90 McConachie, *Melodramatic Formations*, pp. 226–7.

91 Jeffrey Richards emphasises this aspect in his comparison of both films and argues that Baker's film reflects dominant aspects of the British character, such as a 'sense of humour, a sense of duty, a sense of stoicism, a sense of tolerance and a sense of individualism'. See Richards, *A Night to Remember*, p. 74. Peter Hutchings, on the other hand, points out that 'Britishness is not some stable essence waiting to be discovered in its various manifestations by perceptive critics. Instead it exists as a set of ideas and discourses that circulate within a number of different contexts and which are subject to contestation and endless negotiation': Peter Hutchings, *Terence Fisher*, Manchester: Manchester University Press, 2001, p. 5.
92 See Richards, *A Night to Remember*, p. 60.

'A morbid sensibility': 1947–61　　3

Raymond Durgnat, in 1970, wrote that Baker's 'best films are in the class of Dickinson and Losey'.[1] He divided British directors into 'moralists' and 'romantics' and classified Baker, along with Thorold Dickinson, Joseph Losey and the Boulting Brothers, as a 'moralist'. Michael Powell, David Lean and Terence Fisher were, on the other hand, 'romantics'.[2] Baker's films, he concluded, were characterised by doubt, disgust and despair and he perceived him as an '*auteur* whose spiritual attitude, a kind of fair-minded pessimism, precludes open revolt as it precludes acceptance'.[3]

Durgnat formed this view from the films Baker directed before the first phase in his career ended in 1963. The darkness that Durgnat perceives can be explained, to some degree, by the type of film offered to Baker in the late 1940s. This was the peak period of the 'morbid film', the film noir in Britain and Hollywood. A feature of (some) of these films was the way they assimilated psychological problems and mental torment into their storylines. The alienation of the protagonist from an uncaring, hostile society accompanied this shift away from stories based on a simple good/bad dichotomy. Evil, or at least problems, emerged from within as well as without. As Durgnat writes, in not just his crime films but also his naval melodramas, the 'barbed force of Baker's films lies in his feeling for evil as being *both* result of injustice, *and* an impersonal force which, lurking in the nature of man, takes him over'.[4]

This perception complements Baker's own view that he was interested in placing people who 'lead comparatively ordinary lives' in situations involving 'enormous crises'.[5] While this is the dramatic basis of many different types of melodrama, Baker's films often focused on the flawed individuals forced to confront not only externalised problems, such as suspicion of murder (*The October Man*), a controlling wife (*Night Without Sleep*), starvation (*Inferno*), the sea (*Passage Home*), a Mexican bandit

(*The Singer Not the Song*), the need for new blood (*The Vampire Lovers*) or the control of one's own body (*Dr Jekyll and Sister Hyde*). But these obstacles are also combined with inner disturbances that expose the vulnerability of the protagonist. Redemption, or regeneration, was often physical *and* psychological. Sometimes the protagonist is successful, sometimes not.

The October Man (1947)

Towards the end of the Second World War, and in the first four or five years after the war, Britain and Hollywood released a small cycle of films that dramatised the psychological problem of the male protagonist. Richard Maltby suggests that the 'maladjusted veteran' is a pivotal aspect of these films who, either literately or metaphorically, has trouble adjusting to society.[6] In some of these films the trauma was directly linked to the war; in others the war provided an unspoken context to place the mental turmoil, as in *The High Wall* (1947). An early example of this cycle was RKO's *The Fallen Sparrow* (1943), starring John Garfield. However, a low-budget British film *The Night Has Eyes*, starring James Mason, preceded this film, and both films trace the mental instability of their protagonists to the Spanish Civil War. In the final years of the war there were more examples. In the United States combat films, such as *A Walk in the Sun* (1945), focused not just on the enemy but also the state of mind of the soldiers. This pattern continued through films such as *Pride of the Marines* (1945), culminating in 1949 with *Twelve O'Clock High*.

In Britain, Lance Comfort's *Great Day* (1945) dramatised the psychological breakdown of a First World War ex-serviceman, Captain John Ellis (Eric Portman). Ellis, who lives in the quiet English village of Denley, has trouble coping with life outside of the army and this remarkable film shows how the 'pleasures' of actually fighting a war are, for some men, preferable to the simple virtues of peace. After a series of seemingly trivial, but humiliating, incidents Ellis contemplates suicide. *Great Day* was released in the same year as Britain's most popular film of that year, *The Seventh Veil*. This film, which begins with a suicide attempt by a young pianist (Ann Todd), was followed by a succession of films concerned with psychologically disturbed and/or psychotic male protagonists in a variety of genres – *Wanted for Murder* (1946), *Brighton Rock* (1947), *They Made Me a Fugitive* (1947), *Daybreak* (1948), *Corridor of Mirrors* (1948), and *The Small Back Room* (1949).[7]

Baker's first feature film, *The October Man*, can be seen as part of this cycle. Its narrative features can be refined even further to a small group of British films in which, as Andrew Spicer points out, 'the protagonist returns or re-engages with his present life after a period away, only to find that he can no longer cope'.[8] In this cycle the protagonist may be a veteran, as in *Mine Own Executioner* (1947), or just someone who suffers from a traumatic incident, such as *The October Man*. Other films sharing these characteristics include *The Small Back Room* (1948), *The Small Voice* (1948) and *Forbidden* (1949).

'Film noir', as a concept applicable to the British film industry, has a much shorter history than its American counterpart. For a long period the films now grouped together under the heading 'British noir' were, as Spicer notes, 'forgotten, undefined or ignored, part of the "lost continent" of British film-making: vulgar, unruly, and critically despised'.[9] American film historian William Everson was one of the first to explore this area[10] and Robert Murphy followed with a general overview.[11] Murphy also noted that the British reviewers at the time, the late 1940s, were not sympathetic to these films and he cites Arthur Vesselo's criticism of *They Made Me a Fugitive* for its 'morbid burrowings'. Vesselo went even further to present a sweeping criticism of the 'unpleasant undertone' and 'groping into the grimier recesses of the mind' in many post-war British films.[12]

Most of the British critics, however, praised *The October Man* after its general release in September 1947. Some of it was qualified, with regard to this 'type' of film and most of it was directed towards the film's producer and writer, Eric Ambler, rather than Baker. For example the *Tribune* reviewer (5 September 1947) wrote:

> There are two kinds of film, the film you watch and the film in which you are involved. *The October Man* belongs to the second class. Its success is partly a matter of creating the right kind of audience sympathy for its characters, partly a matter of filling the action with significant points which the audience feel excited to pick up. ... *The October Man* belongs to the class of film we might call the psychological thriller, but it is both characterised and motivated with such care that it rises also into the class of serious drama. ... The film is written and produced by Eric Ambler, and must, I suppose, be considered creatively his film.

The review also acknowledged Erwin Hillier's photography, William Alwyn's 'fine' score and Roy Baker's direction as they 'all worked with him [Ambler] most successfully to achieve that unity of effect which is the basis of a good film of any kind'. The film's ability to successfully involve the viewer on an emotional level, through its 'unity of effect', a key characteristic of the classical cinema, meant that the *Tribune* reviewer 'found it completely absorbing so much that I was in no mood to analyse the parts which had been so carefully calculated to make up the whole.'

The *Daily Herald* (4 September 1947) and the *Spectator* (19 September 1947) both emphasised Eric Ambler's role in the production, although the latter described *The October Man* as 'a film in the early Hitchcock tradition, with the superimposition of the currently fashionable frills of psycho-neurosis'. Joan Lester in *Reynolds News* (7 September 1947) gave praise to both Baker and Ambler as did Fred Majdalany in the *Daily Mail* (5 September 1947). This view was shared by David Lewin in the *Daily Express* (6 September 1947), calling the film excellent, with special praise to John Mills and Kay Walsh, and the *People* review (7 September 1947) noted the film's 'intelligent direction'. The *Manchester Guardian* (6 September 1947), on the other hand, found the film 'slightly disappointing' while the *New Statesman* (6 September 1947) gave it qualified praise. This review, as noted in the Introduction, compared *The October Man* with *Journey Into Fear*, and Roy Baker with Orson Welles. Welles, however, was not the credited director on the RKO film as Norman Foster directed most of it under Welles's 'supervision'. The head of RKO, Charles Koerner, was so irritated with the film's lack of narrative coherence that he delayed its release for a year while Mark Robson shot additional footage and re-edited the film. For Baker, this review was the first in many not to appreciate his subtle style and clever reworking of familiar conventions. While the *New Statesmen* may have preferred the 'wonderful bluff' of Orson Welles, *The October Man* is a far better film than *Journey Into Fear*.

A number of newspaper critics also categorised *The October Man* as part of a cycle of films linked by the use of 'psycho-neurosis' (*Spectator*), 'psychological tension' (*New Statesman*) or 'psychological thriller' (*Tribune*). Fred Majdalany in the *Daily Mail* went further and recognised that this film was 'another of these Grade One melodramas which the Rank producing companies are now turning out with gratifying frequency'. Majdalany's use of the term 'Grade One melodramas' would seem to indicate that he, at least, was able to distinguish between simple melodrama and films, such as *The October Man*, which, in terms of more complex motivation and characterisation, differ from the simple variety but still remain within this dramatic mode.

The narrative structure merges a relatively conventional murder mystery – who killed model Molly Newman (Kay Walsh), and how is the killer going to be apprehended – with a psychological drama involving a troubled industrial chemist, Jim Ackland (John Mills). In other words, the simple, external melodrama, involving the murder, is assimilated into an internalised drama involving a man prone to suicidal tendencies. This aspect prompted one reviewer, Joan Lester in *Reynolds News*, to credit the film with a sense of 'realism': 'the new type of thriller in which tension is heightened by the vivid realism of its setting and the complete credibility of its characters'.

The reviewer for the *Tribune*, on the other hand, emphasised not the 'realism' of the film but its use of expressive devices including moral symbols, such as Ackland's handkerchief (which alternates between its shape as a rabbit and a strangulation device that mirrors the scarf that killed Molly Newman), or the train whistle which is deployed so as to expose the fragile state of Ackland's mental condition. At one point in the film, when Ackland believes that he may have murdered Molly, a train whistle is heard while he contemplates suicide. This sound is used a number of times to puncture Ackland's stability.

Jim Ackland suffers physical and psychological trauma after surviving a bus accident in which a young girl (Juliet Mills) is decapitated whilst in his care. He spends a year in rehabilitation in a hospital in the Midlands, and on the day of Ackland's release his doctor, Dr Martin (Felix Aylmer), discusses his patient's condition with an insurance representative. The insurance man, indifferent to Ackland's health, complains that they cannot go on paying out money indefinitely to Ackland. Martin, however, is unsure as to whether Ackland will be able to cope in the outside world: ' If the world is kind to him he'll be all right. If it isn't ... he will probably commit suicide'. This brief exchange establishes both the essence of the drama – will Ackland commit suicide? – as well as foreshadowing the kind of world he can expect – a hostile world that has little sympathy for the vulnerable. Later, Ackland articulates his fear of living in this kind of world to Jenny Carden (Joan Greenwood) as there is 'something in my mind, a sort of fear, as if it's dangerous to be alive'.

Ackland leaves his home in Sheffield for a new start in London, where he moves into a second-rate establishment, the Brockhurst Common Hotel. Andrew Spicer describes it as a 'microcosm of traditional British society, a world of decaying middle-class gentility united by its hostility to outsiders'.[13] Inside the hotel Miss Selby (Catherine Lacey), its sad, overworked manager, has to endure the complaints from Miss Heap (Esme Beringer), an elderly woman who can never keep warm, and the gossip of Mrs Vinton (Joyce Carey) and her pathetic offsider Miss Parsons (Ann Wilton). The other residents include a cash-strapped model, Molly Newman, who is in love with a married man, timid insurance agent Mr Pope (George Benson), and Mr Peachey, a retired businessman who only stays in this 'middle-class filth' so that he can be close to Newman.

A plaque in Ackland's room informs its inhabitant that 'From ghoulies, ghosties and long-legged beasties and things that go bump in the night, good Lord deliver us'. The 'monsters' in the film, however, are not 'ghoulies, ghosties and long-legged beasties' but 'ordinary people' – in the hotel, at work and, especially, the police. Even his 'friend' at work, Harry Carden (Patrick Holt), assumes that Ackland is guilty after Molly is murdered. Similarly, authority figures, such as Dr Martin, and society's representatives, such as Detective Inspector Godby (Frederick Piper), provide little comfort and, in terms of the police, cause only grief. When Godby learns from Detective Sergeant Troth (John Boxer) that Ackland 'used to be a mental case' he immediately assumes that he has caught the murderer.

Early in the film, just after he leaves Brockhurst Common Station at night, there is a scene on a bridge over a railway track that is repeated three times. The first begins with Ackland accidentally bumping into a woman and man, who tell him to 'watch it'. As he stands on the bridge the camera is positioned behind him to show the oncoming train. This is interspersed with reverse shots of his face as the light hits the pupils of his eyes and his hair blows wildly. The chiaroscuro lighting, expertly edited images and strategically inserted close-ups combine with the noise of the train, its whistle, and a dramatic release of steam against the dark background. His inner torment is obvious and William Alwyn's music is delayed until the sequence reaches its climax and then the pounding score maximises the emotional intensity of the moment. This scene – with slightly different set-ups – is repeated twice in the film to mark a new phase in the narrative. Each visit to the bridge represents, within the Manichaean structure of melodrama, a primal moment where virtue undergoes 'an experience of the unbearable'.[14]

Tony Williams argues that *The October Man* 'directly relates its portrayal of male hysteria to postwar issues of masculine dilemma'[15] and that it depicts 'the sterility and viciousness of a stagnant postwar class system'.[16] This 'viciousness', personified by Mrs Vinton, is evident when Ackland meets some of the other guests in the hotel. After he declines an offer to join Vinton, Pope and Parsons in a game of bridge, Vinton tells him: 'You won't play, that's very unsociable'. More personally devastating to Ackland is the lack of support from Harry Carden, who tells his sister Jenny (Joan Greenwood) to stop seeing Ackland after Newman's death.

Ackland, after the accident, suffers from a low self-esteem and Andrew Spicer argues that whereas 'an American hero would strive to prove his innocence, Jim is plunged into an existential nightmare, assailed by crippling self-doubt'.[17] Tony Williams and Peter Hutchings also emphasise this aspect. Williams argues that, despite the positive ending, with Peachey's arrest and Ackland's conquest of his suicidal tendencies, a 'sombre note remains'.[18] He argues that the film's happy ending appears contrived as it does not flow logically from the body of the film: 'Jim's salvation is accidental, the result of arbitrarily convenient *deus ex machina* circumstances rather than of any change in the minds of the accusers'.[19] Hutchings similarly argues that the 'film's morbity is especially insidious and seems to linger in Baker's work much longer than it does in the work of his contemporaries'.[20]

This emphasis on Ackland's trauma and the hostility he encounters is warranted but it also overlooks, or minimises, the fact that he does overcome the physical (being framed for murder) and mental obstacles that confront him. Jim's salvation is not accidental, nor the 'result of arbitrarily convenient *deus ex machina* circumstances' but the reward for not succumbing to his personal demons, of overcoming his desire to commit suicide. Within this over-arching theme of regeneration, there is a pattern of trauma, followed by struggle and (tentative) consolidation. While regression marks the end of each stage, with Ackland on the bridge, he never gives in.

The first phase, following the first scene on the railway bridge, sees him gradually assimilating himself back into society. Initially, at work, this is successful and after three months at his new job he accepts an invitation to attend the company's spring dance, where he meets Jenny. Molly's murder causes a setback, with Vinton's gossip worsening the situation by provoking the police into investigating Ackland. This is compounded by Carden's loss of faith but, with Jenny's support, he confronts Molly's (married) lover, Wilcox. After Wilcox knocks Ackland to the ground outside the Brockhurst Commons Hotel, Jim confronts him at the Crown Hotel where he sets up the device – Molly's letter – that will eventually implicate Peachey and clear Ackland. Jim also knocks Wilcox down in the bar of the hotel. He confronts Vinton, and the other guests, at breakfast and learns that Peachey has been spreading the lie that Ackland was in Molly's room most nights. He decides to take an active role in the investigation at this point by visiting Detective Inspector Godby. Ackland: 'I'm, seeing them [the police] this time'.

When Godby refuses to believe Jim (Godby: 'What do you say old man. Another statement, the real one this time'), Ackland regresses until he even begins to think he may have killed Newman (Ackland: 'I couldn't have done it, could I?' as he twist his handkerchief into a strangulation configuration). His despair is captured by a high-level crane shot looking down on him as he leaves the police station. The camera slowly moves down into a close-up to show his anguish as he enters the dark street. This is followed by the sound of a train whistle and a sudden flash of light across his face as he returns to the railway bridge for the second time.

He doesn't succumb and begins, again, the process of clearing his name. Peachey, aware that anything he tells Ackland cannot implicate him without a witness, confesses that he strangled Molly with her scarf. When Ackland reports this to the police they refuse to believe him. Again, Jim continues to fight on and takes Jenny to Peachey's room where they find a British European airline label. This is significant because Peachey had told the police he was going to Glasgow. When police, again, ignore Ackland's evidence and try to arrest him, he knocks one of them down and escapes to Paddington Station where he learns that Peachey is flying to Lisbon under the name of Hatfield. Ackland phones Godby with this news but the Detective Inspector appears uninterested.

Seemingly defeated, he returns to Brockhurst Common and the railway bridge for the final time. However, the police act on his information, detain Peachey, and Molly's letter confirms Jim's story. As Harry Carden leaves the police station he reminds them that everybody, including himself, has behaved badly. Jenny, fearing that Jim may have jumped under a train, rushes to the railway bridge only to see his symbolic alter ego, his handkerchief twisted into the shape of a rabbit, falling onto the tracks. Jim, however, remains on the bridge. Proudly, he tells Jenny 'I didn't give in'. The film ends with the 'rabbit' lying battered on train tracks, not Jim, and the two lovers come together in one of Baker's most intense endings.

The fact that the film ends on the railway bridge, and not in a more conventional manner with the capture of the killer, indicates that the most significant narrative strand is the internalised battle involving Jim's psychological problem. The external problem, the murder, only serves as a catalyst to deepen this strand. The *Spectator* (9 September 1947) argues that the film is characteristic of the 'early Hitchcock tradition, with the superimposition of the currently fashionable frills of psycho-neurosis'. This aspect is more than just a 'superimposition' but the heart of the drama. Jim's regeneration is not just social but psychological.

Mine Own Executioner, directed by Anthony Kimmins and released in the same year as *The October Man*, is superficially similar to Baker's film. Protagonists in both films suffer psychological trauma due to a relatively recent experience. While Kimmin's film offers no hope for the regeneration of its damaged ex-pilot, Baker's film documents Ackland's regeneration. A brief comparison will show the fact that while Baker's film remains within the parameters of melodrama, especially with regard to its function of establishing moral legibility, *Mine Own Executioner* presents a morally problematic world – particularly with regard to its central character Felix Milne (Burgess Meredith).

Felix Milne, a highly competent but formally unqualified psychiatrist working in a London clinic, is asked by a young woman Molly Lucian (Barbara White) to treat her husband Adam (Kieron Moore) after he has tried to choke her. Milne is hesitant to accept Lucian as a patient because of the intensity of his schizophrenia, a condition caused by guilt when he was unable to withstand torture by the Japanese during the Second World War. Initially there seems to be an improvement in Lucian's condition but this is illusory and he soon deteriorates. Milne, who is distracted by his own marital and professional problems, fails to prevent Lucian killing Molly. Lucian, despite the belated efforts of Milne, shoots himself in the head while standing on the ledge of a tall building.

Mine Own Executioner, scripted by Nigel Balchin,[21] challenges the moralising function of melodrama.[22] The climax of the film, with Milne failing to prevent Lucian's suicide, is one of the bleakest moments in British cinema and is compounded by Milne's behaviour prior to the murder/suicide. On the day Lucian kills Molly, Milne terminates a session with him as he is not feeling well. He is under pressure because a government body has indicated that Milne's lack of formal qualifications will prevent them from funding his clinic. Distressed, Milne heads off to a nightclub to see Barbara Edge (Christine Norden), his mistress. Meanwhile, Adam mistakes his wife, while he is romancing her, for a Japanese prison guard and shoots her. This takes place as Milne makes love to Edge and the film, by crosscutting between them, implies a connection between the two events. A phone call from Milne's wife interrupts him with Edge, and she tells him that Lucian has killed Molly. Milne tries to redeem himself but the film ends in an inconclusive manner with his relationship to both his wife and mistress, and his professional standing, unresolved.

Importantly, the film suggests that Milne is morally responsible for Molly's death. His 'open' marriage and periodic need for Edge, despite his wife's misgivings, distracts him from delivering appropriate care to his patient. Lucian's demise is not balanced by any compensating display of virtue from Milne, his supposed saviour. While there are victims and villains in *Mine Own Executioner*, the film does not, unlike *The October Man*, specify who they really are.

Paper Orchid (1948)

Baker followed *The October Man* with *The Weaker Sex*, a sentimental celebration of those left to fight the Second World War on the home front. His next film, and the only independent film he directed until *The*

Valiant in 1962,[23] was the little-seen *Paper Orchid*. The film was produced by an independent company, Ganesh, with financial support from Columbia Studio's British division. The producer was American William Collier Jr, otherwise known as Buster Collier. Collier was an actor at Columbia in the early 1930s. Although it is one of Baker's most morbid films, unlike *Mine Own Executioner*, this quality is softened by the use of pathos in the last act. The fact that the film was produced outside of the studio system may have contributed to the intensity of its morbidity. Or this may be due to the contribution of Val Guest, who scripted the film,[24] or the fact that it was based on a novel by Arthur La Bern,[25] who also wrote *It Always Rains on Sunday*. Whatever the reason, *Paper Orchid* remains more than just a curious footnote to Baker's career and it has the most fluid narrative structure of all his films. It refuses to follow just one or two characters and the story oscillates between various narrative strands.

The film begins with images of Fleet Street and the printed title: 'where only a newspaper is put to bed ... and ink is thicker than blood'. The light-hearted titillation in this prologue is not indicative of the rest of the film, where deceit, ruthlessness, sexual repression and an extraordinary lack of communal spirit characterise the fictional inhabitants of Fleet Street – the only character who expresses any sense of concern for another human commits murder. It begins with a blonde Stella Mason (Hy Hazell) who bluffs her way into a job as a gossip reporter on the *Daily National*. Although the reporters, and editor Frank McSweeney (Hugh Williams), are cynical about her capabilities they are not prepared to challenge the 'old buzzard's homework' – a reference to Mason's claim that she was an 'acquaintance' of the newspaper's owner, Lord Croup.

At this point Stella, it seems, will be the film's protagonist as she even receives a voice-over early in the film describing the nature of her column, 'Orchids to You'. Her prominence, however, quickly recedes as the film shifts across to the paper's editor, McSweeney, and his battles with Lady Croup (Ella Retford), who starts interfering in the daily operations of the newspaper after the death of her husband. When the highly religious proprietor receives news from one of her spies on the paper, Eustace Crabb (Ivor Barnard), that McSweeney is planning to reduce her input, she fires McSweeney and replaces him with Crabb. McSweeney joins a rival newspaper, the *World Record*, as associate editor, and he is determined to push the sales of his new paper past the circulation of the *Daily National*.

Other issues are introduced and then pushed into the background. For example, Jonquil Jones (Vida Hope) visits both papers hoping to promote the endeavours of struggling artist Peter Pastamen. A murder, relatively late in the film, brings some of the strands together when Stella finds Pastamen, who is renting the loft in her apartment, with his throat slashed. Stella, having lost her position at the *Daily National* after offending Lady Croup, takes the story to McSweeney, hoping that he will give her a job on the *World Record*. McSweeney wants the story to boost this paper's circulation but is less interested in Mason's welfare or moral reputation. He tries to force her to write the story under her own by-line, knowing that the other papers are less likely to steal it as she has no credibility. The editor of the *World Record* describes her as a 'stupid girl'. Mason passes the story on to a novice reporter, John Dean, at the *Daily National*. Dean is then told by the news editor to relinquish it to the paper's crime reporter, Freddy C. Evans (Sidney James).

Evans, however, is the murderer and the last act, with Evans investigating his own crime, has some of the resonance of the 1948 Hollywood film noir *The Big Clock*. The film's ending allows Baker to indulge himself in a sequence of full-blown pathos. Evans, after writing his last newspaper report – his confession – commits suicide by jumping under a train at Charing Cross Station. Evans, who loves Mason, is a pathetic figure as she is unaware of his feelings. Early in the film they are shown drinking together but otherwise there is little indication of his desire, except for a couple of inserts of Evans reacting to Mason, including her surprise when he kisses her hand. In their last scene together his feelings finally erupt as he suddenly kisses her on the mouth. But it is too late: he has killed Pastamen. Just as the audience helplessly watch people die on the *Titanic* in *A Night to Remember*, the audience in *Paper Orchid* watch Mason's futile attempts to contact the reporter as he heads towards his death.

Baker exploits this sense of 'too late' in a prolonged sequence at the end of the film. Evans declares his love for Stella in a variety of situations – including a mannequin in a dress shop window and a cat, which he calls 'Tommy'. At the station, as the camera dollies into a large close-up of Evan's face, he murmurs 'I'm thinking of you Stella, I've loved you since the beginning, I'll love you till the end', before jumping in front of a train. Stella, on the other hand, is last seen in a dark telephone box ringing his apartment. The film's epilogue returns to the harsh world of Fleet Street and the fact that nothing really matters except the story. As McSweeney overrides objections from the newspaper's lawyer and goes ahead and publishes Evans's last story, his confession, he pauses when he hears of the reporter's death: 'Poor old Freddie. He never would tell us what the "C" stood for'.

Paper Orchid presents a cynical view of relationships and institutions. The film also takes pleasure in exposing the machinations of Fleet

Street and the moral hypocrisy of the reporters. For example, Evans taunts Harold Croup (Lady Croup's nephew), the 'Daily National's 'spiritual' reporter, when he catches Croup dancing with a brunette in a nightclub. He suggests to the righteous reporter that he should write a series of articles under the headings, 'I Found Valhalla at Wopping' and 'Saving Souls in the Parrot'.

Morning Departure (1950)

The ending in *Morning Departure*, as three men – Lieutenant Commander Peter Armstrong (John Mills), the captain of the submarine the *Trojan*, Stoker Snipes (Richard Attenborough) and Able Seaman Higgins (James Hayter) – recite the naval prayer and wait to die from a lack of oxygen, would seem as bleak as the ending in *Paper Orchid*.[26] But it isn't. The ending is heroic and uplifting. It is, unlike the noirish qualities of despair and futility in *Paper Orchid*, a celebration of sacrifice and courage. Even Snipe, the only selfish character in the submarine, redeems himself by allowing another sailor to escape the submarine.

Morning Departure is an exercise in stoicism. Or, as Raymond Durgnat explains, it is a 'stiff upper lip naval drama'.[27] While the story may be ostensibly bleak, with chance destroying many lives, it is not a bleak film – as the *Star* reviewer noted on 23 February 1950: although the film is 'concerned with a group of men in the grimmest situations, it is somehow not a grim film'. It is not a film about alienation from the community, as in *The October Man*, but of men who represent the best qualities of their community. Their problems are not due to human weakness or psychological trauma, but are the result of external factors beyond their control. As Commander Gates (Bernard Lee) concludes at the end of the film, the deaths were due to the enemy of all seamen – bad luck and bad weather.[28]

Morning Departure was a crucial film in Baker's career and, in effect, was his ticket to Hollywood and Twentieth Century Fox. The film was well received by the public in Britain and most Commonwealth countries. In Melbourne it ran for seven weeks in late 1950 in a city theatre (Savoy), without a co-feature, followed by lengthy periods in most of the suburban theatres. The British newspaper critics were almost unanimous in their praise for the film – and Baker's contribution. The *Daily Telegraph* (27 February 1950), for example, claimed that the film 'confirms the promise of Roy Baker's "October Man". Mr Baker, at 32 [33], is one of the white hopes of the British screen'.

The film's popularity was affected by the sinking of the *HMS*

Truculent in the Thames estuary, in vaguely similar circumstances, just prior to the film's release. The Admiralty supported the release of the film and the similarities between the film and the real-life disaster were mentioned in most reviews. The *News Chronicle* (26 February 1950), for example, maintained that it 'is right that, in seeing it [*Morning Departure*], filmgoers should especially remember the men of the Truculent'. Similarly, the *Star* (23 February 1950) linked the film to the *Truculent* disaster and argued that 'it is impossible to see it [*Morning Departure*] without thinking of that dark night in the Thames Estuary when 64 men lost their lives'.

Other critics emphasised, as does Jeffrey Richards, that the 'film was in tune with the cultural sensibilities of that post-war decade',[29] that it, somehow, expressed a distinctly British outlook. The *Evening Standard* (23 February 1950) was the most effusive in this regard:

> This is a magnificent picture. Not only is it a tribute to the Navy, but it revives in any doubting mind the sure knowledge that there is no people on earth as dear and as wonderful as the British. ... It would be interesting to hear how a foreigner would react if confronted with a dialogue so charged with unspoken undertone, with silences so simple, and yet so complicated. Perhaps it would seem merely phlegmatic.
>
> ... The agony of not knowing whether the salvage operations will be successful is shared by the audience, but with not nearly so much fortitude. Oh, the gentleness of Englishmen in peril!

Caroline Lejeune in the *Observer* (26 February 1950) praised *Morning Departure* 'as honest a naval film as we have had since "In Which We Serve"'. Everything in the film, she argues, 'feels right to me; it feels very right: I can believe in everything that happens and I can believe that it happened just as the picture says it did'. The ending was crucial in convincing Lejeune that this was an important film:

> There was a suggestion, I understand, that 'Morning Departure' should be given a happy ending. I am glad that wiser counsels prevailed, and the writers made no attempt to compromise with a situation implicit in the story. No botched-up job of last-minute rescue could have consoled the people who have lost their own men in actual naval disasters: and any such device would have seemed impudent, almost in a curious way indecent, in this forthright and singularly philosophic picture.

Scripted by former naval Lieutenant Commander William Fairchild, and based on Kenneth Woollard's play, *Morning Departure* begins with an early morning domestic scene: Lieutenant Commander Peter Armstrong (John Mills) is trying to evade suggestions from his wife Helen (Helen Cherry) that he consider leaving the navy to join his father-in-law's vacuum-cleaner factory. The amicable middle-class banter between Peter and Helen provides a contrast to the uneasy relationship between the working-class couple, Snipe and his wife Rose (Lana Morris). Rose's infidelity and greed provide the motivation for her husband's behaviour on the submarine as Snipe learns that his wife has been receiving presents from her boss. While both women want something from their husbands, only Helen's request to have a permanent home is presented as legitimate. Rose, on the other hand, merely wants more money. Yet as Armstrong drives off, there is a slight premonition on the face of his wife that there is trouble ahead, a feeling reinforced by the sound of a baby crying in their house.

The 'trouble' is a mine that the *Trojan* hits sending the submarine to the seabed and leaving only twelve of the sixty-five men alive. Their difficulties are compounded by the news that there are only enough suits for eight men to escape through the conning tower and the gun hatch. The remaining four will be forced to wait for the salvage team. Little, in the terms of action, happens after this as the film focuses on the reaction of the four men to the disaster – Armstrong, Snipes, first officer Lieutenant Harry Manson (Nigel Patrick) and Able Seaman Higgins. When bad weather foils the salvage attempt, with a cable snapping in a heavy storm, the submarine falls back on to the seabed leaving the men with no hope of survival. The film ends on a Sunday morning with the men resigned to their deaths.

Dilys Powell, writing in the *Sunday Times* (26 February 1950), claimed that of all the films about submarines that she had ever seen *Morning Departure* was the best. She appreciated that the film was not a 'documentary', which she generally finds dull, and to make such a film 'about life in a submarine which is neither boring or melodramatic' she praised Fairchild's script, Desmond Dickinson's camerawork, the excellence of the settings, and 'the direction and playing of the actors ... John Mills gives one of the subtly understated performances which have made his reputation: you can feel the tensions beneath the surface of behaviour, but the behaviour itself is controlled, business-like and even'. Her only criticism was directed at Attenborough's performance for relying 'too much on tricks of characterisation', thereby, in Powell's view, rendering him a dramatic stereotype rather than a 'real' person. Powell's criticism of Attenborough, however, was not shared by the other reviewers, and the *Star*, reflecting the majority, argued that in a 'difficult role as the hysterical stoker, Richard Attenborough exactly suggests a man fighting a battle with his nerves which he wins only after a near defeat'.

Snipes is the only person in the group who fails to control his feelings – the rest are professional and express a stoic reaction to the disaster.

Snipes, who suffers from claustrophobia, only volunteered for submarine duty to gain the extra money for his wife to spend. When Armstrong learns of his condition he explodes: 'You're useless to me and a menace to everybody on board'. Snipes also behaves poorly during the game of chance to determine which men will be allowed to wear the equipment that will enable them to escape the submarine. Armstrong asks another sailor, Marks (George Cole), to stand down. Although Marks agrees, Snipes redeems himself and agrees to stays behind.

Manson, who is popular with women and lives, compared to Armstrong, a less responsible life, is relieved when he has to stay behind. His passive, compliant nature contains a fatalistic streak due to an earlier incident when he survived whilst a friend died. Manson, however, dies when he inhales chlorine gas and during his brief illness Snipes cares him for. Both men, Snipes and Manson, are redeemed by their willingness to die and the film's use of pathos, especially at the end, is subtle, but evident. It concludes with the camera pulling away from Armstrong as he reads the naval prayer to Snipes and Higgins. To reviewers, such as in the *Daily Telegraph*, this was an 'authentic' ending as it presented 'fighting men seen as they are, without false heroics or sickly sentiment'.

Highly Dangerous (1950)

In 1947 the inquiries of the House Committee on Un-American Activities into communism in the American film industry resumed and the studios began production of anti-communist films. Twentieth Century-Fox was the first with *The Iron Curtain* in 1948. Howard Hughes followed the next year with the infamous *I Married a Communist* (also known as *Woman on Pier 13*) and 41 anti-communist films were released between 1951 and 1953. This cycle was less pronounced in Britain, although Roy Boulting wrote, with Frank Harvey, the script in the late 1940s[30] for *High Treason* (1951), which he also directed. Roy Baker's *Highly Dangerous*, scripted by Eric Ambler, was part of this cycle, although the tone of the film was less paranoid and political and more comedic. In fact, *Highly Dangerous* veers, at certain points, towards a parody of the hysteria that characterised these films.

At the beginning of the film, entomologist Frances Gray (Margaret Lockwood), who works for the Biological Control Laboratory in Brockhurst, is shown supervising the transport of live insects to Sierra Leone. She tells the operator (Anthony Newley) that it is important to maintain the correct temperature and feed the insects a glucose solution every three hours. Failure to do so will, Gray warns, will result in the insects turning on each other and eating their fellow insects. This warning comes to fruition at the end of the film when the insects do begin eating each other. While this is not a fully developed metaphor concerning the Cold War and the anti-communist witch-hunt, it can be interpreted as a comment on the finger-pointing and accusations of betrayal in the United States and Britain at that time.

The film resembles a comic strip as Gray assumes dual identities. For most of the time she is the serious, repressed,[31] scientist who, reluctantly, agrees to help the British Government investigate the possibility that an East European country is breeding insects as part of a germ warfare campaign. Her inhibitions dissipate when she listens to the radio serial 'Frank Conway, Secret Agent'.[32] Early in the film she discusses the possibility that Frank Conway may exist in real life with her young nephew Adam who suggests that Frances shares certain qualities with the secret agent:

ADAM: But he may be real.
FRANCES: I don't think so.
ADAM: Why not. You're just as clever aren't you? You always know what he [Conway] is going to do.
FRANCES: That's not the same thing.
ADAM: Why not?

Adam is sent to bed and, as a consequence of the serial and her discussion with Adam, Frances changes her mind and agrees to assist the government. She travels to an East European country under the guise of being a European representative of an American travel agency. Her false passport shows her name as Frances Conway.

After she arrives, the film reinforces the Cold War stereotype of the totalitarian communist regime as tightly controlled and all-powerful. Gray's cover as a travel agent is exposed right from the start. She is accompanied on her journey by the Chief of Police, Commandant Anton Razinski (Marius Goring), and he notices a microscope in her handbag while guards divert her attention. Later, Frances's East European contact 'Alf' (Eugene Deckers) is murdered by the police after his first visit to her hotel room.

Gray is accused of 'Alf's murder and interrogated by Razinski. When she fails to reveal anything under a battery of bright lights, a 'truth drug' is administered so that they can 'search her mind'. The drug, however, only succeeds in transforming the meek scientist into 'Frank Conway, Secret Agent'. Suddenly, her persona changes into that of an adventurous spy and Gray, with the assistance of an American journalist Bill Casey (Dane Clark), infiltrates the laboratory of the East European country. She takes samples of the insects. Casey, wishing to get out of his appointment to this backwater, agrees to accompany Gray as they flee the country. However, even Casey has misgivings about her reckless behaviour ('it's like a soap opera on the radio') and he worries why she constantly calls him 'Rusty' (the name of Frank Conway's sidekick in the radio serial).

They board a train that will carry them out of the country. However, Razinski and his police wait for them at the border and, at this point, the film loses its semi-comic tone. Razinski's guards murder a young couple during the inspection and Casey and Gray, disguised as peasants, provoke a fight with the authorities which allows them to escape undetected. However, they are detained by British Customs when they try to bring the insects into Britain and, in a comic parallel to the situation at the East European border, Gray becomes alarmed when the insects start to devour each other. In a desperate attempt to save them she approaches the attendant (Gladys Henson) at the airport café who refuses to supply her with the sugar needed to save them: 'If they're [the ants] entitled to sugar then the Ministry will issue the necessary coupons'. Casey is also told that he will not be able to publish the story of their exploits because of security. This epilogue provides a (comic) parallel to the same sort of censorship, and rigid government bureaucracy, that they thought they had left behind in the totalitarian state.

Highly Dangerous received a mixed, and often confused, reception from the newspaper critics. Dilys Powell, writing in *Britain Today* (February 1951), objected to the film's mixture of seriousness and comedy and while admitting there 'are moments ... when hilarity breaks in ... the film falls between two stools ... [and] the irony is constantly being interrupted by straightforward excitement. *Highly Dangerous* ... refuses to rely, as the best American thriller relies, on fast action, solid backgrounds and good playing, and insists on calling waggishness to its aid'. Paul Rotha (*Public Opinion*, 15 December 1950) similarly argued that the comedy weakened the overall film: 'I really thought that here was the best British thriller in years ... Unhappily, the last third of the film wholly collapses'. The review in *The Spectator* (15 December 1950) thought that Roy Baker has expanded an 'amusing idea' into 'quite an entertaining film. He should, though, have been a little more certain as to whether it was a farce or a tragedy he was directing. Grimness and giggles do not mix happily and leave the audience uncertain as to how to behave'.

Others, such as the *Times* reviewer (11 December 1950), claimed that the humour, the 'Dick Barton parody' was the only thing that made the film 'bearable': 'About halfway through a film of quite dreadful inanity, considering the script is by Mr Eric Ambler, [it] suddenly breaks into a joke, and not a bad joke either'. Similarly, the *Daily Mail* (8 December 1950) argued that the film 'is a melodrama with its tongue in its cheek – sometimes in both cheeks' and that it gave Margaret Lockwood a chance to reprise her early success as the assertive heroine in Hitchcock's *The Lady Vanishes* (1938). The reviewer agreed that she 'has succeeded pretty well'. This view was also shared by Reg Whitley in the *Daily Mirror* (8 December 1950) although some critics objected to her credibility as a scientist ('Miss Margaret Lockwood doesn't seem the scientific type and her eye-lashes are too long for close work with a microscope').

Don't Bother to Knock (1952)

Roy Baker directed three films in Hollywood. Baker's other film for Twentieth Century-Fox, *The House on the Square*, was filmed in London. These three films are among his best. There are probably many reasons for this – he was at the peak of his skills as a director, the facilities were better in Hollywood and each script had a distinctive edge to it. As Raymond Durgnat points out, 'the limiting niceness of the quality British films abruptly disappeared when [Baker was] at Fox'.[33] *Don't Bother to Knock* gave Marilyn Monroe her strongest dramatic role to date as a mentally disturbed baby-sitter, and *Night Without Sleep* extended the romantic fatalism of film noir beyond most other examples of this sub-genre. *Inferno*, on the other hand, was the pick of the three films as it provided Baker with both a technical challenge (it was filmed in 3D), as well as a formal challenge in involving the audience in the plight of a selfish businessman left to die in the desert with a broken leg.

Don't Bother to Knock, together with *A Night to Remember*, is Baker's most well-known film largely because it co-starred Marilyn Monroe. Based on Charlotte Armstrong's novel (*Mischief*) and scripted by Daniel Taradash, it was a significant film for Monroe as her studio, Twentieth Century-Fox, had little faith in her as a dramatic actress. It was also important in confirming Richard Widmark's status as a leading man, as opposed to the psychotic villain in which he made his name in Hollywood, in films such as *Kiss of Death* (1947).

These charismatic actors, and their prevailing screen image (in 1952), are important to the film. The dangerous persona of Richard Widmark provides sufficient motivation for his girlfriend, singer Lyn Lesley (Anne Bancroft), to end their relationship at the start of the film. The first image of Widmark, as pilot Jed Towers, lying on a hotel bed, smoking a cigarette with a sour look on his face (he has been reading the goodbye note from Lyn), with Lyn's voice drifting into his room via the hotel radio, is typically noir. Towers rips up Lesley's note and then goes down to the hotel's nightclub to confront her. On the way down from his room on the eighth floor, Towers shares the elevator with Peter Jones (Jim Backus) and his wife Ruth (Lurene Tuttle). This cleverly introduces the film's two plot strands. One involves the Joneses, who have employed Nell Forbes (Marilyn Monroe) to look after their daughter Bunny (Donna Corcoran) – following a recommendation from the elevator man Eddie Forbes (Elisha Cook Jr) – Nell is Forbes's niece and she has just arrived in New York from Oregon. The other strand involves Towers and his relationship with both Nell and Lyn.

In the nightclub Lyn tells Jed that she wants to end the affair because of his attitude to life in general and her in particular; Jed, on the other hand, tells her that he thought she shared his easy-going lifestyle (Jed: 'I believe in a drink, a kiss and a laugh.') Later, when a female photographer (Gloria Blondell) wants to take a picture of the 'happy couple', Jed tells Lyn that the photographer reminds him of a 'chicken thief I use to know'. Lyn flares at this crack as she despises the way he treats people. Although he can be sweet and fun, underneath he is cold and hard and lacks 'an understanding heart'. Lyn's evaluation of Jed is a dominant motif in the film. Hence, the film is another story of regeneration as Jed, finally, convinces his girl friend that he does care for somebody beside himself.

The film dramatises his regeneration through his concern for Nell. Initially, after rejection from Lyn, all Jed sees in Nell is the possibility of a good time – especially after he sees her dancing in a negligee in the hotel room opposite to his. Soon he is in her room with a bottle of rye whisky. Baker records the change in his attitude in a subtle, but effective, camera movement. It shows Nell applying lipstick as the camera dollies in to reveal scars on her wrists. Now Jed begins to appreciate that she is not flirtatious but a deeply troubled woman due to years of physical and mental abuse from her parents. He learns that after her boyfriend Philip died during the Second World War, she suffered a nervous breakdown and was sent to a mental institution for three years.

Jed's total regeneration takes time and his initial interest in Nell confirm Lyn's judgement that he is an opportunist caring only for his own pleasures (Nell: 'You came over to flirt'). However, after noticing that the initials on the suitcase in the room don't match her name, and also that there is a pair of men's shoes under the bed, he decide to get away from her ('I ran out of girls like you when I was 14'). Baker brings this first part of the film to a strong climax, which is conveyed visually. The two protagonists are shown, in slightly tilted composition, in a long dress mirror, with Nell in the foreground and Jed in the background. When she learns that Jed, like Philip, is a pilot, her psychosis returns and, believing that her boyfriend has returned, she kisses Jed. He reciprocates until he notices Bunny, the young girl in Nell's care, standing by the door watching them.[34]

Jed, unnerved by Bunny's presence and Nell's strange behaviour, goes to leave but Nell stops him by recounting her troubled upbringing. This is a turning point — it marks the beginning of Jed's regeneration — and it provides the basis for the subsequent suspense involving the threat to the young girl from her baby-sitter. Nell resents the way Bunny interrupts her relationship with Jed. She first contemplates pushing Bunny out of the eighth-floor window and, later, binds the young girl to the bed. This provides another of the film's arresting images as the camera pans across Bunny bound and gagged while Jed, who is unaware of the situation, leaves the darkened hotel room. In the film's climax, Jed rescues the young girl from Nell and then protects the baby-sitter, who has a razor blade in her hand, from onlookers in the hotel foyer. Jed's actions convince Lyn that he does have an 'understanding heart'.

All this takes place in less than two and a half hours of screen time. A clock shows the time as 7.48 pm at the start and another clock reveals it is 10.05 pm near the end. When asked about the film's short running time Baker replied: '[I]t was written that way. It's one of the few pictures which takes place in real time. There are no dissolves. No lapses of time, no fade out/fade ins, it's all straight cuts. Everything is happening as you see it.'[35]

Night Without Sleep (1952)

Night Without Sleep, Baker's third film for Twentieth Century-Fox and the second he directed in Hollywood, was one of his bleakest and comes towards the end of a long cycle of films noirs that focused on male weakness and internal torment.[36] Although the film has its castrating woman, Emily Morton (June Vincent), she disappears early in the film and the other women, especially Lisa Muller (Hildegarde Neff), are either troubled or a source of comfort to the 'hero', Richard Morton (Gary Merrill). For much of the film Morton cannot comprehend what he may or may not have done. Towards the end he cries out in the darkness of his wealthy Long Island mansion, 'What is real? What happened? What did I do?' Fearing that he has killed the woman that he loved, Julie Bannon (Linda Darnell), he is reassured when she phones him minutes later. Earlier he thought he might have killed his mistress Lisa Muller. Relieved, Morton rushes on to his patio and vows to leave his wealthy wife Emily and resume his career as a writer of musicals. Rushing upstairs, with his dog, to pack his bags he finds out that he has killed somebody. The camera slowly tracks across the devastation of his bedroom, across the bow tie that Emily tied around his neck the night before, across the wine bottle, past his expensive clothes to Emily's body lying at the foot of their bed. Suddenly, all his plans are rendered futile.

Richard Morton is a combination of the obsessive romantic Freddie Evans in *Paper Orchid* and the psychologically troubled Jim Ackland in *The October Man*. He is, basically, a decent man who has been damaged by two women. First, his mother and her determination that he will be a successful pianist, whatever the cost. Second, his dominating, wealthy wife who 'buys' Morton when he is at the peak of his fame. Morton's psychiatrist warns him that as a result of these experiences, in certain situations involving excessive alcohol, he is capable of murder.

The film begins in the dark living room at 5.15 am in his Long Island home and the camera slowly dollies in on a dishevelled Morton lying on the couch suffering from a nightmare – the sounds of police sirens, car horns, a woman screaming ('don't, please don't, you're hurting me') abruptly cease when he wakes up and screams 'No!' before knocking a lamp over. As he walks across the lounge room he accidentally steps on a picture of his wife, and as he picks up the shattered image he remarks to himself: 'Dear Emily, I didn't mean to step on you. Or did I? Six years ago I would have known the answer.' This provides the cue for the first flashback in the film – overall there are five, including a flashback within a flashback – as the film goes back six years to Morton's creative period, having just written the successful musical 'Purple Like Grapes'. Morton, who is having trouble financing the production, agrees to Emily Fletcher's bargain that she will finance the show and, in return, he will marry her if it is a success. Morton, aware that he is being purchased by a wealthy woman, lets Emily know that he doesn't really love her – 'always remember that you talked me into it'. Emily, on the other hand, is unconcerned that he does not love him: 'I should have warned you I am very good at picking winners'. The film returns to the present and Emily's shattered picture: 'You won the bet, Emily: the play was a hit but you didn't pick a winner'.

Another flashback follows his discovery of deep scratches on his wrist and he remembers his fight with Emily the day before, as she prepares to fly to Boston for her father's birthday party. When she tells him he was much more fun six years ago, and that he should get back to writing, Morton explains that he wants her to be interested in him as a person, not an artist. Morton then kisses her passionately on the mouth and pleads with her not to fly to Boston. When Emily refuses, he tries, unsuccessfully, to arouse her jealousy by telling her that he has a date (with Lisa). She only laughs at him, refusing to be 'a little suburban wife':

> EMILY: Don't be such a child!
> MORTON: Stop using that tone. I can stand anything but you mothering me.
> EMILY: Don't be silly darling, you couldn't live a week without me mothering you.

Morton then flings the bow tie, which Emily attached to his neck, on to the floor and tells her that 'I should have left you long ago'. This is followed by another flashback, which includes a warning from Dr Clarke (Donald Randolph), of Morton's potential for murder. Back to the present and when he spills coffee on a tie that belongs to his friend, John Harkness (Hugh Beaumont), this triggers the longest flashback involving memories of the night when he meets actress Julie Bannon, who is flying the next day to London to make a film. Their romance, interspersed with two hostile encounters with his mistress Lisa, occupies the bulk of the film. It ends the next morning with his fear that he has killed someone as, during the night, he threatened both Julie and Lisa when they tried to 'mother' him.

The film was expertly photographed by Lucien Ballard, who worked on all of Baker's Hollywood films, and scored by Cyril Mockridge, who, with Alfred Newman, wrote 'Too Late for Spring'. This melancholy tune is a key motif in the film as it reinforces the prevailing mood, pathos, through its theme of 'too late'. For Morton, having killed Emily the night before, it is too late; for Julie, who loved Morton years ago, without him knowing it, it is also too late; similarly for Lisa, who remained Morton's mistress throughout his troubled marriage, it is also too late.

This quartet of 'lost' people is archetypal noir. The themes of failed dreams and personal weakness are smoothly assimilated into the distinctive noir style. The low-key lighting in most scenes, the use of tight close-ups and the cold atmosphere of the Long Island mansion together with the heightened sounds of his nightmare, shift the dramatic focus to Morton's fragile state of mind. Consistent with film noir, this is primarily due to the women in his life, especially his mother.

Night Without Sleep is an example of a film noir sub-genre, a cycle of 'male weepies' produced in the 1940s and early 1950s. The most famous exponent of this type of film noir was Cornell Woolrich.[37] There is a similarity between Cornell Woolrich's 1943 novel *Black Angel*, which was filmed by Universal in 1946, and *Night Without Sleep*. At the climax of the 1946 film the man assisting a woman in her hunt for a killer realises that he is the murderer: he committed the act whilst drunk. Morton in Baker's film also discovers that he murdered Emily whilst drunk. June Vincent, who plays Emily in *Night Without Sleep*, also starred as the wife trying to save her philandering husband in *Black Angel*.[38] There is another connection between *Night Without Sleep* and earlier films in this cycle. RKO's *Stranger on the Third Floor* (1940) was scripted by Frank Partos, who also wrote, with Elick Moll, *Night Without Sleep*. Both films use prolonged flashbacks and voiceover to communicate the inner desperation of their protagonists. Morton's vow to leave behind the emasculating presence of Emily, and her money, comes too late. In fact, it never was a possibility but just a sad dream. It is, however, consistent with the melancholic pall that pervades the film.

Inferno (1953)

Unlike most of his films, *Inferno* was a project that Baker actively sought.[39] It is also one of his finest films.[40] This melodrama shares the same narrative premise as *Double Indemnity* (1944) although it is set in a desert and not urban California. The wife of a wealthy, selfish businessman plots with her lover to kill her husband. After the attempted murder the ardour between the couple cools until they finally turn on each other. This premise, which is archetypally film noir, is modified in *Inferno* by beginning the film after the affair has been consummated and the husband, who has a broken leg, is left to die in the desert. This premise gives Baker the opportunity to demonstrate his mastery of the medium. *Inferno*, his second film in colour, has the longest running time of his films made in Hollywood. This allows an almost leisurely narrative rhythm with long stretches of the story focusing on one man, Donald Whitley Carson III (Robert Ryan), alone and incapacitated in the desert. Within this context Baker has fun devising simple visual associations – such as cutting between Carson, suffering from a lack of food and water, to his wife Geraldine (Rhonda Fleming) and her lover Joe Duncan (William Lundigan) wallowing in the luxury of the 'Circle T Guest Ranch'.

The early scenes set up the characterisations and basic plot. Geraldine (Gerry) Carson and Joe Duncan spend time hiding the actual whereabouts of Carson from any future search party. The problem facing Carson is neatly signalled by the film's opening image, a close-up of a sign warning people 'not to attempt this route without ample supplies of water and gasoline'. This sign, against the background of a barren desert, indicates his chances of survival are slim.

This situation, survival against the elements, is clearly melodrama. The film updates this simple premise by presenting the wife and her lover as physically attractive, seemingly reasonable people – not stereotypical villains. It is possible, the film implies, that they have a good reason to kill Carson – especially after the first time we see him: unshaven, with an ugly hat pulled over his face, drunk and firing wildly at a bottle, while complaining that he is low on cigarettes. His wild behaviour is interspersed by screams of 'where are they?'. This image is reinforced when Carson's business manager Dave Emory (Larry Keating) confirms that nobody really likes him. Emory explains to the local sheriff (Robert Burton) that although Carson has been married for five or six years, he does not get along with anybody:

> EMORY: He's [Carson] unpredictable, impatient, unreasonable and sometimes even vengeful. He avoids even personal relationships when money doesn't give him an edge. And he can be pretty rough with it.
> SHERIFF: Doesn't sound like a very popular fellow at that. Or, [a] very happy one either.
> EMORY: No, he's not. You see I think he's had the fear that without his money he'd be nothing. Helpless!

Emory's assessment provides the main focus of the film – Carson's regeneration from a pampered, vindictive businessman to a man who expresses pride in his ability to survive the desert. As no help comes his way[41] Carson learns that he can survive without money and power. He even loses his desire for retribution. Society is no help and the search party never finds him – he has to do it alone.

Cinematographer Lucien Ballard again worked with Baker and the result was a visually stunning film. Although Paul Sawtell's lacklustre score, which is reminiscent of his formulaic music for numerous B westerns in the 1940s and 1950s, marginally weakened the film this was more than offset by the casting of Robert Ryan, arguably one of the finest actors of his generation. Baker was pleased with acquiring his services as he considered Ryan a 'good actor' and judged his performance as 'outstanding'.[42] His lean, craggy face and intense persona meant that he, more often than not, was cast as a morally problematic character, often with a hint of mental instability. This image was indelibly forged after his powerful performance as an anti-Semite in *Crossfire* (1947). Prior to *Inferno* Ryan was cast as the troubled policeman in Nicholas Ray's *On Dangerous Ground* (1952) as well as the principal villain in two westerns, *Horizons West* and *The Naked Spur*, both 1952.

Ryan considered *Inferno* one of his finest films.[43]

Baker is able to turn the inherent difficulty of *Inferno*, the lengthy sequences showing Carson alone in the desert, to his advantage. He involves the viewer, for example, in Carson's plight by combining his narration with a series of clever point-of-view shots. This technique allows the audience to perceive the changes in the businessman's outlook. His early bouts of self-pity and desire for revenge ('Wonder what they [Gerry and Duncan] are doing now? Probably laughing at me. If only I hadn't made it so easy for them') dissipate and are replaced by his self-deprecating humour ('By the time I get out of here I can qualify as a first-class campfire girl') and his determination to survive. His failure to obtain food, when he misses a bird with his revolver, only causes him to remark 'Goodbye lunch'. Baker makes sure that the audience is involved in his regeneration every step of the way.

Initially Carson's determination to survive is fuelled by his desire for revenge and this is expressed in his fantasy to leave his wife and her lover in the desert to die. Later, they become irrelevant to him as his physical journey out of the desert parallels his spiritual 'journey'. Expressions of rage, self-pity and thoughts of suicide weaken until they no longer occupy his consciousness. The defining moment comes as he plans to leave a message by an abandoned mine establishing the culpability of Gerry and Duncan in his plight. However, realising he is in a basin, and that water may lie beneath the sand, he digs in the soil until the finds a muddy patch. Water is followed by food as he shoots a small deer. Just at this moment rain falls to mark his 'rebirth'.

Moral and social regeneration through direct contact with nature is a familiar theme in American literature and *Inferno* reiterates this ethos. While it can be punitive and fatal, it also offers the possibility of recuperation.[44] The film's climax, however, shifts away from the philosophical implications and returns to elemental melodrama. This shift was primarily due to the intervention of Darryl F. Zanuck. Zanuck, who was impressed with most of the film, objected to the film's climax where Gerry, after betraying Duncan, is left to die in the desert as he heads off to Mexico. Meanwhile a 'desert rat' picks up Carson[45] and they eventually collect Gerry waiting by the side of the road. They head off to the nearest town – where Baker postulates – Carson will obtain a divorce and go his own way.[46] Duncan, on the other hand, is allowed to wander, unpunished, towards Mexico.

Zanuck disliked this low-key ending and insisted on a more conventional (melodramatic) climax involving retribution and action. He also wanted greater usage of the cheap thrills associated with the 3D format with objects hurtling towards the camera.[47] Baker, therefore, had to reshoot the climax and, at Zanuck's insistence, include a series of contrived shots to exploit the fact that it was filmed in stereo photography (3D). While most of the film is devoid of such visual gimmicks, the climax almost appears as part of a different film. The fight between Carson and Duncan in a small hut provides the motivation for objects to start flying through the air and it ends in Duncan's death when the roof falls on him after catching fire. This is presented in a spectacular point-of-view shot. Baker, however, retains his epilogue and there is no last-minute reconciliation between Carson and Gerry, nor is there any conflict. As Carson (and Elby) drive along a dusty track they pick up Gerry waiting by the side of the road. After an exchange of glances Carson quietly asks her whether she would 'rather have the sheriff come back out for you or come back with us'. She climbs on to the back of the car and they drive off. 'The End' – no emotion or histrionic behaviour, just two people with different futures.

The British newspaper critics were impressed with *Inferno*. Dilys Powell in the *Sunday Times* (27 September 1953) praised its 'well constructed' story, which she found 'extremely exciting'. Although C.A. Lejeune in the *Observer* objected to 'these stereoscopic pictures' which she couldn't consider as 'other than freaks', and the 'director's whim in mixing up the plot with the credit titles', she rated *Inferno* as 'something out of the ordinary' and singled out 'Robert Ryan's acting [in] that he never allows a part which largely consists of talking to himself while inching slowly from rock to rock to become in the least bit tedious'. Similarly, Baxter in the *Evening Standard* (12 November 1953), objected to the 3D process, but praised the film because

> this film demolishes the threat of 3D. It loses nothing – absolutely nothing – by being reduced to the normal two dimensional medium of sight and sound ... Now let me extend my congratulations to 20th Century-Fox – congratulations not unmixed with awe – that they decided to make a picture with an ending that is wholly tragic.
>
> This is a merciless story that never reaches the softening mood of pity ... You must see *Inferno* if only to realise that films are not only a medium for picturing a story but as a permanent expression of the tragi-comedy of the human race.

Critics in the United States also praised the film and Baker's contribution. H.H. Thomson in the *New York Times* (8 December 1953) argued that the 'restrained treatment of Roy Baker [which] turns a simple, grim story idea with conviction, irony and chilling crescendo. Mr Ryan's portrayal of the gritty, determined protagonist, is, of course, a natural'. Similarly, Philip T. Hartung in *Commonweal* (9 April 1953) argued that '*Inferno* is the best of the 3–D pictures thus far. Its Technicolor of the Mojave Desert in three dimensions is stunning, and the story is more adult than most of the pap which the movies have been exhibiting in 3–D. Roy Baker has given the whole film an atmosphere of reality'.[48] Later, in 1971, Gordon Gow praised Baker's film as 'the most fascinating of the 3–Ds':

> Roy Baker's *Inferno* (1953): the first and only example of the dramatic value of depth, with Robert Ryan isolated in a desert which stretched away towards a distant horizon. This had the very feel of space, heightening our perception of the character's insecurity, and alerting us to the fact that a useful technical advance had been squandered in a short-lived bonanza [by other directors].[49]

Passage Home (1954)

Manuela (1957), based on William Wood's novel and directed by Guy Hamilton, is a startling film in the context of the British cinema in the 1950s. It dramatises the liberating effect of the sexual relationship between a middle-aged, burnt-out sea captain, James Prothero (Trevor Howard), and a young woman, Manuela Hunt (Elsa Martinelli). After the woman is smuggled aboard a miserable tramp steamer by one of the sailors, Mario Constanza (Pedro Armendariz), Prothero threatens to put Manuela off at the next island. During the voyage, however, he becomes infatuated with the seventeen-year-old and the intensity of their highly sexual relationship not only rejuvenates the old sea dog but also causes him to neglect his duties – even after the ship, literally and symbolically, catches fire.

The ship is destroyed and when one of Prothero's officers, Evans (Donald Pleasance), threatens to report Prothero to the shipping company, he is murdered, without consequences, by Constanza. In the final moments, when it appears that the film will conform to the tenets of conventional/conservative moral standards, it suddenly takes a new tack. Prothero, after appearing to let Manuela believe that he is dead, changes his mind and heads back to his young lover. Roy Baker's *Passage Home*, released three years before *Manuela*, shares a similar narrative premise but endorses a different moral sensibility. While *Manuela* ends on hope and the potential for sexual release, *Passage Home* closes on a strange melancholic moment that only intensifies what Peter Hutchings argues is 'one of British cinema's most relentless portrayals of sexual repression'.[50] In a similar vein, Raymond Durgnat claims that this 'sadly underestimated British movie' is 'worthy of George Orwell, as a study of a man in the spiritual prison of his class'.[51]

Captain 'Lucky' Ryland (Peter Finch) is the skipper of the merchant ship S.S. *Bulinga* sailing from Villamonte in South America to Britain at the height of the depression in 1931. The film begins 20 years later at Ryland's retirement 'celebration' of his 'proud service' to the shipping line, as the director presents him with a painting of his first command, the *Bulinga*. A flashback to the Villamonte sees Ryland reluctantly accepting a cargo of pedigree bulls. The bulls, in turn, function as a metaphor for the sexual tension that builds throughout the voyage after a young English governess, Ruth Elton (Diane Cilento), comes on board the all-male ship after she has been abandoned in Villamonte.

Ryland is a martinet and a loner, despised by his first officer, Llewellyn (Duncan Lamont) and barely tolerated by the second officer, Vosper (Anthony Steel). While Llewellyn waits for Ryland to make a mistake so that he can take over command, Vosper tries hard to avoid confrontation with his captain. He resembles the classic western hero who avoids involvement in disputes – until Ryland goes too far and threatens Ruth. A revealing secondary plot concerns the strange relationship between the captain and his steward, Bohannon (Cyril Cusack). While Bohannon remains with Ryland for his entire career, he hates him and takes delight in spreading malicious gossip. The remaining major character, Ruth Elton, has little to do in the film and Diane Cilento was not impressed with her role.[52] Her function, similar to the heroine in many westerns, is to mediate between the captain and the crew while attracting the attention of both Ryland and Vosper. Her moment of glory comes when she is able to cajole the drunken captain into performing his duty by leading the funeral for the bosun, Ike (Geoffrey Keen).

The film begins in a similar manner to *Manuela*, with the crew cavorting in a hotel in Villamonte. The captain and Vosper remain on the ship as they have no interest in the cheap pleasures of a bawdy hotel. Ryland interrupts their leave, after accepting a cargo of bulls, as he is keen to make the trip home in record time. However, the ship's engineer, Pettigrew (Hugh Griffith), has a shady deal with the local coal merchant and there is some doubt whether the *Bulinga* has sufficient coal to make the 30–day journey. Ryland, ambitious, and eager to secure the bonus for a quick trip home, pushes on. He has little rapport with his crew and only his desire for Ruth fractures his hard exterior. Llewellyn, on the other hand, relishes the prospect of Ryland cracking under the pressure of his desire. The first mate tells Vosper 'when those frosty-faced types crack they really crack': 'The only sort of woman he has ever known is the sort you pay for and forget about. This one's different. She's got him.' He predicts that when she rejects him Ryland will start hitting the drink and 'when he has cooked his goose I'm next in line for his job'.

The alienated community Baker depicts on the *Bulinga* depicts a class war, as the crew have little affection for their captain, especially after he purchases rotten potatoes for their meals to keep costs down. Ike battles hard to keep the men under control but, following his death, the discontent escalates. After Ruth rejects Ryland's marriage proposal he tears open her dress exposing her bra, and only the intervention of Vosper prevents Ryland from raping the young woman. Vosper, carrying news of Ike's death, enters the captain's cabin and punches Ryland in the face after witnessing the attack.

Ryland's action, the legacy of years of frustration and loneliness, provides the most obvious demonstration of the film's basic theme – the alienation and 'unnaturalness' of a life at sea. There is little sense of communal solidarity on the ship and only necessity and a sense of grievance against the system in general, and Ryland in particular, unify the men. *Passage Home* reveals, in different ways, what the men miss out on. For most of them, however, it is not a matter of choice but a life born of necessity as jobs are scarce in the 1930s depression. While Ryland is trapped by his desire, they are trapped by the economic situation and their pain is evident. For example, Ike's death coincides with the birth of his seventh son and after he dies, two sailors (Sam Kydd and Gordon Jackson) point out that he rarely saw his children or his wife. Kydd also wonders what his own wife is doing at that moment and whom she is going out with, saying 'Still, she's always there when I get back. You can't ask for more than that, can you?'

As Llewellyn predicts, Ryland turns to alcohol after Ruth's rejection and neglects his duties. While the captain, reluctantly, performs his duty with Ruth's assistance at Ike's funeral, he nearly allows the ship to sink during a violent storm. However, when Llewellyn's nerve fails during the crisis, Ryland takes over and saves the ship. He is the best sailor on board and the worst human being. His inability to inspire loyalty from his crew is perfectly captured in Bohannon's display of sadism and cowardice just prior to this act of heroism. When Bohannon brings Ryland his dinner and finds him drunk, he relishes the opportunity to unleash his pent-up hatred: 'And I hope it [the dinner] chokes you, you cold-blooded son of a ...'. However, realising that Ryland is not totally incapacitated, the steward stops his verbal attack on the seemingly defenceless captain and quickly departs.

The perverse nature of Bohannon's relationship with his captain parallels, in some ways, the 'strangeness' of Ruth's final scene with Ryland. Instead of closing the film in a conventional manner with husband (Vosper) and wife (Ruth) sharing an intimate moment as a way of highlighting, and taking pleasure in, Ryland's bleak future, Baker ends the film in a wordless exchange between the captain and the woman he tried to rape twenty years before. Ruth, standing at the top of the stairs leading down to the deck, is clearly distressed as she looks down on Ryland – not at his assault on her but at what might have been. Does this, the film implies, mean that she made the wrong decision in marrying Vosper? What is clear is that this nautical melodrama does not close in an upbeat manner but on a moment of strong pathos, of being 'too late'. The film fades on this image of shared pain. Durgnat argues that the 'wreckage of his [Ryland's] love affair is not so far, after all, from Sartre's, and Marx's, theories of alienation from society being alienation from others and from one's self'.[53] Alienation is not, it seems, confined to just Ryland.

Tiger in the Smoke (1956)

Tiger in the Smoke reunited Baker with Leslie Parkyn, who co-produced *Morning Departure*, and Geoffrey Unsworth, one of Britain's top cinematographers, who had photographed *Passage Home* and *Jacqueline*, as well as working with Baker on *A Night to Remember*. *Tiger in the Smoke* is based on Margery Allingham's 1952 novel, which was part of a long series of crime novels involving her gentleman detective Albert Campion and the Lady Amanda, sister to the Earl of Pontisbright, wife to Campion and director of Alandel Aircraft Limited. Although Anthony Pelissier's[54] script omitted Campion and Amanda, it followed closely the events of the novel. Baker completed the script, without credit, when Pelissier left the film to direct a television event.

Allingham, who wrote her first Albert Campion crime novel in 1928, was part of the British detective tradition rather than the American hard-boiled style, which also had its practitioners in Britain. Her novels, for example, were less influenced by the moral relativity in the flawed protagonists of Dashiell Hammett, Raymond Chandler, James M. Cain, Cornell Woolrich, or even home-grown British hard-boiled writers such as Peter Cheyney, John Creasey and, especially, James Hadley Chase (René Raymond).

Instead of evil and corruption being represented as an endemic, and pervasive, part of modern society, as in the hard-boiled tradition, in Allingham's *Tiger in the Smoke* they are perceived as an aberration, a condition that can be isolated and eradicated by the determined behaviour of 'good' people. Similarly, instead of the deeply suspicious view of the police and the judiciary presented in the hard-boiled novels, the police in *Tiger in the Smoke* are shown to be the agency fighting to save society from those who threaten it. The community is presented as good, but vulnerable. Within this tradition the novel, and the film to a lesser extent, use the generic elements as a pretext to present a treatise on Good and Evil. The 'surface of upper-middle-class English life', Durgnat argues, provides a context to present the 'spiritual struggles between good and evil, considered as metaphysical forces'.[55] Considerations of the Manichaean, and its emphasis on the 'true' morality that is concealed by the surface of everyday life, is a major element in this crime story. The film, to its credit, eliminates some of the more obtuse 'philosophical' passages from the novel, a position endorsed by Durgnat who agrees that Baker's film is less 'specific, and therefore more interesting in tracing out this near-banal opposition'.[56]

The atmospheric opening scenes are superb in generating a sense of unease and mystery, as Phil Hardy writes: 'Its opening sequence, a gang of embittered war veterans masquerading as a Dickensian set of street musicians tramping through a dream-like London swathed in fog searching for their former boss – the pointedly named Jack Havoc – is superbly staged, announcing a film that is clearly marching towards *Brighton Rock*, even if it never quite gets there.'[57] Hardy was impressed by the fact that the film was able to rise above 'the naturalism that infects most British films of the period' and he credits this to 'Baker, who directs with a fine sense of atmosphere, and cinematographer Unsworth'.[58] These atmospheric scenes showing London enveloped in fog are accompanied by the sounds of a church bell, cars, and street noises. They introduce the band of war veterans who will play a prominent role in the film, as well as Geoffrey Levett (Donald Sinden) and Meg Elgin (Muriel Pavlow). Levett and Elgin arrive at a large London railway station and their enigmatic conversation plunges the viewer into a drama that, seemingly, has begun some time ago:

GEOFFREY: I'd rather you didn't have a husband.
MEG: I know it can't be Martin, but if it is, I wonder how he is feeling?

After Duds Morrison (Gerald Harper) is captured by Chief Inspector Luke (Christopher Rhodes) and Detective Sergeant Pickett (Wensley Pithey), they discover that he was dressed in Meg's late husband's coat. This coat provides the linkage to Meg's family and, eventually, to Jack Havoc (Tony Wright), a psychotic killer. Havoc, when he was a young boy, lived opposite Meg. Meg married Martin Elgin in the early 1940s and during the Second World War Elgin and Havoc, while on a mission in France, visited Elgin's home at St Odile sur Mer where, as Elgin informs Havoc, a 'priceless treasure' is located. Prior to his death Elgin sends a letter to Will Talisman (Charles Victor), who works for Meg's father, Canon Avril (Laurence Naismith). The letter comes with instructions to pass the information on to Meg's second husband if he (Martin) dies in the war. Havoc, who knows the existence of this the letter, begins murdering people in order to locate it.

This storyline only becomes apparent to the audience late in the film. For much of the time the audience is left wondering as to the motivation of numerous events as two plotlines are developed. One strand concerns Levett, who is held prisoner by the war veterans. This, we learn, is due to their desire to locate Havoc. The second plotline follows the trail of bodies left by Havoc, having escaped gaol, as he tries to take possession of Elgin's letter. Both parts come together when Havoc joins up with the veterans and Levett escapes. The second half of the film is more conventional, and less interesting, culminating in a conventional climax as Levett and Havoc wrestling for control of the 'treasure', a religious statue, on the top of a cliff in Brittany. Allingham's climax, on the other hand, is based less on action, and more on metaphor, as Havoc commits suicide by dropping off the cliff to a deep pool of water two hundred feet below. In both, the 'priceless treasure' has no monetary value.

Durgnat was impressed with the film:

> Baker transcends the intrinsic limitations of allegory by its skilful dialogue and atmospheric toughness. For all its melodrama, it comes, at moments, nearer the fuliginous lyricism of Bernanos than the Greene films. The opening sequence particularly, with its street-band of wretched and embittered ex-servicemen tramping through London fogs, dogging the city-gent with scrannel music, are a superb image for a world 'possessed' by the equal and complementary evils of unaware complacency and craven spite.[59]

However, the British critics, in 1956, were less kind. Paul Dehn in the *News Chronicle* (23 November 1956) wrote that it 'is often hard to tell whether fog or plot is thickening faster. Plot, I think'. He concludes that the 'film is recommended as a thriller only to those who find "Sapper" too modern'. Dilys Powell in the *Sunday Times* (25 November 1956) pointed to one of the film's weaknesses when she wrote that 'Tony Wright, playing what is heralded as evil incarnate, turns up as Goldilocks' and she finds the film a 'disappointing muddle to admirers of Margery Allingham'. Robert Kennedy in the *Daily Worker* (24 November 1956) and Ross Shepherd in *The People* (25 November 1956) also singled out Wright. Shepherd, however, argues that 'Wright, in his first big part, is a real find'.

The problem facing the film emanates from the novel's determination to be a philosophical treatise on Good and Evil. Once Tony Wright makes his appearance in the cellar there is a let down, as Dilys Powell points out. When he is just a shadowy figure causing mayhem, the excitement and sense of atmosphere is strong. Early, the film spends considerable time building Havoc into a figure of evil incarnate. Assistant Commissioner Oates (Alec Clunes), for example, warns Chief Inspector Luke that Havoc is not a 'normal' man:

> OATES: Havoc is an evil man, Inspector. You ever meet a truly evil man?
> LUKE: Can't say I have.
> OATES: I've met three in my lifetime and they all had something in common. Something [pause] I can't describe exactly, but oh you'll recognise it if you see it, [pause] if you have time. It's like seeing death for the first time.

Similarly, Canon Avril, who knew Havoc as a young boy when Havoc was known as Johnny Cash,[60] describes him as 'cruel and wicked'. Later, when he confronts him in his church in a futile attempt to save his soul, Avril nearly loses his life when Havoc stabs him in the back.

The film's best scene presents Havoc as a malevolent, almost supernatural, presence and it takes place when Meg and Will visit the empty house she is planning to live in with Levett. The house is dark as the electricity has been turned off. When Meg sees a shadowy figure (Havoc) she calls out and he pursues her in the darkness with his knife. The police arrive just when Will restores the power and as the lights come on, Havoc, seen only in outline behind a window, stretches his arms in a bird-like fashion and jumps from the top floor. This is the one area that the police did not guard, thinking that it was impossible for a man to escape via a steep drop across a spiked railing. A policeman describes Havoc's presence as 'just like a dark shadow ... a shape, like in a nightmare' – as if he had 'dark wings'. Unfortunately, fresh-faced, blond Tony Wright fails to fulfil the expectations generated by such a build-up. His first appearance, in full lighting, is disappointing and it is left to Beatrice Varley, as Havoc's mother, to convey a sense of evil that would seriously threaten society. Her scenes, however, are brief.

Baker also included another demonstration of his mastery of the medium in a wordless sequence involving mime, music and rhythmic editing. It shows Levett's rescue and Meg's reaction to the news that he is safe. The sequence begins when Police Constable Perkins (Stratford Johns), suspicious of the men in the cellar, obtains a key from a grocery attendant (Dandy Nicholls) in the shop above the cellar. He enters the room at the top of the stairs as a close-up of Geoffrey's face (he is bound and gagged and hidden behind a garbage stack) shows that he is aware of the policeman's presence. If he does not reveal himself somehow he will be killed when Havoc returns. After Geoffrey pushes away the rubbish and papers with his feet, Chief Inspector Luke is shown on the phone followed by the police rounding up various suspects. The sequence culminates with Geoffrey shaving, Meg picking up the phone and then smiling broadly. It closes on triumphant note with Geoffrey and Meg kissing each other passionately.

The Singer Not the Song (1960)

The Singer Not the Song was, in Baker's view, the film that effectively killed his career as a major British director. He loathed it.[61] The exact basis of his repulsion to it ('it just gives me the horrors'[62]) is not completely clear. When the film was suggested by Rank's head of production, Earl St John, Baker rejected it on the grounds that the story of a girl falling in love with a priest had 'been done to death'[63] and that the Rank organisation, associated with the well-known Methodist views of J. Arthur Rank, was not an appropriate company to make a film that could be interpreted as critical of the Catholic Church.

The basis of Baker's opposition – the 'forbidden' desire' of a young woman for a priest – was foregrounded in the promotion of the film, as the advertisements show:

> A new and powerfully different kind of motion picture story.
> One by one the people die, in alphabetical order.
> Only the girl and the priest fight back, to stop the senseless murder.
> But then the girl, who has only love in her heart, becomes more deadly than a gun.

This text was placed above three photos – Dirk Bogarde in a black shirt, Mylene Demongeot looking distressed, and a pensive John Mills dressed as the priest. A thick black border around each photo links the three characters.

Another advertisement, with the same photos, increased the emphasis on the girl's relationship with the priest while also including a reference to the 'strange and deadly combat of two men':

> IT IS ABOUT VIOLENCE AND DEATH AND HUMAN FRAILTY.
> IT IS ABOUT THE STRANGE AND TERRIBLE COMBAT OF TWO MEN IN A STRANGE AND TERRIBLE TOWN.
> ONE OF THESE MEN IS A PRIEST. A DOGGED, COURAGEOUS, BATTLING PRIEST. IN THIS DEADLY STRUGGLE HE MUST NOT LOSE.

'A MORBID SENSIBILITY' 129

BUT THEN A BEAUTIFUL GIRL DOES THE ONE THING THAT CAN BRING HIM
DISASTER ...

A third, with the same photos, plus a photo of a smiling Bogarde holding a worried Demongeot, intensified the power of the young woman by creating a scene, with dialogue, that is not in the film:

> Before the priest came, the young bandit ran the town with a whip. Now the priest was a gun at his head ... Would he kill the priest? 'No,' he said. 'That would create a martyr. Besides,' he smiled, 'I like him.'
> Then what?
> He smiled again at the girl. 'I have noticed how you look at the priest. You are the loveliest weapon I have ever known!'

While one 'forbidden desire' is openly acknowledged, indeed, highlighted in the promotional material, the other 'forbidden desire', the homosexual desire of the bandit for the priest, and the possibility that his feeling are reciprocated, is never stated explicitly. But there are a few hints in this material that the film is also about something that cannot be directly acknowledged, something 'strange and terrible': 'the strange and terrible combat of two men in a strange and terrible town' and, in the third advertisement that the bandit 'liked' him. In the press kit that accompanied the film's release through Warner Bros in the United States, an interview with Baker is included that acknowledges not only the desire of the young girl but also that there is a level of meaning in the film involving a 'tremendous depth of feeling for those who care to look':

> In this film the young girl, played by Mylene Demongeot falls in love with the priest, John Mills. I cannot believe this never happens in real life. Young girls fall in love all the time – with older men, with headmasters, even with headmistresses ...
> What I hope comes over strongly in the film is the relationship between the priest and the bandit, played by Dirk Bogarde. Each man could, in different circumstances, have been the other.
> In strength of character they are very similar; but in the way they use that strength completely opposed.

The plot follows the basic narrative employed by countless westerns involving the arrival of the new settler, sheriff or gunman hired to break the corrupt power of an entrenched villain. Along the way he invariably wins the love of a young woman. In *The Singer Not the Song*, Father Keogh (John Mills) is sent to the remote Mexican village of Quantana to restore the influence of the church from the tyranny of a local bandit, Anacleto (Dirk Bogarde). Keogh reopens the church but the locals are too afraid to come to his service until he challenges the bandit with a church service in the main street. Keogh receives assistance in his battle to restore the church and assist the locals from Locha (Mylene Demongeot), the daughter of a wealthy landowner. She is of special assistance to Keogh in the dispensary. Anacleto makes two attempts on Keogh's life and when they fail, fearing that he will create a martyr, he decides to put pressure on the priest by killing the locals in alphabetical order. When a member of the bandit's gang, Old Uncle (Laurence Naismith), tells Keogh during a drunken bout that Anacleto is responsible for the killings, he tries to make amends by attempting to murder the priest. Anacleto, however, kills Old Uncle.

Anacleto leaves Quantana when the Chief of Police (John Bentley) threatens to put him in gaol but, after a short period, he returns and asks the priest if he may stay with him so that he can learn more about the principles of the of the Catholic Church. Once inside Keogh's house he discovers that Locha loves the priest and he disrupts the forthcoming wedding between Locha and a young American, Philip Brown (Philip Gilbert). Locha leaves Brown at the alter and flees the church with the bandit and this provides Anacleto with an opportunity to exploit Keogh's relationship with Locha by attempting to blackmail the priest into endorsing the bandit's control of Quantana. The priest agrees, providing he can see Locha, and when they meet she declares her love for him. However, the priest betrays the bandit by denouncing him in church – after the police have freed Locha. Anacleto is taken into custody and during a gun battle between the police and his gang the priest and the bandit die alongside each other.

Audrey Erskine Lindop's best-selling novel *The Singer Not the Song* was published in 1953. Although Lindop was not a Catholic, and had never been to Mexico, she was convent-educated and checked details in the novel with the Mexican Embassy. When Rank acquired the film rights in the late 1950s, they wanted Baker to direct it as the follow-up to *A Night to Remember* and they cast Dirk Bogarde, hoping that he would renew his contract as this was the last film in his contract. Bogarde, on the other hand, warned Roy Baker that if they went ahead and cast John Mills as the priest he would 'make life miserable for everyone concerned'. When Mills was cast, Bogarde lived up to his threat and Baker described his conduct as 'outrageous'.[64] Bogarde, however, was right. Mills, despite his fine performance, was too old and there is something incongruous in watching 24-year-old Mylene Demongeot as Locha, who is described as, variously, 15 or 16 years of age in the press material, lusting after 52-year-old John Mills as the priest.

Although Baker later claimed that the film 'deviated hardly at all from the original book'[65] there are a number of significant changes in the film. Whereas the novel is wordy and philosophical, the film is direct and melodramatic. For example, the book spends the first eleven pages establishing Father Keogh's credentials with the Bishop and the likely problems he will face in Quantana. The film covers the same ground during the credits: the bus arrives at the village and as Father Keogh gets off the bus the driver tells him 'around here people say that's where the Devil lives'.

As Keogh walks towards the village he meets Doreta Rosalia Teodora Maria-Christina de Cortinez y Ketter – Locha – who warns the priest that Anacleto Gonzeles Flores Comachi Alvarez (she calls him Malo), will kill him as he hates the Catholic Church. When Keogh asks why the bandit has not murdered the current priest, Father Gomez (Leslie French), Locha tells him that there is no need as Gomez has no power in the village. The novel, on the other hand, although it contains the exchange presents Locha as a pre-teenager. Instead of depicting Locha's infatuation with the priest, it shows the interest of Locha's bored, sexually frustrated mother, Doña Marian, in Keogh. The priest is not interested, as Lindop establishes in their first meeting:

> When Father Keogh came into the room he was greeted by 'Pagan Heaven' [Doña's overwhelming perfume]. He saw an ageing bright young thing and he thought that it was the pleasures of a rag-time world that had stamped the hard lines on her face.
>
> He managed to escape after five minutes. Against her name in his little notebook he wrote – 'Gushing and *very* hard-boiled'.[66]

In the film Doña Marian (Jacqueline Evans) is relegated to a minor role, as the film is more interested in Locha's feelings for the priest. In the novel, on the other hand, after there is a lapse of five years while Anacleto is in gaol, Locha flees the village leaving behind incriminating love letters that Doña Marian takes to Keogh:

> I love him. I've always loved him, and nothing and no one can help. I know he isn't meant for me, and I know I'm not allowed to love him. 'Convention' has placed us apart. There are a thousand barriers that could never be broken down. Think of the scandal! Think what people would say! It doesn't bear thinking about. Sometimes I touch my own hand with my eyes closed because I must never touch him. I touch it and I stroke it and put my lips against it.
>
> Sometimes I think I must be mad. I can't think when I loved him first, but I was certainly still a child ... [67]

Both Keogh and Doña Marian make the mistake of believing that the letters are addressed to Anacleto, not Keogh. However, when Locha abandons her 'suitable' young man (Dyke Brown in the novel and Philip

Brown in the film) and leaves him at the altar she openly acknowledges her love for Keogh. This is a critical moment and the novel and film differ. In the novel:

> Locha lay white-faced and wretched across the bed. She raised herself up when she saw Father Keogh. He crossed over and sat beside her ... It was close in the tiny room. Where the hair grew down to a peak, Locha's forehead was damp ... Only Malo appeared to feel no heat ... Her chin was uppermost and her throat ran down from it long and supple and palely skinned. Her breasts made no blatant outward thrust ...but they made a soft and sweet impression ... Father Keogh was still looking at her when she put herself into his arms. She sighed against him – as if it were an almost unbearable relief to be in his arms at last ...
> She drew her lips across his cheek and brought them tenderly back to lie quietly on his mouth ... She clung again to him, her chin driving into him as if it were not enough to feel him next to her, as if she felt unsafe outside him and must force her whole body inside his [68]

Lindop is careful to show that Keogh does not return Locha's feelings as he tells her: 'When you were a child I loved you, Locha – and to me you have never grown up'.[69] Thus, while he 'felt her kisses against him ... above her head he stared at Malo [Anacleto]'.[70] It is the bandit and his salvation that interests the priest and even when Anacleto forces him to kiss Locha in public, Keogh realises that 'there were no sins that he felt he had committed ... [as] he loved only the child'.[71]

The film is more ambiguous. Just prior to Keogh's arrival Locha is shown to be naked in bed although when the priest enters her room she is dressed and standing. She begs Keogh to take her away. He responds by asking her to hold on for a few more days, to which she replies: 'A few days! And then after that what! Nothing! And then more days and days until the end of my life.' She then asks him to give her a 'real kiss, a love kiss, the sort of kiss that can be a sin' as then she will know all through her life that he loved her so much that he had sinned for her. Keogh agrees and kisses her on the mouth after telling her: 'Yes Locha, I love you. In my conceit I didn't realise, didn't know it could happen to me. I failed you as I failed everybody.' As they kiss, a reaction shot of Anacleto appears and the lighting catches the triumph in his eyes.[72]

This aspect, the possibility that Keogh also desired Locha, did not occupy the attention of many reviewers in 1961.[73] Nor have commentators since been very interested in it. Instead, the bandit's desire for the priest, and the possibility that Keogh may share these feelings, has been integral to the perception of the film as somehow 'subversive'. Within the context of 1961 this is a possibility – especially at certain points, such as the ending. Here style, camera movement, composition, colour, mise-en-scène, especially costume and body language, combine to suggest another meaning, one that repudiates the 'innocent' meaning conveyed only by dialogue. Here, the subtext that has excited reviewers and audiences since 1961 is expressed by those elements, such as composition and costume, which could not be totally constrained by institutional censorship strictures.

These same devices also suggest that Keogh has sexual/romantic feelings for Locha. This is best illustrated by the scene where they passionately kiss. But an earlier scene just before Locha's wedding ceremony foreshadows this moment. Here Baker includes an ambiguous camera movement that shows the effect the young girl has on the priest. Disturbed by her strange mood just prior to her wedding, Keogh asks her if she loves the young American Phil Brown. Locha tells him: 'I am quite sure that Phil loves me. I'm quite sure that I love him – as much as I could love any man that I could *possibly marry*.' Baker emphasises the effect of her statement with a subtle, but surprising, movement of the camera which, assisted by a music motif from Philip Green, emphasises the impact of her statement. As she walks out of the frame the camera slides past the side of Keogh's face until it frames the back of his head as he turns and looks at Locha walking away. This camera movement, coupled with the music and the reverse image of Locha is excessive in terms of its narrative function – which is merely to reassure Locha that the wedding is a good idea. Instead it confirms that Keogh is aware of Locha's love for him and, perhaps, suggests that he has similar feelings for her.

Baker was aware that the kiss between the priest and the young girl would be controversial, especially in countries with large Catholic populations. In an attempt to defuse any controversy he refused to allow the distribution of stills of this scene.[74] The filmmakers, on the other hand, never directly acknowledged the possibility of homosexual desire although the British press, who were fascinated by Bogarde's black leather trousers, quickly seized on this aspect. Yet such an interpretation hinges, in many ways, on the costume and the ending as there is little in the dialogue to sustain such a view. The closest reference to such a possibility comes when a member of his gang tells the Anacleto that 'you like this priest too much'. His costume is a different matter. Bogarde wears black pair leather trousers, a black shirt, black leather gloves, a black gun and a black hat in many scenes. This is not a homage to William Boyd, who wore a similar outfit in his Hopalong Cassidy films for Paramount and United Artists in the 1930s and 1940s.[75] Nor is Bogarde dressed in such a manner as a way of merely reinforcing the western stereotype of the black-garbed villain – particularly in such overly redundant, excessive scenes where he carries a whip and, in one scene, strokes a white cat and, in another, a black cat.

In the death scene, Anacleto falls first and then Keogh is shot in the back as he leans over to tend him. The priest dies in a 'Christ-like' gesture with his arms outstretched and then falls so that his face is close to the bandit. Keogh pleads with Anacleto to say an act of contrition before he dies and when the priest tells him that he can no longer hear, he asks the bandit to press his hand so as to acknowledge that he is begging God's forgiveness. Anacleto complies with Keogh's request and a close-up shows the priest smiling as he dies. The film ends showing Anacleto's leather-clad body and his gloved hand holding Keogh's hand before releasing it. While it is not as obvious as Sue Harper suggests when she writes that 'Father Keogh gasps his last with his hand clutching Anacleto's leather groin',[76] there is certainly something going on here. Bogarde acknowledged as much when he admitted that he played the bandit as camp.[77] It is difficult to believe that only Nigel Balchin, the film's scriptwriter, and Bogarde were privy to this interpretation.

Certainly many British critics seized upon the 'strange' attraction of the bandit for the priest when the film was released in London in January 1961. Peter John Dyer, reviewing the film in the *Monthly Film Bulletin* (February 1961), claimed that it was 'as startling as a muffled scream from the subconscious' while Raymond Durgnat, writing in *Films and Filming* in November 1961, described it as 'lyrically homosexual without mentioning the dread word':[78]

> *The Singer Not the Song* is a lyrical, guilt-haunted study of the relationship between a priest (John Mills) and a killer (Dirk Bogarde) whose unrealised passion for each other leads to their joint death. Although the men's concern for each other is translated into terms of souls and guns, it can escape no one's notice that the death of priest and killer, holding hands in the dust, echoes the climaxes of *Duel in the Sun* and *Ruby Gentry*. A powerful nostalgia comes from the fact that both men, abnormally dressed, John Mills in his cassock, Dirk Bogarde in black leather trousers, also, without realising it, are yearning to be loved by Mylene Demongeot, yet reduce her to a helpless pawn in their moral battle.[79]

The British critics were divided in their overall assessment of the film and most emphasised its 'odd' nature. For example, William Whitebait in the *New Statesman* (13 January 1961) singled out screenwriter Nigel Balchin's contribution to the 'year's whackiest film' and finished his review by quoting the reaction of the lady in front of him in the cinema who remarked to her companion that the film was 'unusual'. Whitebait also described the film as a 'film noir à l'anglaise'. Clancy Sigal in *Time 'Tide* (13 January 1961) was less complimentary but pointed to the film's 'Spiritual Relationship With Homosexual Overtones', while the *Times* reviewer (6 January 1961) wrote of the 'slightly lunatic mood of the piece' and cited the 'hallucinatory moment' where Dirk Bogarde as Anacleto 'appears tightly sheathed in black leather and carrying a white Persian kitten for all the world like a latterday Queen Kelly'. Bogarde's black leather trousers featured in nearly every review, with the *Times* claiming that the trousers were 'the real star of the film'.

While many of Baker's films end on a slightly ambiguous note, especially *Passage Home* and *The Vampire Lovers*, or bitter-sweet pathos, such as *Paper Orchid*, *Night Without Sleep* and *The One That Got Away*, his films rarely concluded in abject failure. In *The Singer Not the Song*, the priest fails to save Anacleto's soul and his mission to Quantana, from this point of view, was a failure. Although Keogh dies with smile on his face, we immediately learn, after he dies, that this was only a gesture by the bandit, that he believed only in the singer (Keogh), not the song (the doctrine of the Church). To save Locha and the village Keogh has to break his word and this provokes a sense of despair in the priest: 'I taught him that the power of good will always defeat evil. Yet I could only defeat him by trickery.' This follows Anacleto's virulent denunciation of the Keogh and Catholic doctrine during a church service when he spits on the floor and tells the congregation that although he never believed in the doctrine, he believed that the priest was a 'completely good man' and that the 'goodness of you has failed us both'.

From this point of view, as Durgnat points out, Anacleto has won: 'Good has revealed its helplessness, its dependence on lies, on evil'.[80] His assessment of the priest is harsh:

> [T]he priest's kindly indifference towards Locha's love for him assumes strong overtones of an inadequacy like perversity. He doesn't *know* heterosexual temptation. He loves only God, is ice-cold to human love. Anacleto, killer that he is, loves both the girl (although she rejects him) and the priest (although he rejects him). Of the two men, he is incomparably the most generous and vulnerable lover, and, as a man, the priest's superior.[81]

The novel, on the other hand, is less morbid. Whereas the film closes on three 'lost' characters – with the priest and the bandit dead, Locha has no one left – in Lindop's novel, Locha drives off with Dyke Brown, and although Keogh dies his death has meaning in that it persuades Sam Frankenson, a character not in the film, to accept the power of prayer.[82] The novel ends with the Bishop reading a letter from Keogh informing him that if he is successful in outwitting Anacleto then he [Keogh] will surely die. But he will die happy if Frankenson will pray and if he could arouse in Anacleto 'one single moment's awakening to pity'. This he achieves, unlike the film.

The Singer Not the Song is not one of Baker's outstanding films but it is one of his most fascinating. Its faults reside mainly in decisions made by others during pre-production, especially in the casting. Durgnat criticised the film for its 'Englishness creeping into the playing' and that through 'English restraint, the metaphysical conflict lacks, at times, during this engrossing and admirable film, the continuous intensity which Baker might well have reached more easily with an American cast'.[83] Its lack of 'superficial verisimilitude'[84] is due, in part, to the misconceived casting of John Mills, and Laurence Naismith as Old Uncle. Bogarde was right when he argued that a younger actor, such as Paul Newman,[85] would have made the romantic triangle between the bandit, the priest and the girl more believable. Although Bogarde, who was 39 when the film was shot on location near Malaga in southern Spain, passes for 29, Anacleto's age, Mills, at 52, is far too old for the young priest. Despite a characteristically sincere performance, he cannot project himself as a believable object of sexual desire to a young girl who is described in the press kit as either 15 or 16. As the promotional material stressed, she has to pose as a believable moral danger to the priest, as 'the loveliest weapon I have ever known!'.

When Baker was asked to direct the film he tried to extricate himself by suggesting to Earl St John that the film should be made as an Italian or Spanish co-production with Luis Buñuel directing it.[86] If Rank had accepted Baker's idea, this would have produced a different type of film – perhaps not a melodrama. Baker's film, however, retains the melodramatic excess while trying to make it more plausible, or more 'real'. Durgnat claimed that although the film confirmed 'Roy Baker as one of the most individual English directors, with a quietly intense feeling for a theology of evil',[87] it was not as successful as some of the director's other 'studies of evil and despair'.[88] It remains one of his oddest films in an odd career.

Notes

1 Durgnat, *A Mirror for England*, p. 240.
2 *Ibid.*, p. 206.
3 *Ibid.*, p. 239.
4 *Ibid.*, p. 241.
5 See the Roy Ward Baker interview in McFarlane, *An Autobiography of British Cinema*, p. 49. Jeffrey Richards also cites this as evidence of Baker returning 'again and again to the theme of ordinary people put into extraordinary situations, pushed to the edge and tested to the limit': Richards, *A Night to Remember*, p. 47.
6 See Richard Maltby, 'Film Noir: The Politics of the Maladjusted Text', in Ian Cameron (ed.), *The Movie Book of Film Noir*, London: Studio Vista, 1992.

'A MORBID SENSIBILITY' 137

7 Tony Williams adds *Dear Murderer* (1947) to this list although its protagonist's murderous plan is, similar to Robert Newton in *Obsession* (1949), motivated more by a desire for revenge rather than the result of a mental breakdown. Williams sees these films as examples of the 'relatively unexplored contemporary British cinematic "male hysteria" syndrome'. Tony Williams, *Structures of Desire: British Cinema, 1939–1955*, Albany: State University of New York, 2000, p. 99.
8 Andrew Spicer, *Film Noir*, Essex: Longman, 2002, p. 184.
9 *Ibid.*, p. 175.
10 See William Everson, 'British Film Noir', *Films in Review*, Volume 38, Numbers 5 and 6, 1987.
11 See Robert Murphy, *Realism and Tinsel: Cinema and Society in Britain 1939–1948*, London: Routledge, 1989, Chapter 9.
12 *Ibid.*, p. 168.
13 Spicer, *Film Noir*, p. 185.
14 See Brooks, *The Melodramatic Imagination*, p. 35. Brooks argues that this experience is comparable to 'Freud's structure of pathogenetic trauma'.
15 Williams, *Structures of Desire*, p. 115.
16 *Ibid.*
17 Spicer, *Film Noir*, p. 185. There are, however, a number of Hollywood films, such as John Farrows' *Where Danger Lives* (1950) and Otto Preminger's *Angel Face* (1953), both starring Robert Mitchum, where the protagonist is as passive and accepting of his intolerable situation, if not more so than Ackland.
18 Williams, *Structures of Desire*, p. 115.
19 *Ibid.*
20 Hutchings, 'Authorship and British Cinema', p. 183.
21 Balchin also wrote *The Small Back Room*, which was filmed in 1949 by Michael Powell and Emeric Pressburger. The protagonist in this story suffers from trauma due to the loss of his right foot.
22 See Williams, *Playing the Race Card*, p. 16. Williams perceives melodrama as a 'mode of representation with a particular moralizing function operating across many genres'.
23 *Morning Departure* is generally seen as a Rank film but it could qualify as an independent production as Jay Lewis Productions produced it, with a financial contribution from the British Film Finance Corporation.
24 In 1964 Val Guest wrote and directed *The Beauty Jungle*, a powerful exposé of the beauty contest industry, and a film that shares the same cynical attitude towards the newspaper industry and other institutions as *Paper Orchid*.
25 La Bern also contributed additional scenes and dialogue to the film. La Bern also wrote *Night Darkens the Street*, which was filmed in 1948 as *Good Time Girl*.
26 Peter Hutchings argues that *Morning Departure* is a 'prolonged – and morbid – meditation on the futility of action': Hutchings 'Authorship and British Cinema', p. 184.
27 Durgnat, *A Mirror for England*, p. 240.
28 The only hint of a fatalistic character is Lieutenant Manson (Nigel Patrick), who exhibits, in an understated way, a vague death wish due to his involvement in a similar incident some years before.
29 See Richards, *A Night to Remember*, p. 44.
30 See McFarlane, *An Autobiography of British Cinema*, p. 74.
31 Gray has just emerged from a failed romance and, at time of her invitation to become a spy, was planning to take her holidays in Torquay, designated as 'Queen of the English Riviera', so she could meet somebody who would tolerate her work with insects.
32 A reference to Dick Barton, a popular British radio serial at that time.

33 Durgnat, *A Mirror for England*, p. 240.
34 Bunny's intrusion represents, literally and metaphorically, the film's primal scene. In this example, the situation mirrors Peter Brooks' use of this concept as an adaptation from Freud's analysis of infantile neurosis and the traumatic aftermath of an infant who witnessed sexual intercourse between his parents. See Brooks, *The Melodramatic Imagination*, p. 34. See also 'The Dream and the Primal Scene', in J. Strachey (ed.), *The Complete Psychological Works of Sigmund Freud, Volume XVII (1917–1919)*, London: The Hogarth Press, 1978.
35 Dixon, 'Twilight of the Empire', Part One, p. 34.
36 See, for example, *The Stranger on the Third Floor* (1940), *I Wake Up Screaming* (1941), *The Fallen Sparrow* (1943), *Detour* (1945), *Dark Angel* (1946), *Fear in the Night* (1947), *Pitfall* (1948), *Secret Beyond the Door* (1948), *In a Lonely Place* (1950), *Where Danger Lives* (1950) and *On Dangerous Ground* (1952).
37 His novels were adapted into films such as *The Black Curtain*, which was released by Paramount as *Street of Chance* (1942); *Black Alibi* became RKO's *The Leopard Man* (1943). Universal retained Woolrich's title for *Phantom Lady* (1944) and it was followed by *The Black Path of Fear*, which became *The Chase* (1946), *Fear in the Night* (1947), *Night Has a Thousand Eyes* (1948), *The Window* (1949) and *No Man of Her Own* (1950). There were also numerous radio versions of his works in the 1940s and 1950s.
38 Frank Krutnik notes that 'Woolrich's work contains tortuously elaborate passages of masochistic delirium'. Frank Krutnik, *In a Lonely Street: Film Noir, Genre, Masculinity*, London: Routledge, 1991, p. 41. James Naremore also described Woolrich's fiction as 'doom-laden and slightly crazed'. See James Naremore, *More Than Night: Film Noir in its Contexts*, Berkeley: University of California Press, 1998, p. 145.
39 Author interview with Roy Ward Baker, September 2000.
40 Baker considered it the best film he made for Twentieth Century-Fox. *Ibid*.
41 An old miner, Sam Elby (Henry Hull), provides some assistance late in the film after Carson has left the mountains.
42 See Baker, *The Director's Cut*, p. 84.
43 See Franklin Jarlett, *Robert Ryan: A Biography and Critical Filmography*, Jefferson, NC: McFarland & Company, 1990, p. 71.
44 This theme is central to the ideas of historian Frederick Jackson Turner, and others. The distinctive American character, they argue, was formed by stripping away its European attributes through contact with nature. See Frederick Jackson Turner, *The Frontier in American History*, New York: Holt, Rinehart and Winston, 1962.
45 Baker's term for Henry Hull as Sam Elby. Baker also praised his performance. Baker, *The Director's Cut*, p. 84.
46 *Ibid*.
47 Author interview with Roy Ward Baker, September 2000.
48 Quoted in Jarlett, *Robert Ryan*, p. 219.
49 Gordon Gow, *Hollywood in the Fifties*, New York: A.S. Barnes & Co., 1971, p. 16.
50 Hutchings, 'Authorship and British Cinema', p. 181.
51 Durgnat, *A Mirror for England*, p. 41.
52 Author interview with Roy Ward Baker, September 2000.
53 Durgnat, *A Mirror for England*, p. 42.
54 Anthony Pelissier was also a director of films such *The History of Mr Polly* (1949) and the bizarre *Rocking Horse Winner* (1950), both of which were produced by, and starred, John Mills.
55 Durgnat, *A Mirror for England*, p. 240.
56 *Ibid*.

57 Phil Hardy (ed.), *The BFI Companion to Crime*, Berkeley: University of California Press, 1997, pp. 325–6.
58 *Ibid.*, p. 326.
59 Durgnat, *A Mirror for England*, p. 240.
60 This involves a complicated plot twist concerning the Canon's wife and Johnny's mother (Lucy Cash – Beatrice Varley), with Havoc assuming a new identity after his mother claimed he had died when he was 15.
61 Author interview with Roy Ward Baker, September 2000.
62 McFarlane, *An Autobiography of British Cinema*, p. 52.
63 Baker, *The Director's Cut*, p. 106.
64 Author interview with Roy Ward Baker, September 2000.
65 Baker, *The Director's Cut*, p. 112.
66 Audrey Erskine Lindop, *The Singer Not the Song*, London: The Reprint Society, 1954, p. 88.
67 *Ibid.*, p. 241.
68 *Ibid.*, pp. 322–4.
69 *Ibid.*, p. 323.
70 *Ibid.*, p. 324.
71 *Ibid.*, p. 336.
72 There is a similar image in *The October Man* when Peachey confesses to Jim Ackland that he murdered Molly.
73 For example, see Durgnat's comments on the film below where he claims that both men, Anacleto and Keogh, are yearning to be loved by Locha, without realising it, and she is sidelined in 'their moral battle of wits'. Raymond Durgnat, 'Saturnalia in Cans', *Films and Filming*, November 1961, p. 33.
74 Baker, *The Director's Cut*, p. 112.
75 Bogarde also rides a white horse similar to Cassidy's 'Topper'.
76 See Sue Harper, *Women in British Cinema: Mad, Bad and Dangerous to Know*, London: Continuum, 2000, p. 104.
77 See McFarlane, *An Autobiography of British Cinema*, p. 70.
78 Durgnat, 'Saturnalia in Cans', p. 33.
79 *Ibid.*
80 Durgnat, *A Mirror for England*, p. 241.
81 *Ibid.*, p. 242.
82 'Okay, I never said a prayer before ... here's prayer coming up. This is Sam Frankenson – praying!' See Lindop, *The Singer Not the Song*, p. 350.
83 Durgnat, *A Mirror for England*, p. 242.
84 See *Ibid.*
85 See McFarlane, *An Autobiography of British Cinema*, p. 70.
86 Baker, *The Director's Cut*, p. 106.
87 Durgnat, 'Saturnalia in Cans', p. 33.
88 *Ibid.*

1 Dirk Bogarde in *The Singer Not the Song*

2 Mylene Demongeot and Dirk Bogarde in *The Singer Not the Song*

3 Dirk Bogarde and John Mills at the climax of *The Singer Not the Song*

4 John Mills in *The Singer Not the Song*

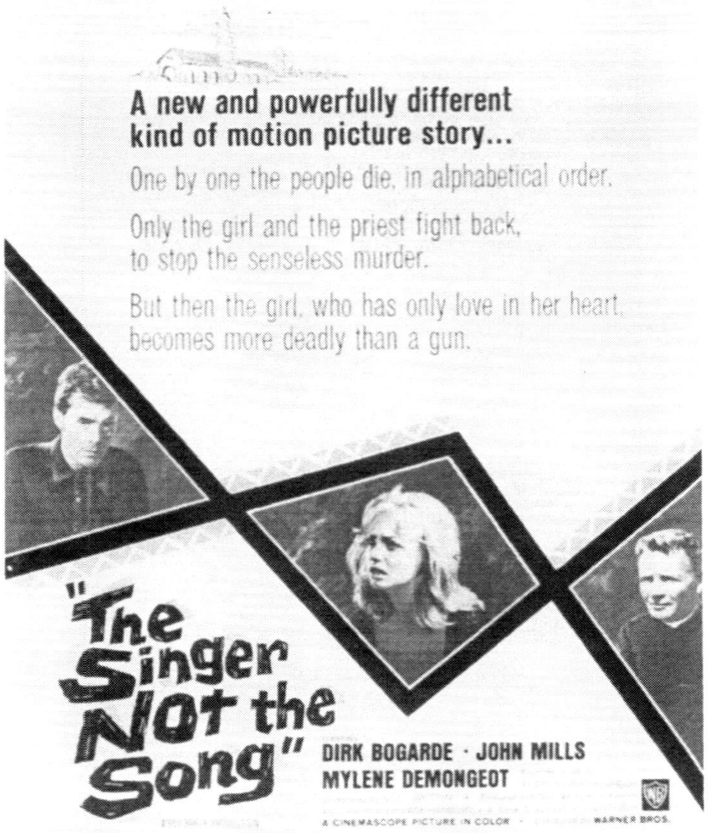
A new and powerfully different kind of motion picture story...
One by one the people die, in alphabetical order.
Only the girl and the priest fight back, to stop the senseless murder.
But then the girl, who has only love in her heart, becomes more deadly than a gun.
"The Singer Not the Song"
DIRK BOGARDE · JOHN MILLS
MYLENE DEMONGEOT
A CINEMASCOPE PICTURE IN COLOR
WARNER BROS.

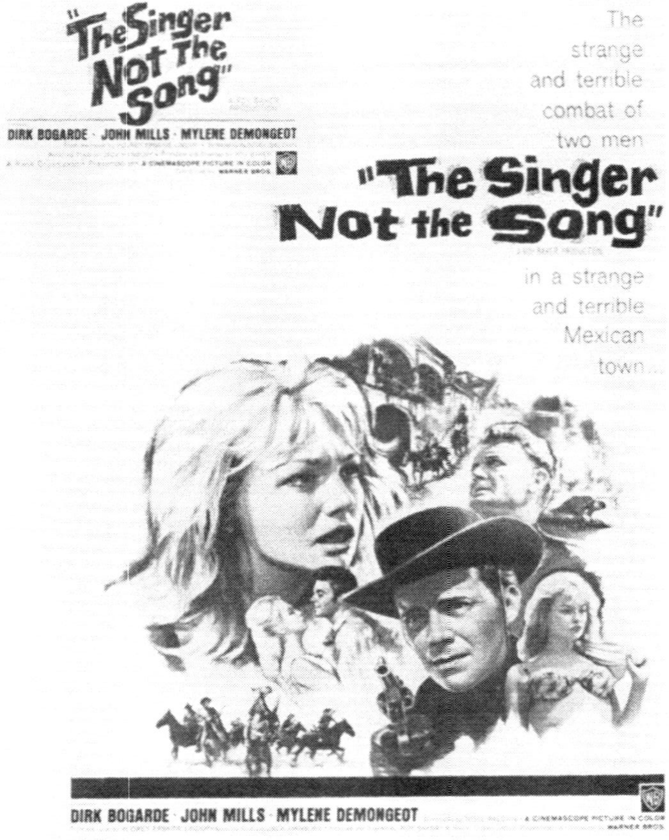
"The Singer Not The Song"
DIRK BOGARDE · JOHN MILLS · MYLENE DEMONGEOT
A CINEMASCOPE PICTURE IN COLOR
WARNER BROS.
The
strange
and terrible
combat of
two men
"The Singer Not the Song"
in a strange
and terrible
Mexican
town...
DIRK BOGARDE · JOHN MILLS · MYLENE DEMONGEOT
A CINEMASCOPE PICTURE IN COLOR
WARNER BROS.

facing] **5, 6** Posters for *The Singer Not the Song*

7 Poster for *The Singer Not the Song*

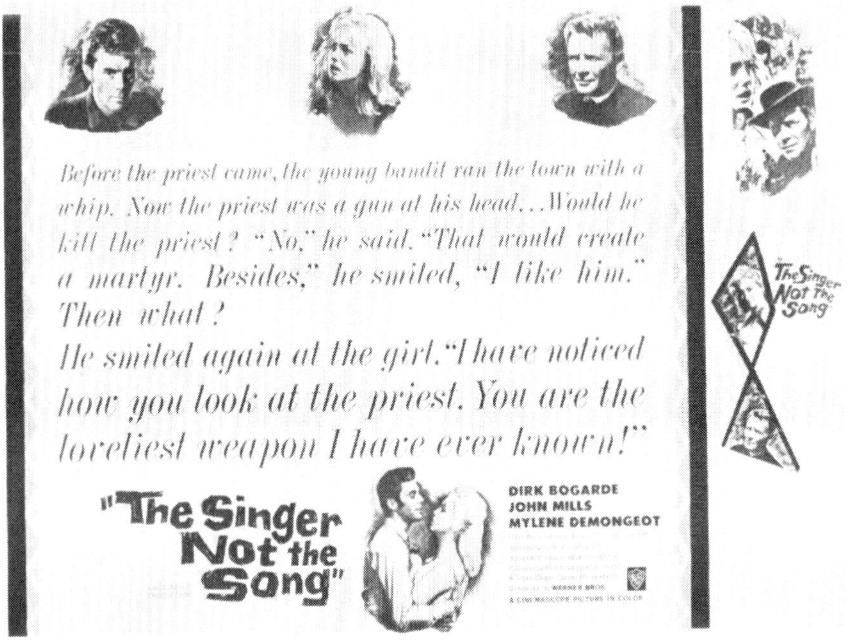

MAY WE HELP YOU?

Stereos of the 65-screen blocks illustrated on this sheet can be supplied free of charge direct to a newspaper for editorial use. Order from Rank Film Distributors Ltd., Press Dept., 11, Belgrave Road, London, S.W.1. Phone : Victoria 6633. You are free to lift or adapt any of the material printed here. Matrices are supplied for overseas use. Order from Ad-Sales Dept., Rank Overseas Film Distributors Ltd., 127 Wardour St., London, W.1.

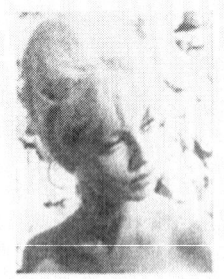

Block SNS-1
Mylene Demongeot plays Locha, a young Mexican girl who falls in love with a priest in "The Singer Not The Song". Dirk Bogarde and John Mills also star.

Block SNS-2
Dirk Bogarde, the bandit in "The Singer Not The Song", a Rank Organisation film, has a contrasting role. Here he comes to Father Keogh's (John Mills) rescue when Old Uncle tries to kill the priest (right). Mylene Demongeot also stars.

Block SNS-3
But not all is violence. Dirk takes Locha (Mylene Demongeot) in his arms and kisses her.

8 Press book for *The Singer Not the Song*

Block SNS-4

Anacleto (Dirk Bogarde) sees Father Keogh (John Mills) praying in the market place and the people of Quantana listening to his prayer. Anacleto strides towards the priest and at his approach the frightened people disappear. A scene from "The Singer Not The Song" which also stars Mylene Demongeot.

Block SNS-5

For the first time in his long career John Mills plays a priest in "The Singer Not The Song". He plays Father Keogh, co-starring with Dirk Bogarde and Mylene Demongeot.

Block SNS-6

In "The Singer Not The Song" Dirk Bogarde plays Anacleto, a cold, ruthless, calculating bandit who terrorises the small Mexican town of Quantana. John Mills and Mylene Demongeot also star.

Block SNS-7

The Chief of Police (John Bentley) is determined to take Anacleto—dead or alive. Father Keogh (John Mills) begs him not to shoot. A scene from the Rank Organisation film "The Singer Not The Song" which also stars Dirk Bogarde and Mylene Demongeot.

9 Press book for *The Singer Not the Song*

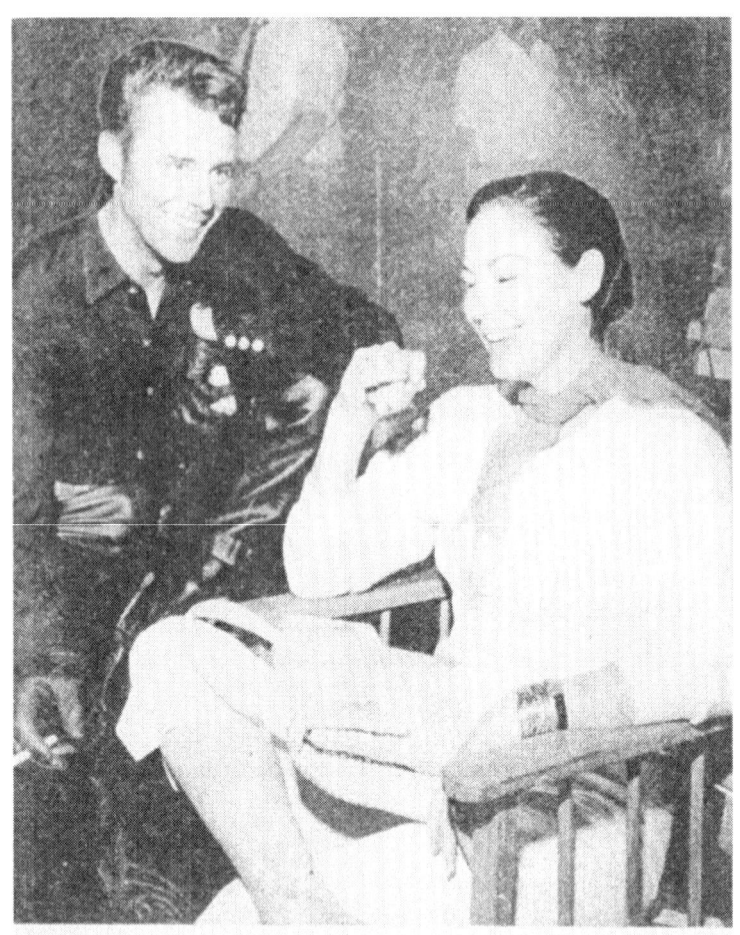

BRITISH actor Dirk Bogarde enjoys a joke with Ava Gardner when she visited Pinewood Studios to watch him working on his latest film, "The Singer Not the Song."

10 Ava Gardner visits Dirk Bogarde on the set of *The Singer Not the Song*

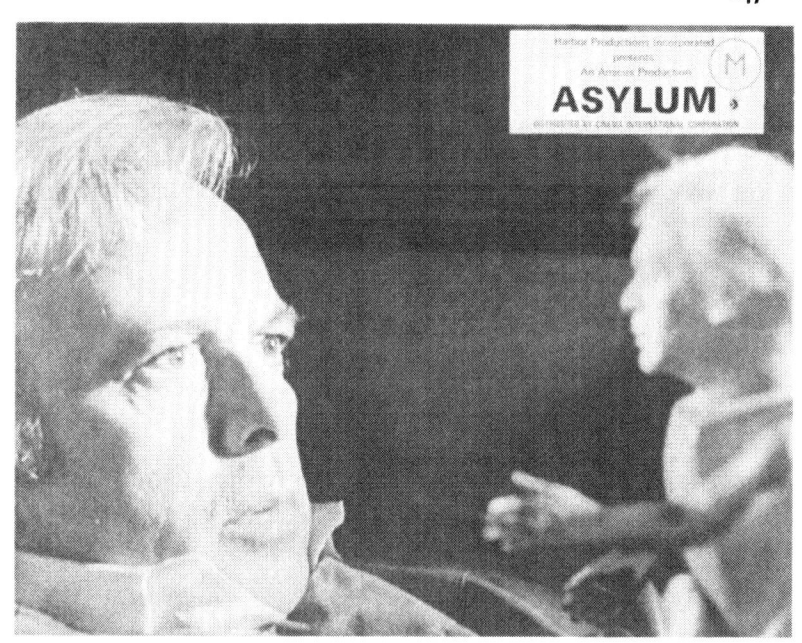

11 Lobby card for *Asylum* featuring Herbert Lom

12 Lobby card for *Asylum* featuring Babara Parkins

"AND NOW THE SCREAMING STARTS"

And the suspense.
And the drama.
And the horror.

Technicolor

Starring Peter Cushing
Patrick Magee
Herbert Lom
Stephanie Beacham

You've got to hand it to this movie.
It's a classic. It's bizarre.
It's spine-chilling.
It's shocking, and still
it remains a classic!

facing] 13 Lobby card showing Ian Ogilvy in *And Now the Screaming Starts!*

14 The American poster for *Operation Disaster*, which was released in Britain as *Morning Departure*

YOUNG AND BEAUTIFUL... SHE WAS CAUGHT IN A DESPERATE BATTLE BETWEEN GOOD AND EVIL !
IN COLOUR
THE SINGER NOT THE SONG
NOT SUITABLE FOR CHILDREN
STARRING
DIRK BOGARDE
JOHN MILLS
MYLENE DEMONGEOT
A CINEMASCOPE PICTURE
Produced and Directed by Roy Baker
This film is made under licence from Twentieth Century-Fox Film Corporation the registered proprietor of the trade mark "Cinemascope"

facing] **15** Poster for *The Singer Not the Song*

16 Poster for *The Vampire Lovers*

17 Poster for *Inferno*

'Roy Ward Baker' : Hammer and Amicus

Hammer

After five years in British television Roy Baker resumed his feature film career when Anthony Nelson Keys invited him to direct *Quatermass and the Pit* for Hammer. At the same time he also changed his name from Roy Baker to Roy Ward Baker.[1] Baker appreciated his return to feature films, although he never regained the status that he enjoyed at Rank in the mid- and later 1950s. He was a professional, a working director, and Hammer, and later Amicus, gave him the opportunity to make films again. Conditions at Hammer, primarily in terms of resources and shooting schedules, were different and the film at which Baker excelled in the 1940s and 1950s, the medium-budget genre film, had largely disappeared by the late 1960s. With the exception of *The Anniversary*, the only feature films for a theatrical release he was offered after 1962 were science fiction or horror.[2] These were commercially profitable genres, especially with regard to the American market, but Baker, the industry and the critics generally considered them to be less prestigious than other genres.

This perception was often reflected in the less-than-serious attitude to Baker's post-1967 films. For example, the term 'hokum' appeared in number of reviews over the next six years. Paul Errol's response to *Quatermass and the Pit* in the *Evening Standard* (5 November 1967) was typical of the prevailing ethos at this time: Errol described the film as a 'well-made, but wordy, blob of hokum' and 'mildly amusing rubbish'. Similarly, William Hall in the *Evening News* (2 November 1967) described it as 'entertaining hokum' with an 'imaginative ending'. Dilys Powell, on the other hand, was a little more circumspect in her review but a slightly patronising tone is evident: 'Let me hasten to separate myself from any tendency to scoff. The film is produced and directed with dash – and an absolutely straight face' and she conceded that it was 'pretty smart'.

Penelope Mortimer, in the *Observer* (5 November 1967), called it 'good nonsense': 'this nonsense makes quite a good film, well put together, competently photographed, on the whole sturdily performed. What it totally lacks is imagination'. *Quatermass and Pit* was one of the more complex science-fiction films of the 1950s and 1960s: what sort of imagination was Mortimer seeking? In terms of its ideas, if not its execution and budget, it rivals Stanley Kubrick's *2001 – A Space Odyssey* (1968).

Quatermass and the Pit (1967)

The film had its genesis in screenwriter Nigel Kneale's story, which was serialised by the BBC between December 1958 and January 1959. Baker, in effect, had 97 minutes to deal with ideas that were developed during a six-part television serial. This hampered the film, as Kneale's thesis was complex. When workmen discover a number of skulls and skeletons inside a cavity wall during extensions to the Hobbs End underground station,[3] anthropologist Dr Matthew Roney (James Donald) and his assistant Barbara Judd (Barbara Shelley) are called in. After examining the ape-like creatures, Roney speculates that this discovery indicates that mankind roamed the earth as early as five million years ago. Further excavations uncover a large metal object and, fearing that it is an unexploded bomb, the army is called in under the command of Colonel Breen (Julian Glover). Breen, who has just been appointed commander of Professor Quatermass's (Andrew Keir) rocket project, allows the scientist to accompany him to the site.

Quatermass uncovers evidence that the site, originally called 'Hob's Lane' (suggesting a link to the Devil), has been the centre of strange incidents since Roman times. After insect-like aliens are found inside the metal object he concludes that the creatures are from Mars. The site is shown to be dangerous after a worker returns to the craft at night to retrieve his tools. He is sent spinning wildly into the street and Quatermass and Judd investigate his condition. Their conclusion that the skeletons are genetically altered apes provokes only ridicule and anger from Breen and Minister of Defence (Edwin Richfield). They also reject Quatermass's fear that the space capsule is still alive and is radiating electricity and telepathy to those who are susceptible to its messages.

Judd agrees to act as a conduit for messages from the craft. They discover that the horned demons, which have been recorded in this area for centuries, are Martians who, in a desperate attempt to save their dying planet, took apes from earth and instilled them with Martian memories. This represented a more complex variation of the 'alien invasion' story that was popular in American and British science-fiction films in the 1950s, where Martians, and others, attempted to establish a colony-by-proxy on Earth. However, Kneale's ideas were considerably more complex than the relatively simple fears of the 1950s films. Martian memories in *Quatermass and the Pit* remain dormant within humans for millions of years until the excavation work at Hobbs End triggers their release through exposure to the spacecraft.

The army and the government reject Quatermass's warnings and allow the media into the excavation site, thereby allowing the spaceship to acquire a huge surge of energy. This unleashes the latent Martian instincts, provoking a murderous frenzy amongst the humans. To disperse the alien energy force, Roney climbs up on a large crane and pushes its metal arm into the 'Devil'. Although the chaos subsides, the film closes on a downbeat note with a disconsolate Quatermass and Judd framed by the fires still burning in London.

Quatermass and the Pit, Kneale's most ambitious story, combines a radical theory of evolution with telekinesis. It also proposes that many occult beliefs emanate from the fear of Satanic Martians. Devising a workable script, together with problems relating to the American financing, delayed the project for many years. Kneale claimed that this delay was deliberate on his part: 'They had wanted me to do it for some time but I think I held off because I didn't want to see Mr Donlevy on the screen again. I was very happy with Andrew Keir ... and very happy with the film.'[4]

Unlike the simple good/bad paranoia of many 1950s science-fiction films, Kneale's script was unusually abstract and, as a consequence, it offered fewer opportunities for suspense and tension. This provoked a negative review from Richard Davis in *Films and Filming* (February 1968), who complained that Kneale's 'complicated premise' was 'very wild and woolly and fails to carry one tenth of the unnerving credibility of the Quatermass predecessors'. This was harsh, as the confrontation between the scientists and the army/government provided some drama but the overall story was more thought-provoking, and less formulaic, than its predecessors. *Quatermass 2* (1957), for example, was based on an alien conspiracy to take over the British Government and, as directed by Val Guest, was similar in tone to the paranoia of many Hollywood films. Baker, however, made the most of the film's few action sequences, such as the drill operator caught up in a psychic whirlwind and the chaos unleashed by the Martian craft. He was assisted in this by Tristrum Cary's eerie score, which was influenced by his work with the BBC Radiophonic Workshop. There are similarities between the score and the music for the *Dr Who* television series.[5]

There was also a significant difference between the climax in the film and the teleplay. While the BBC series concluded inside the pit, as Roney flings a weighted chain into the image of the Devil, the film provides a more visually spectacular scene of the scientist riding a crane into the concentrated image of the Martian devil. The teleplay, on the other hand, also included a warning to the audience from Quatermass that is not found in Baker's film:

> If another of these things should ever be found, we are armed with knowledge. But we also have knowledge of ourselves ... of the ancient, destructive urges in us, that grow more deadly as our populations approach in size and complexity those of ancient Mars. Every war crisis, witch-hunt, race riot, and purge ... is a reminder and a warning. We are the Martians. If we cannot control the inheritance within us ... this will be their second dead planet!

The film, produced in a different social and political context, jettisons the scientist's plea and shows only despair at the destruction caused by humans acting on their primeval instincts. The guarded optimism, and social criticism, of the 1950s teleplay is replaced by a more fatalistic acceptance of the dark side of human nature.

The Vampire Lovers (1970)

> Sometime after an hour of apathy, my strange and beautiful companion would take my hand and hold it with a fond pressure, renewed again and again; blushing softly, gazing in my face with languid and burning eyes, and breathing so fast that her dress rose and fell with the tumultuous respiration. It was like the ardour of a lover; it embarrassed me, it was hateful and yet overpowering; and with gloating eyes she drew me to her, and her hot lips travelled along my cheek in kisses; and she would whisper, almost in sobs, 'You are mine, you *shall* be mine, and you and I are one for ever.'
>
> Then she has thrown herself back in her chair, with her small hands over her eyes, leaving me trembling.[6]

Roy Baker and Eric Ambler planned to film J. Sheridan Le Fanu's *Uncle Silas* as soon as they were demobilised from the army, although they never worked on the project, moving on to *The October Man* instead. Baker, however, was familiar with Le Fanu's novels and short stories.[7] In 1969 Hammer offered him one of Le Fanu's best-known novellas, *Carmilla*, which was serialised in the magazine *The Dark Blue* between December 1871 and March 1872. By the late 1960s the tightly knit Hammer group was forced, through financial exigencies, to admit new people and new ideas. Independent producer Harry Fine, with his new partner Michael Style, took a story outline for a film based on Le Fanu's story to James Carreras who immediately approved the project.[8] This proved to be Baker's most controversial, and misunderstood, film and he has expressed his own unease with it in recent years ('This one was full of traps for the unwary'[9]).

The Vampire Lovers was not the first film to feature a female vampire. Aside from the vampire women in the 1931 version of Dracula, and pseudo-vampires such as Carol Borland, in Mark of the Vampire (1935), the first sound feature film showing a female vampire with lesbian tendencies was Dracula's Daughter (1936), Universal's excellent follow-up film to Dracula. The first version of Le Fanu's story was, ostensibly, Carl Dreyer's Vampyr (1930) although he jettisoned virtually all of Le Fanu's story. Thirty years later another French film Et Mourir de Plaisir (Blood and Roses), directed by Roger Vadim, adapted and updated Carmilla although censorship restrictions limited the lesbian activities between Annette Vadim and Elsa Martinelli. Vadim also changed the setting to Italy. In 1963 the low-budget Italian horror film, La Cripta e l'Incubo (also known as Terror in the Crypt) borrowed aspects of Carmilla and cast Christopher Lee as Count Ludwig von Karnstein. The Vampire Lovers, however, remains the most faithful, and best, version of Le Fanu's story.

Baker's concern for the project emanated from his suspicion that producer Fine and Style wanted only a soft-core porn film with lashings of female nudity and lesbianism. Baker wanted to remain faithful to the sad, melancholic tone of Le Fanu's tale and its subtle rendering of female desire. The potential for exploitation is obvious – as the quote from Carmilla above indicates. Baker's determination not to accede to the prurient objectives of his producers and keep most of Le Fanu results in a strong film, far better than the rest of the so-called 'Karnstein trilogy'.[10] Lust For a Vampire and Twins of Evil, the other two films in this 'trilogy', were more explicit with regard to nudity and sex.

In an interview in Bizarre (Number 3) in the early 1980s, Baker explained his approach to The Vampire Lovers:

> Hammer rang me up and said, "We're thinking of doing a horror picture ... [if] they had offered me a Dracula or Frankenstein at that time I doubt I would have accepted ... Then they asked me if I had ever read the book CARMILLA by Joseph Sheridan Le Fanu. I said I had read it and I liked it very much. In fact the first time I read it was when I was 14 years old. So I became more interested. They said 'We've developed it into a script. We feel that there are lesbian overtones and we have brought these out.' ... well I stuck my head right out and decided that in my own way I would try to save the book's dignity by at least toning down the lesbianism and

doing it seriously and tastefully. Hammer had some doubts but the one person who agreed with me was Ingrid Pitt ... People are what they are, and as far as I'm concerned, any character has got his own rights, his own status in life ...
This point is something I am very intense about; something that holds true in all my films. I am not going to push the characters around like cardboard because if I do, they are going to be cardboard. That is no good.[11]

The two nude scenes appear to have unduly influenced the attitude of British critics to the film – at the time of its release and in recent years. It was the most graphic Hammer film to up to this time. This was due to the liberalisation of censorship and Hammer's need to arrest the declining popularity of their films. Yet it is appropriate that this should occur in the vampire film because of all the genres, both literary and film, it has the strongest historical basis for the inclusion of erotic material as it traditionally functioned as an 'oral-sadistic metaphor'.[12] The vampire was, in the late eighteenth and nineteenth centuries, part of the Gothic Romance, a mode of sentimental literature concerned with a cluster of macabre themes involving death, terror and the supernatural. The prevailing mode was anti-mimetic and examples, such as Horace Walpole's *The Castle of Otranto* (1764) and M.G. Lewis's *The Monk* (1796), provided a compensatory function in their persistent 'attention to anything assumed to be noncivilized or taboo, for example, necrophilia, incest, domestic violence, or murder'.[13] Such stories mixed generic elements with an affinity to the marvellous, or the fairy tale, and they provided a dramatisation of the 'rational mind grappling with – resisting, explaining away, allegorising – that marvellous'.[14]

A characteristic feature of such stories was their 'self-indulgent eroticism'. This was combined with strong emotions involving terror and a sense of revulsion – as in Lewis's *The Monk*. Critics of this novel, for example, were repelled by its 'overly "strong colours" – lurid scenes of sex, violence and death, all told in perfect hyperbole'.[15] *The Monk* was a significant publication and it told the story of the downfall of a stern abbot (Ambrosia) because of his fatal attraction to an evil spirit in the form of a beautiful woman (Matilda). Matilda, who enters his convent in the guise of a male novice, leads him into rape, incest and matricide. When Ambrosia views the bared breast of Matilda he does so 'with insatiable avidity ... A raging fire shot through every limb; the blood boiled in his veins, and a thousand wild wishes bewildered his imagination'.[16]

Le Fanu's *Carmilla* also utilises the Gothic motif of the 'fatal woman' as the basis for his story although he modifies it by emphasising

Carmilla's loneliness, languid movements, beauty, and, above all, her 'melancholy expression': 'There was a coldness, it seemed to me, beyond her tears, in her smiling melancholy persistent refusal to afford me the least ray of light'.[17] Carmilla is an aristocrat, the Countess Mircalla Karnstein, who, 150 years after her funeral, reappears to insinuate herself into the home of a Stryian aristocrat. The tale is narrated by the aristocrat's daughter Laura, who first encounters Carmilla in a dream when she is six years old: 'She caressed me with her hands, and lay down beside me on the bed, and drew me towards her, smiling: I felt immediately delightfully soothed ... I was awakened by a sensation as if two needles ran into my breasts'.[18] Years later, when Carmilla's coach breaks down near Laura's house, she is invited to stay and the young girl's disturbing dreams return while her health deteriorates. When a neighbour, General Spielsdorf, tells the family that his daughter died after they had invited a young woman, Millarca, into their house, they realise that Carmilla and Millarca are the same person: the Countess Karnstein. Baron Vordenberg confirms this and the three men visit the abandoned Chapel of Karnstein to stake the Countess:

> The body, therefore, in accordance with the ancient practice, was raised, and a sharp stake driven through the heart of the vampire, who uttered a piercing shriek at the moment, in all respects such as might escape from a living person in the last agony. Then the head was struck off, and a torrent of blood flowed from the severed neck.[19]

The tale concludes on an ambivalent note. Although 'that territory has never since been plagued by the visits of a vampire'[20] Laura cannot forget her dead lover: 'to this hour the image of Carmilla returns to memory with ambiguous alternations – sometimes the playful, languid, beautiful girl; sometimes the writhing fiend I saw in the ruined church; and often from a reverie I have started, fancying I heard the light step of Carmilla at the drawing room-door.'[21]

Baker's film version closely follows Le Fanu's story although General Spielsdorf's (Peter Cushing) story is placed at the start of the film where, unaccountably, his daughter is renamed Laura (Pippa Steele). Laura dies early in the film and the bulk of the story concerns the relationship between Emma (Madeline Smith), the daughter of Roger Morton (George Cole), an English landowner living in Styria, and Carmilla. The casting of Ingrid Pitt as Carmilla reinforces the tale's eroticism as Carmilla is clearly older and more sexually aware than Emma or Laura.

This is in accord with the nineteenth-century melodramatic motif involving the violation of the 'space of innocence'. An important aspect of this tradition, as Peter Brooks notes, is the opening scene where the villain, 'either under the mask of friendship (or courtship), or simply as an intruder', will insinuate him- or herself into a household leading to the fall and (temporary) expulsion of virtue.[22] This *topos* is repeated twice in *The Vampire Lovers*. Carmilla, after moving into Laura's house and, after a 'violated banquet',[23] killing her, insinuates herself into Morton's home and befriends Emma.

The film presents Carmilla as both a fiend and a victim of her condition. The first aspect emerges in her violation of innocence (Laura and Emma). This is reinforced by the casting of wide-eyed Madeline Smith as the ultimate sign of innocence (Emma). On the other side, the film shows both women as suffering from the constrictions of patriarchal society. Hence Carmilla's ability to wrest control of the Morton household from the patriarch could be perceived as admirable – she seduces Emma's governess, Mademoiselle Perrodot (Kate O'Mara), and the family's butler Renton (Harvey Hall) after he makes a vain attempt to save Emma with garlic flowers and a crucifix.

The classical narrative structure of the film includes a number of 'parallel' characters, such Emma and Laura. Similarly, Perrodot and her need for Carmilla parallels Carmilla's repressed desire for the young girls. Both are presented as figures of pathos, due to their inability to satisfy their desires. Eventually, after the governess pleads with the vampire to take her away, Carmilla kills her. Perrodot's vulnerability is a quality shared by Carmilla. When a funeral passes her as she sits in the shade ('The sun hurts my eyes')[24] the vampire becomes traumatised by the religious iconography of the procession and her awareness of Emma's mortality. She screams at her young lover 'You must die, everybody must die!' before pleading with Emma to 'hold me, I beg you, hold me tight'.

Le Fanu concludes his story with the young girl's wish to 'hear the light step of Carmilla at the drawing room door'. Baker's film concludes in a similar manner by suggesting that Emma is somehow attuned to Carmilla even though they are miles apart. This link is established by showing both women in the same position, lying down, and, through editing, a psychic connection between Carmilla in her coffin in Karnstein castle and Emma on her bed in the Morton house is suggested. Just prior to the staking of Carmilla, Emma yells 'dear God, no!' and then screams as the stake is driven into vampire's heart by General Spielsdorf.

The film retains a sense of sympathy for Carmilla's sadness to the end – an emotion that is strengthened by the sadism of the men and their self-righteous attitudes. Spielsdorf tells them there's 'no other way' as he drives a stake into Carmilla's heart and the film's climax is, in effect, a reprise of the prologue. Prior to the credits Baron Joachim von

Hartog (Douglas Wilmer) avenges the death of his sister by staking all of the vampires, except one (Carmilla), in Karnstein Castle. When he starts to lose his nerve, the breast of a young female vampire touches his crucifix and he regains his strength to decapitate the woman. Near the end of the film he describes this moment to Spielsdorf and Morton as the film flashes back to the prologue:

> But face-to-face my limbs seemed paralysed. I prayed to God to give me back their strength. But when the moment came I could not move [the young woman approaches him]. That moment has been a nightmare all my life. I was saved by a cross I wore. As it touched the vision of beauty ... I felt a shock of evil [the woman's breast touches the cross hanging across his chest] as God in his mercy gave power to my arm [Hartog decapitates the woman].

This poetic sequence invokes a series of moral signs – such as the white gown worn by the young blonde, female vampire, and her breast touching the crucifix. Yet, interestingly, these signs are rendered problematic – not only by an association between purity and virtue and the undead, but also in the excessive violence used by Hartog. This confusion is taken even further at the end of the film due to General Spielsdorf's brutal staking, and decapitation, of Carmilla. Instead of catharsis and joy at the destruction of the vampire, the film closes in a problematic manner that captures the mixed emotions expressed by Laura in Le Fanu's tale.

The Vampire Lovers, made on the relatively low budget of £165,227, was a financial success although few British critics approved or even took it seriously. Dilys Powell, for example, reviewed it in the *Sunday Times* (6 September 1970) under the heading 'Poor Monster' and she lamented the disappearance of 'aesthetic horror' in films such as Dreyer's *Vampyr* and Roger Corman's series of adaptations of the stories of Edgar Allan Poe.[25] On the other hand, Powell expressed a tinge of sympathy for Carmilla who, she writes, 'deserves to join the martyred monsters of the screen'.

Although criticism of the film in recent years has taken it more seriously, many critics failed to see past the film's nudity and lesbianism. The film also suffered from the fact that many writers included *The Vampire Lovers* as part of a 'Karnstein trilogy'. David Sanjek, in his survey of the decline of the British horror film in the period from 1968 to 1975, criticised the 'trilogy because the films failed to

> subvert hegemonic definitions of femininity, but each instead incorporates a number of voracious female characters possessed of unhealthy

lusts and appetites. The loosening of the censorship codes in 1968 permitted the near-pornographic display of female bodies that the fantastic narrative structure rendered 'safe'. Even more dismaying, the eventual destruction of the villainous women allowed audiences implicitly to condemn at one and the same time vampirism and lesbianism, equating the two as crimes against nature.[26]

Ian Conrich, in his overview of the British horror film, argued that the declining fortunes of Hammer in the late 1960s required the company to 'transgress further to compete' and thus the 'three lesbian vampire films' presented scenes of soft-core pornography'.[27] The *Encyclopedia of Horror Movies* also criticises the film for veering from 'an eerily poetic pre-credit sequence to insipid soft-core scenes punctuated by realistically shot Grand Guignol' and for displaying 'a typically English unease with luscious eroticism, which too often makes the picture collapse into restrained, but insipid, girlie magazine imagery'.[28]

Tim Greaves, on the other hand, argues that the film is 'essential viewing' as 'it is transgressive cinema beyond compare ... Hammer may have made better films, but never before or again did they present their audience with one so intensely elegant and provocative'.[29] Bruce Hallenbeck, in praising the film, singled out Baker's contribution: 'Baker, who must be one of the most under-rated directors of all time, did a superb job' as his 'camera set-ups were almost traditional in their elegance, and the whole pre-credit sequence is one of the most atmospheric and visually stunning scenes ever done by Hammer'. Unlike others, Hallenbeck thought that the presentation of the lesbian relationship between Emma and Carmilla was 'extremely tasteful' and the 'film's restraint can only add to its reputation. Its languorous pacing perfectly captures the mood of Le Fanu's story.' Hallenbeck also praised the 'elegant sets by Scott MacGregor' and 'Moray Grant's shadowy, suggestive photography' that 'combine to create a haunting visual treat'.[30]

The Vampire Lovers has little in common with the other films in the so-called 'Karnstein Trilogy'. In the first two films the vampire is called Mircalla – in the third film, *Twins of Evil*, Mircalla is only a minor character as the emphasis shifts to two *Playboy* models, Madeleine and Mary Collinson. Also, the plot of this film, concerned mostly with the activities of a puritanical witch-hunter, Gustav Weil (Peter Cushing), is in no way related to *The Vampire Lovers*. Only Baker's film is based on Le Fanu's story and the melancholic, poetic mood of his film is absent in the subsequent films. For example, after Laura's death, her father (General Spielsdorf) tries to locate Marcilla. His cries echo through his mansion as the camera prowls through the family room to a windswept balcony and, finally, to her coffin. Earlier, she quietly declares to

Spielsdorf and the rest of the household, in a quiet, restrained voice, that they 'may open the curtains. It is daylight now, she is dead!'.

This scene, stripped of emotional excess, captures what Jack Sullivan identifies as the distinctive quality in Le Fanu's stories: 'his work is haunted by a terrifying stillness and loneliness'.[31] Later, when Emma, pale and listless from repeated nocturnal attacks, asks Carmilla if she is dying, the vampire quietly replies 'Yes'. Emma then asks her if she will 'live until father comes home?' Carmilla, holding Emma, looks up and softly tells the young girl, 'Perhaps' as she gently strokes, and kisses, her forehead.

Even the periodic bursts of violence are rendered in a poetic manner. Carmilla's attack on the doctor (Ferdy Mayne), for example, begins when he falls off his horse in a forest at dusk as the vampire is first seen as a reflection in a pond, slowly gliding towards her victim. The wind, blowing her white nightdress, transforms Carmilla into a spectre emerging out of the trees. Baker also captures the poetic terror of Le Fanu's juxtaposition of beauty and blood as Laura wakes from a dream to see Carmilla standing at the foot of her bed 'in her white nightdress, bathed, from her chin to her feet, in one great stain of blood'.[32] This is recreated near the end of his film after Carmilla has killed Mademoiselle Perrodot. Emma looks up to see the vampire's mouth covered with the governess's blood.

The most persistent criticism of the film relates to the charge that it is, or comes close to, 'soft-core pornography'. In the context of the changes in the horror film in the early 1970s this is difficult to sustain. There was in 1960s in the vampire film a growing tendency for more sexually explicit material that was often combined with a graphic representation of violence. This was particularly evident in European films such as Jean Rollin's *Le Viol du Vampire* (1967), although Hammer was not immune, as reflected, for example, in *Taste the Blood of Dracula* (1970). In the early 1970s this trend escalated although there is a considerable difference between Baker's film and, for example, Joseph Larraz's ultra low-budget (£42,000)1974 exploitation film, *Vampyres* (aka *Daughters of Dracula*).[33] Both films share a similar premise – involving sexual domination by a female vampire, or two vampires in Larraz's film – but there the similarities end. Whereas Larraz's film is literal, with graphic scenes of copulation and extended bloodletting, Baker's film is, mostly, symbolic and poetic. While Larraz combines full-frontal nudity with graphic bloodletting in a number of scenes, Baker allows only one scene of female nudity, not full frontal, when Emma is invited into Carmilla's room while she is bathing.[34]

Most critics, except David Pirie and Bruce Hallenbeck, failed to consider Baker's film in the context of Le Fanu's novella. Pirie argues, for example, that if the film 'seems to be adopting the whispered, excited tone of a women's magazine romance'[35] it may well be that Le Fanu's novel, narrated by a naive young girl with no experience of sex, adopts the same tone. As Le Fanu writes:

> She used to place her pretty arms about my neck, draw me to her, and laying her cheek to mine, murmur with her lips near to my ear,
> 'Dearest, your little heart is wounded; think me not cruel because I obey the irresistible law of my strength and weakness; if your dear heart is wounded, my wild heart bleeds with yours. In the rapture of my enormous humiliation I live in your warm life and you shall die – die, sweetly die – into mine. I cannot help it; as I draw near to you, you, in turn, will draw near to others, and learn the rapture of that cruelty, which yet is love; so, for a while, seek to know no more of me and mine, but trust me with all your loving spirit.'
> And when she had spoken such a rhapsody, she would press me more closely in her trembling embrace, and her lips in soft kisses gently glow upon my cheek.[36]

Laura responds with both excitement and disgust to Carmilla's gentle ministrations: 'I experienced a strange tumultuous excitement that was pleasurable, ever and anon, mingled with fear and disgust. I had no distinct thoughts about her while such scenes lasted, but I was conscious of a love growing into adoration, and also of abhorrence.'[37]

The nineteenth-century mode of Gothic Romance, which included the vampire story, was able to indulge in socially 'unacceptable' themes and behaviour largely because such themes and behaviour are rendered acceptable when they were mediated through the symbolic codes of the genre. As Jack Sullivan argues, the Victorian vampire tale is

> virtually a textbook case of sexual repression emerging as horror. The bite on the neck, usually in the victim's bedchamber, is a carnal gesture, signalling a simultaneous horror and fascination with the sexual act. Bloodsucking becomes a perverse metaphor for sexual embrace, just as the losing and gaining of blood represents the losing and gaining of sexual power. When Carmilla pants 'You are mine forever' over her young victim, she articulates a fantasy of unending pleasure and domination.[38]

Baker's approach to *The Vampire Lovers* may have been more suited to a period when censorship, and social norms, insisted that the entire film be presented in a symbolic and oblique way. He was enthusiastic that the film include an 'element of fantasy'.[39] He was unhappy with the pressure to include more nudity in the film ('If they wanted porn, they'd got the wrong cast and director'[40]). The most effective scenes in the film are the poetic, elegant moments, such as Carmilla stalking the doctor in the woodland and her quiet expressions of desperation and despair. The nudity, which could easily be defended as a contemporary filmic adaptation of Le Fanu's novella, in particular, and the vampire story in general, is a diversion and should not provide an impediment to an appreciation of Baker's skill in bringing Le Fanu's story to the screen.

Censorship in Britain in 1970, although liberalised in the late 1960s, was wary of the genres such as the vampire film. Even after the age restriction of the X Certificate was raised to 18, the BBFC's John Trevelyan threatened to ban *The Vampire Lovers* unless there were deletions in Tudor Gates' script, including the removal of the 'dream orgasm ending in a scream'. Trevelyan was also uncomfortable with the film's depictions of homosexuality and he warned Hammer of the Board's 'firm treatment' of the lesbian elements in *The Killing of Sister George* in 1969.[41] This was not Baker's first encounter with Trevelyan, who tried to interfere with the 'rape scene' in *Passage Home* and the murder of Duds Morrison in *Tiger in the Smoke*. Baker had little time for the secretary, as he had the 'schoolmasterly habit' of distinguishing between what was allowed in 'art cinema' and what was not allowed in 'commercial cinema',[42] with the latter subject to greater restrictions regarding the presentation of sex, violence or anything else considered controversial by the BBFC. Baker's response to Trevelyan's interference with the murder in *Tiger in the Smoke* is revealing. As the killing was not shown it was difficult to 'cut out anything objectionable' – and the scene was 'all the more powerful for that'.[43]

Scars of Dracula (1970)

Roy Baker maintains that the *Scars of Dracula* was his first real horror film, as he considered *The Vampire Lovers* more of an 'exploitation film'.[44] This judgement was formed, partly, on the basis that *Scars of Dracula* was the fifth entry in the Hammer series starring Christopher Lee. Unfortunately it is not one of his best films as the script was cobbled together from elements from earlier films in the series, notably *Dracula* (1958) and *Dracula – Prince of Darkness* (1966). It was also burdened with a tight shooting schedule owing to the small budget, and Baker pushed the narrative along at a rapid pace in an attempt to hide its deficiencies.[45] *Scars of Dracula*, coming near the end of the series, displayed the same, tired tendencies evident in the final years of the Universal horror films in the 1940s, in films such as *House of Frankenstein* (1944) and *House of Dracula* (1945).[46] In both cases the prestige and inventiveness of the earlier films had dissipated into recycled plots and thin, formulaic characterisations.

Although *Scars of Dracula* borrows elements from Dracula (1958), it lacks a key aspect of that film: the moment when 'innocence' contributes, or accedes, to its own 'corruption'. It is this moment that provides much of the vampire film's 'subversive' change. The violation of innocence is an integral element of the vampire story and from its literary origins this basic tenet of melodrama has been imbued with a strong, if symbolically rendered, eroticism.

David Pirie, for example, argues that the success of Dracula as a character is 'no historical accident':

> The novel in which he appears [Bram Stoker's 1897 publication of *Dracula*] is one of the most extraordinary works of popular fiction ever written, an astonishing culmination of the sado-erotic strains and stresses of the entire Victorian age. It is a book of immense unconscious power, weaving a spell of sex, blood and death around the reader, which remains quite unaffected by time. On one level at least, the character of the Count can be construed as the great submerged force of Victorian libido breaking out to punish the repressive society which had imprisoned it; one of the more appalling things that the Count perpetually does to the matronly women of his Victorian enemies (in the novel and in the best of the films) is to make them sensual.[47]

This is a key element in *The Vampire Lovers* as patriarchy, for a large part of the film, is rendered irrelevant. During the course of the film Carmilla not only insinuates herself within its bastion, but proceeds to undermine it as her two lovers are wrested from the control of their fathers. Laura even loses interest in her fiancé Carl Eberhardt (Jon Finch). The same pattern is evident in *Dracula* (1958), and Van Helsing (Peter Cushing) even foregrounds this motif when he dictates the nature of the relationship between the vampire and his or her victim into a primitive recording machine: 'Established that victims consciously detest being dominated by vampirism, but are unable to relinquish the practice, similar to addiction to drugs.'

Thus, Lucy (Carol Marsh), under the influence of the Count, not only waits for his nocturnal visits but disregards, or undermines, her family's attempt to protect her. The most blatant example of this motif, of Dracula's ability to penetrate the Victorian family, occurs when the scientist Van Helsing and the middle-class patriarch Arthur Holmwood (Michael Gough) wait in the garden outside the bedroom window of Holmwood's wife Mina (Melissa Stribling) so as to protect her from the control of the vampire. However, as the two men wait in the cold, Dracula, unknown to them, is spending the night with Mina in her bedroom as he is already living inside the house, in the cellar.

This motif is foregrounded in all of Christopher Lee's Dracula films for Hammer up to, but not including, *Scars of Dracula*. After the 1958 version Christopher Lee did not play the Count again until 1965, when he starred in Terence Fisher's *Dracula – Prince of Darkness*. In this film two English couples, travelling through northern Europe, find themselves in Dracula's castle after their guide abandons them. Both women, Helen (Barbara Shelley) and Diana (Suzan Farmer), fall under the Count's spell and although the transformation of the severely repressed Helen into a snarling vampire is spectacular, the Count's seduction of Diana is more sensual. He exposes his chest and rips his nail across it so as to draw blood. He then invites Diana to suck it and only the intervention of her husband (Francis Matthews) prevents consummation of this act. This scene appeared in a lobby card to advertise the film.

Similarly, in *Dracula Has Risen From the Grave* (1968), directed by Freddie Francis, while a young woman, Maria (Veronica Carlson), is clearly tempted by the Count's offer, another women, Zena (Barbara Ewing) is positively eager to accommodate him. This motif is repeated in *Taste the Blood of Dracula*, released six months before the *Scars of Dracula*. However, Baker's film lacks this aspect and remains, as a consequence, a simple melodrama involving pure polar concepts of Good and Evil without the necessary intensity to bring them to life. The film is a minimalist shadow of the earlier films.

The first part of the film, for example, borrows plot incidents from the 1958 version. After dallying with the burgomaster's daughter, young Paul Carlsen (Christopher Matthews) arrives at Dracula's castle where he receives the same greeting from a female vampire as did Jonathan Harker (John Van Eyssen) in the 1958 film. In both films the man is approached by an attractive brunette in a low-cut dress who asks for his help to get away from Dracula. In the first film she is merely designated as the Vampire Woman (Valerie Gaunt), while in Baker's film she is called Tania (Anouska Hempel). Whatever her title, her status as the dangerous, fatal woman is clear. When Harker shows sympathy and comforts her she bites him in the neck. The same action thirteen years later is preceded by Carlsen taking her to bed. Next morning, however, when Tania sees his exposed neck, she cannot control herself and attempts to bite him. In both films Dracula intercedes at this point. The only difference is the degree of violence he uses to take the woman away. In the 1958 film he merely carries her away. In the 1970 film Dracula places Tania on the bed, stabbing her repeatedly before drinking blood from her mutilated body.[48] Tania's body is then dismembered by Dracula's slave Klove (Patrick Troughton). Later, Dracula brands Klove, a character taken from *Dracula – Prince of Darkness*, with his red-hot sword. Baker, in justifying this graphic violence, pointed out that John Elder's (Anthony Hinds) script was 'brutal and cruel' and 'if that was what they wanted, they should have it'.[49]

While the first half of the *Scars of Dracula* borrows from *Dracula*, the second half is a limp variation on *Dracula – Prince of Darkness* with the Count luring Sarah Framsen (Jenny Hanley) into his castle while Paul's brother Simon (Dennis Waterman) tries to protect her. Yet, considering this premise, the film fails to show the seductiveness of evil – even when Sarah finds herself in bed in Dracula's castle with the Count threatening her. Instead of exploring the possibilities that follow when the desires of innocence become complicit with the desires of the Count, the film merely recycles one of the genre's most overused elements, the protection of the crucifix, to save her. By disregarding this key motif involving the corruption of innocence, Baker's film regresses to pre-Hammer presentations when the genre consisted primarily of Evil threatening Good – without the rich subtext introduced by Terence Fisher's 1958 version.

Just prior to the production of the Scars *of Dracula*, Christopher Lee speculated that Hammer was planning to start a new series of Dracula films without him.[50] He noted, for example, that this was the only film in the series, up to that time, not to include an explanation at the start as to how the Count was resurrected from his seeming demise in the previous film. Also Baker's film, unlike the Victorian England setting of *Taste the Blood of Dracula*, goes back to the mid-European atmosphere of Stoker's novel and Lee speculated that *Scars of Dracula* was, in effect, a return to the beginning. However, Baker's film was no match for the 1958 version. The film lacks, among other things, a strong presence to balance Lee's dominance. There is, for example, no Van Helsing or any of the 'Van Helsing prototypes' used by Hammer in subsequent films – such as Andrew Keir's Father Sandor in *Dracula Prince of Darkness* and Rupert Davies as Monsignor Ernst Muller in *Dracula Has Risen From the Grave*. Instead it is left to a weak priest (Michael Gwynn) and an insipid couple, Simon Carlson and Sarah Framsen, to oppose the prince of darkness. Baker admitted that Waterman was miscast as Carlsen 'and it wasn't really him'.[51] He is hardly a match for Dracula in the film's climax at the top of the castle and only a lightning strike, which hits the metal shaft in Dracula's hand, sending him over the side in a ball of fire, saves Carlsen and Sarah.

This was a perfunctory ending to a disappointing film, as Baker acknowledged:

I'm not very pleased with the film. We needed a more experienced cast and a bigger budget would have helped. There should have been more set-ups, but we just didn't have the time. After I ran SCARS OF DRACULA I viewed DR. JEKYLL AND SISTER HYDE. Now that's a much better film. It's an original concept and a better cast. I know which one I prefer. The problem with SCARS OF DRACULA was that we were just rehashing old themes. I tried to get back to the book. There are some good moments, but not enough of them.[52]

Taste the Blood of Dracula was the last of the important Hammer vampire films starring Christopher Lee and it was financed by an American studio (Warner Bros-Seven Arts). EMI provided limited finance for *Scars of Dracula* and a short shooting schedule – Baker felt that the film was extremely rushed.[53] When Warner Bros saw the film they declined to distribute. It may have been because the receipts of the previous film 'weren't impressive' although the general consensus was that *Scars of Dracula* looked 'cheap'.[54] A small independent company, American Continental Films, picked up the American distribution rights. Although the film did reasonably well in Britain, grossing £55,385 in London when released on a double bill with *The Horror of Frankenstein*,[55] it failed in America, grossing only an estimated $51,000.[56] This may have been due, at least in part, to American Continental's small advertising budget.

Dr Jekyll and Sister Hyde (1971)

In October 1971 Hammer released two films – *Hands of the Ripper*, directed by Peter Sasdy, and *Dr Jekyll and Sister Hyde* – which were variations on the Jack-the-Ripper story. While both films use the Whitechapel murders in the late 1880s as background for their stories, Baker's film also assimilated characters and situations from Robert Louis Stevenson's 1886 story, *The Strange Case of Dr Jekyll and Mr Hyde*.[57] Both films, however, are very different. Baker's film is, in terms of its unwillingness to breach social and cultural norms of the 1960s and early 1970s, a mainstream Hammer horror film, visually elegant and, wherever possible, oblique in terms of its presentation of violence. Sasdy's film is thematically confronting, only functional in terms of its visuals, and graphically violent.

These contrasting qualities are evident in the opening scene in each film which shows the murder of a woman. In *Dr Jekyll and Sister Hyde* there is a concerted effort to intensify the effectiveness of the sequence, and to heighten audience involvement, through the association of images and sounds that are directly related to the murder. The sequence begins with a huge close-up of the eye of a dead rabbit which is replaced by a close-up of a butcher sharpening his knife, followed by the exterior of the butcher shop. The butcher's preparation of the rabbit, while geographically located to the main action, is unrelated to the killing. Baker, however, inserts the mutilation of the rabbit at a pivotal moment in this sequence. The camera pans with a woman walking by the butcher's shop and it keeps moving to the back of a man in a black cloak, tall hat and walking stick standing near a poster advertising the reward for the identity of the man, wearing a dark cloak and tall hat, responsible for the 'Whitechapel Murders'. He walks towards the pub alongside a street singer and watches a prostitute (Maureen) leave the hotel as her friend yells out: 'Here Maureen, if you find a gent charge him half a crown – tell him it's gone up, everything's gone up [she lifts her dress up]'.

The man follows Maureen and there is an insert of a policeman checking doors and another reward poster. The film briefly returns to the butcher sharpening his knife just as Maureen walks into a close-up. A knife appears from the top right-hand corner of the screen, followed by another image of the reward poster, only this time with blood streaked across it. Maureen's (dead) face is replaced by the killer opening a medical instrument box and taking out a sharp blade. However, instead of showing the removal of an organ from the woman's body, the film shows the butcher cutting the rabbit open. The sequence concludes with a reprise of the blood-streaked reward poster.

While it is clear that a woman has been violently killed and mutilated, this is primarily communicated through the inserts of the butcher and his sharp knife and the gutting of the rabbit. In other words, the audience is prepared for the murder by the first two images. The reward posters provide additional information by contextualising the killing within the well-known actions of 'Jack the Ripper'. One poster is also used to show its aftermath with blood splattered across it. The sequence is stylish and the meaning is clear and efficiently staged with a minimum of explicit violence.

The opening to Peter Sasdy's film, on the other hand, is purely functional and lacks the imagination of *Dr Jekyll and Sister Hyde*. *Hands of the Ripper* begins with a man in a tall hat and dark cloak running along Berner Street, Whitechapel, which is indicated by a street sign, before entering a room where a blonde woman is minding a young girl (Anna). After the woman indicates that the man, the father of the girl, is Jack the Ripper he kills her. The credits follow and sporadically freeze on images of the girl and her mother's murder – including a point of view shot of Anna looking at her dead mother framed against a glowing fire. This pre-credit sequence provides the thematic basis for the film and the motivation for Anna's sudden bursts of violence. The presentation of this violence is exceedingly graphic and includes slitting the throat of a housemaid and pushing hatpins into the eye of a prostitute who tries to befriend her.

There are many possible reasons why the two films differ so much. Part of it may relate to the experience and training of the two directors. Baker, who gained his early experience in film at Gainsborough in the 1930s, adapted the techniques he learned from Carol Reed, Robert Stevenson, Alfred Hitchcock, William Beaudine, Walter Forde and others who passed through Islington during this period. Sasdy, a Hungarian director, did not learn his craft in the studio system but came to feature films via television after attracting attention with his production of *The Caves of Steel* for BBC2.

When film projects dried up for Baker in the early 1960s he also spent a long period working on British television series, such as *The Saint* and *The Avengers*, and this experience, plus the limited budgets of his post-1967 films for Hammer and Amicus, affected his style after 1967. There were, in some films, less elaborate tracking shots, more pans and zoom, less staging in depth.[58] These changes, however, did not represent a repudiation of the mode of cinema that he had practised from the start of his career. It was merely another example of functional equivalents as each device, such as a pan or a zoom instead of a tracking shot, fulfilled the same basic role within the overall aesthetic. Sasdy's film, on the other hand, represented more of a challenge to the classical mode – not so much in terms of its style, but with regard to its moral basis. By focusing on the perverse desires of a respectable psychiatrist (Eric Porter) for a young girl (Anna), and less on a more conventional storyline, such as trying to 'cure' her, *Hands of the Ripper* enters a moral realm that has no comparable example in Baker's filmography. The psychiatrist's decision to ignore the carnage caused by a young woman (Anna) is rationalised by his scientific pursuit of 'knowledge' but, as the film reveals, this decision has more to do with his own obsessions and desires. The incestuous implications of the film's ending, their macabre union on the floor of the whispering gallery of St Paul's Cathedral, takes this film well beyond the morbid fatalism of Baker's cinema.

Yet the 'subversive' possibilities of *Dr Jekyll and Sister Hyde* are also extensive. Brian Clemens's script imbues Robert Louis Stevenson's morality tale of the constant battle between good and evil with the gender twist. Jekyll is transformed into a manifestation of the Victorian fatal woman – sexually powerful, devoid of emotion and determined not to be bound by the restrictions of nineteenth-century patriarchy. At this level, the film efficiently exposes Victorian hypocrisy, mainly through the double standards of Jekyll's mentor, Professor Robertson (Gerald Sim). A seemingly respectable scientist assisting the police in their hunt for the Whitechapel killer, Robertson is prepared to abandon his duties in exchange for the possibility of sex with Hyde (Martine Beswick). After Robertson discovers that Jekyll (Ralph Bates) is responsible for the murders he is prepared to inform the police of his friend's behaviour. But his resolve dissipates at the sight of Hyde in her undergarments, a weakness that leads to his death.

Much of the film is told via a prolonged flashback that is motivated by Jekyll's confession. Preoccupied by developing an anti-virus for each of the major diseases, Jekyll becomes depressed when Robertson tells him that he (Jekyll) will not live long enough to complete his research. Hence, as his voice-over informs, he vows to discover the means to prolong life: 'I saw it as the first step in an exciting scientific adventure. I could not know then it was the first step toward the black abyss, toward the mad horrors, toward self-destruction. I was seized and engulfed by the idea, it became my passion and my obsession.' The arrival of the Spencer family in the apartment above his laboratory, and Susan Spencer's (Susan Broderick) obvious infatuation, does not deflect Jekyll from his research. He even gives tacit approval to the actions of body snatchers Burke and Hare after they murder a prostitute to supply him with body parts. Later, when this supply dries up following the murder of Burke, and Hare's blindness (after a mob throw him into a lime pit), Jekyll begins killing women and ransacking their bodies for human organs: 'Who else', a policeman asks, 'but a madman would do that to a woman?' as the film shows Jekyll working in his laboratory.

The film explores various aspects of gender reversal, largely through the dominating presence of Martine Beswick as Hyde. Some of this is treated in a light-hearted way, such as when Howard Spencer cries out at the height of sexual passion that she [Jekyll] could never imagine the pleasure a man feels of having sex with a woman. Hyde, knowingly, informs him 'but I can imagine it'. Later, Jekyll finds that he is in combat with Hyde over the control of his own body. When he meets Howard in the street he finds himself strangely drawn toward Susan's brother:

> HOWARD: And how is your delightful sister?
> JEKYLL: Fine, excellent, I am in excellent health.
> HOWARD: No, you misunderstand me. Your sister?
> JEKYLL: Howard! [Jekyll goes to stroke Howard's face before he regains control of himself]

This battle within Jekyll occupies the latter half of the film. In Stevenson's story Hyde has no redeeming traits and he is presented as a violent, ugly man: 'There is something wrong with his appearance; something displeasing, something downright detestable'.[59] The unique aspect of the tale was that the battle for moral supremacy was within one man. It struck an immediate response with the public as the first edition of the story sold over 40,000 copies in a short time.[60] Victorian readers, it seemed, 'were fascinated by the idea of the total incarnation of a good man's evil subconscious into a Caliban figure'. This appeal, Richard Dalby argues, came from the portrayal of Jekyll as suffering from the suppression of his natural instincts and, as a consequence, 'Stevenson was attacking the rampant hypocrisy of highly respectable and upright Christian "ideal husbands" who led double lives'.[61]

The clear moral dichotomy in Stevenson's tale is less clear in Baker's film as Beswick's Hyde emerges as a more charismatic figure than the dour, obsessed scientist. It is only when Hyde threatens Susan Spencer that Jekyll objects to the killings. Hyde is presented as a charming sociopath and when Howard asks after Jekyll's state of health, she tells him that 'he [Jekyll] hasn't been himself of late'. Stevenson's story was more concerned with exposing Victorian double standards by showing how a seemingly 'good' man, a pillar of society, could harbour anti-social desires and commit acts of gross violence. The implications of Baker's film, on the other hand, are more psychological rather than social. *Dr Jekyll and Sister Hyde*, as Sue Harper points out, becomes a 'powerful Freudian reading of Stevenson's tale' which suggests 'that the unspeakable Hyde is Jekyll's feminine side, which is dangerous when released and threatening when challenged'.[62]

Beswick, with her tall body and high cheekbones, dominates the film and she attracted the attention of Richard Corliss in his 1972 review, which was titled 'His doppelganger was a lady':

> Hyde (Martine Beswick) has the face of a gorgeous cadaver, thin, muscular arms, a strong, lanky body, and a cool, in-charge smile that castrates even as it invites. She represents an unfamiliar type in 19th-century England: the upper class-libertine, the lady of leisure who is also a lady of pleasure. She enjoys fondling her body, first out of curiosity and then out of carnality. She dips her fingers in brandy and licks them. Divine decadence! There's something about Miss Beswick's physical and behavioral rightness for the role that's weird, off-putting – and riveting.[63]

Ralph Bates as Jekyll is less interesting and he emerges as a weak character. In an attempt to justify his actions, Jekyll seeks Susan Spencer's approval through the story of a lifeboat with six people compared with a steamer with 500 people aboard. Asked whom would she sacrifice if a choice had to be made, Spencer naturally tells him the lifeboat with six lives compared with the 500 people on the steamer. Somehow, he uses this to rationalise his monstrous behaviour under the guise of committing 'an evil' in order to promulgate 'an unquestioned good'. His lunacy is apparent in his subsequent voice-over: 'I decided I must take human life so as to eventually prolong it'.

After Jekyll rescues a prostitute from the boorish behaviour of a couple of sailors, he goes back to the woman's room. While she is undressing she explains that she can always spot a real gentleman: 'I can tell a real gentleman – not by the way he looks – but real gentlemen have such sophisticated tastes in [pause] certain things.' These 'certain things' refer to sexual 'perversions' and the peculiar habits of the upper class. While the specific nature of these 'sophisticated tastes' is not revealed, this exchange reinforces the film's depiction of the inadequacies of the upper-class male. While Jekyll is racked with despair over his inability to control Hyde, she is confident, wilful, and devoid of doubt. Martine Beswick, with her imposing physical presence, reinforces this aspect as the men are no match for her, notably Ralph Bates and 'his pageboy haircut, and ... trace of a flounce in his step',[64] the decadent Gerald Sim (as Professor Robertson) and Lewis Fiander (as Howard Spencer). These men embody what Richard Corliss describes as 'the reserved effeminacy of the genteel Victorian male'.[65] The asexual Jekyll, who would prefer killing women to romancing Susan Spencer, is no match for Sister Hyde, the 'aggressive, sybaritic male'.[66]

The noirish aspects of *Dr Jekyll and Sister Hyde*, as Jekyll despairs over the growing dominance of Hyde within his body, are similar to those shown by such tormented protagonists as Jim Ackland in *The October Man* and Richard Morton in *Night Without Sleep*. Slumped in front of his mirror, Jekyll's voice-over records his inner turmoil: 'I was caught in a terrible trap. To continue my work I needed Sister Hyde. Yet all the time I became more and more aware of her growing dominance. I no longer had the strength to fight, contain or control'. Jekyll is implicated not only in the murder of the prostitutes, but, during Robertson's murder, the battle between Jekyll and Hyde erupts as the film alternates between Hyde and Jekyll plunging the knife into the hapless professor.

Gradually, Hyde assumes control and she walks up to the same mirror, now shattered by a knife, and calls Jekyll weak. She challenges him by saying that 'it will be interesting to see who wins' before stalking the only person he cares for – Susan Spencer. After Jekyll saves the young woman he acknowledges that the desire to wrest control of his body from Hyde is ultimately futile: 'I had won a battle but only just. I knew it could only be a matter of time before Sister Hyde completely took over'. The final battle for dominance takes place as Jekyll is trapped by the police high up on a window ledge. Filmed through the distorted glass of the window, thereby emphasising the demented aspect of the scientist, Jekyll loses control of his body to Hyde as he and she fall to their death. When the police turn the body over, Jekyll is no longer recognisable as the crowd, including Susan Spencer, view a grotesque transsexual figure on the pavement. Unlike the clear morality of Stevenson's tale, the meaning of Baker's film is more problematic. Jekyll has few redeeming qualities – some may even perceive the ending as Hyde's victory over the inequitable practices of the upper class and, hence, a positive ending with Jekyll's death.

Many British critics, grudgingly, praised *Dr Jekyll and Sister Hyde*. Tom Hutchinson in the *Sunday Telegraph* (17 October 1971) pointed to the film's basis in simple melodrama when he argued that the 'penny-bizarre quality of *Dr Jekyll and Sister Hyde* is, in its incredible way, rather fun ... a kind of Jack-and-Jill the Ripper. The director, Roy Ward Baker, gets down to Hammer's usual charnel-house chores with appreciative vigour and a realisation that the way to the public's heart is through a slit stomach'. The *Daily Mirror* (15 October 1971) complained that 'permutations in this sex-swap are not fully developed', a view shared by David Robinson in the *Financial Times* (15 October 1971), who also complained about the 'lack of style in direction'. John Russell Taylor in *The Times* (15 October 1971) thought that the premise was a 'nicely kinky idea' with 'solid, conservative direction from Roy Ward Baker'. Dilys Powell in the *Sunday Times* (17 October 1971) enjoyed the film's 'few sophisticated jokes' and its 'nice mixture of the dedicated and the tongue-in-cheek'. Felix Barker in the *Evening News* (15 October 1971) worried about the historical accuracy of the film and pointed to its historical inconsistencies, such as Burke and Hare who died much earlier in the century. He was also concerned with the way Brian Clemens's script combined Stevenson's tale with the Whitechapel killings, a criticism repeated by Derek Malcolm in the *Guardian* (21 October 1971), who thought that although Baker directed 'with an old-fashioned flourish that keeps things going reasonably', the 'whole thing is irredeemably silly, even by recent Hammer standards'.

Dr Jekyll and Sister Hyde, which was released on a double bill with *Blood From the Mummy's Tomb* in October 1971, was not a financial success and managed to gross only £2,376 in its opening week at London's New Victoria.[67] In the United States it was distributed by American International Pictures, who devised the following campaign:

This film is filled with SHOCK (Once Again He Will Change Sexes and Kill, Kill, Kill!) after SHOCK (Unnatural Laboratory Experiments Performed Behind Barred Doors!) after SHOCK (Victim After Victim Dies Horribly in Throat-Cutting Orgy!)

Below this text there is an image of a naked man metamorphosing into a naked woman with their genitals covered by a sign:

> WARNING! The Sexual Transformation of a Man into a Woman Will Actually Take Place Before Your Very Eyes!

The British campaign, on the other hand, was relatively reserved. The British advertisement for the film merely urged people to come and watch the 'kinkiest experiment of all! Dr Jekyll becomes a beautiful woman with a lust for murder and revenge!'

American writer Richard Corliss, however, took a more serious view of the film compared to most of the British critics. He maintained that *Dr Jekyll and Sister Hyde* could 'stake an early claim to being one of 1972's best English-language movies'. It belonged, he argued, to the 'niche in respectable horror films that produce respectable profits'. While Corliss congratulated Hammer for 'basking in the glory of a retrospective season at the British Film Institute' in 1971, Derek Malcolm in the *Guardian* (21 October 1971) was wondering '[how the] National Film Theatre can launch, with a comparatively straight face, into a season of this largely cheap-jack rubbish defeats me'.

Amicus

During the filming of *And Now the Screaming Starts!* in 1972 Roy Baker was interviewed on the set by Chris Knight, who asked him if he liked 'the challenge of making the unbelievable seem believable'. Baker replied that they 'are interesting to do from that point of view':

> One of my favourite ploys in achieving this is to make the characters interesting. I trap the audience into an emotional involvement with the characters at the very beginning and from then on you can depend on their greater acceptance of everything because they feel involved. I don't believe in cardboard characters. This is very dangerous, no matter how far-fetched or weird the story may be. The more outrageous it is, the harder you've got to work on the characters so that the audience can accept them as real people, and in so doing accept what is happening to them.[68]

While this was possible in *And Now the Screaming Starts!*, as it was a rare single-plot period horror film produced by Amicus,[69] the rigid structure and tight editing favoured by Subotsky for the episodic portmanteau films defeated most directors with regard to audience empathy for the characters and any semblance of character development. Baker directed two portmanteau films for Amicus: *Asylum* (1972) and *The Vault of Horror* (1973).

Asylum (1972)

Asylum, the first, and best, of Baker's portmanteau films, differs from other Amicus film in that the link-narrative does not have a 'horror host', as in *Torture Garden* (1966) and *Tales From the Crypt* (1971). Nor are the stories linked by setting – such as the subterranean room in *The Vault of Horror*. Instead, the narrative structure of *Asylum* creates a little more dramatic space for Baker as there is a narrative connection between the four episodes with the final one, 'Mannikins of Horror', bringing the various strands together. Also, unlike the other Amicus portmanteau films, there is a climax in *Asylum* that is directly related to the enigma, or question, 'who is Dr Starr?'. This issue is introduced at the start of the film when a young psychiatrist, Dr Martin (Robert Powell), is challenged by Dr Rutherford (Patrick Magee) to discover the identity of the former head of the asylum, Dr Starr. Rutherford intimates that Starr is one of four patients at Dunsmoor hospital. If Martin is successful in discovering his identity he will be offered a position at the hospital.

The episodes are scripted by Robert Bloch from his short stories. In the first story, 'Frozen Fear', Martin interviews Bonnie (Barbara Parkins) who tells how her lover Walter (Richard Todd) murdered, and then dismembered, his wife Ruth (Sylvia Syms). Ruth's body parts are wrapped in brown paper and placed in a freezer in the basement of their house. Ruth, who had been taking classes in African spirituality, refuses to die and her body parts kill Walter and attack Bonnie. To loosen Ruth's dismembered hand from her face Bonnie is forced to cut into her own face with an axe.

Although the thematic basis of the episode is dark, the tone is generally light. For example, when Walter places his wife's body parts in the freezer he, mockingly, offers his best wishes – to 'rest in pieces'. Similarly, Bonnie's duplicitous nature is excessively signalled by Baker – as she narrates her story her face is reflected in *three* mirrors on her table. The story ends with the traditional Amicus 'shock' when she lifts her hair away from her otherwise pretty face to reveal the hideous scars on her right cheek caused by the axe.

In 'The Weird Tailor' an impoverished tailor, Bruno (Barry Morse), is approached by a mysterious man, Smith (Peter Cushing), to make a special suit from material that he brings with him. Bruno subsequently discovers that the purpose of the suit is to bring Smith's dead son back to life. However, when Smith fails to pay Bruno, the tailor kills him. Bruno's wife then makes the mistake of placing the new suit on a dummy that comes to life and attacks her husband. The story ends with Bruno warning Martin that he must find the dummy.

The third story, 'Lucy Comes to Stay', has basic similarities to Alfred Hitchcock's *Psycho* (1960), which was based on a novel by Robert Bloch. Barbara (Charlotte Rampling) tells Martin that she was framed for the murder of her brother George (James Villiers) and her nurse Miss Higgins (Megs Jenkin) by her close friend Lucy (Britt Ekland). Barbara resents George's control over her life and her property, the family home. When George leaves the house, Lucy suddenly appears and tells her that her brother is planning to return her to a mental institution. After George and Higgins are murdered, Lucy explains to Barbara that she is finally free and story ends with Barbara protesting her innocence at Dunsmoor. However, when she looks into a mirror she does not see herself, only 'Lucy'. This is a variation on the final scene in *Psycho*, when 'mother' assumes total control of Norman Bates.

In the final story, 'Mannikins of Horror', Martin interviews the most likely candidate for Dr Starr: Dr Byron (Herbert Lom), a neuro-surgeon with an intense hatred of the current director, Dr Rutherford. While Martin is upstairs with Byron, the neuro-surgeon unleashes a homunculus who kills Rutherford. Martin responds by destroying the doll, which immediately kills Byron. The film concludes with the standard Amicus 'twist' which, in this case, is that Starr is none of the patients – it is the hospital orderly 'Max Reynolds'. Reynolds kills Martin and the film ends, in a vaguely similar manner to *Dead of Night*, with Reynolds greeting a new applicant at the front door of Dunsmoor Hospital as the story begins to repeat itself. *Dead of Night* was a favourite film of Milton Subotsky, who claimed that Amicus modelled all of their anthology films on it.[70]

Asylum was one of the best of the Amicus portmanteau films. Nevertheless, Subotsky's 'formula' placed severe restrictions on any director. He explained in 1972 that his films were based on 'four or five stories' of about fifteen to twenty minutes duration, so that 'you don't bore an audience'.[71] Yet this reduced the possibilities of character development and plot exposition, resulting, as David Pirie points out in his review of *From Beyond the Grave* (1973), in severe limitations:

> I[n] general the stale repetition of trite supernatural themes demonstrates the limitations of Amicus' basic approach, and the reason why – despite so many attempts – they have yet to come up with anything as

good as Ealing's *Dead of Night*. A uniquely feeble link-story hinges together a script in which no attention at all is paid to character, exposition or dialogue, with the result that everything is dependent on the limited visual suspense of the material.[72]

Just about everything was affected, or driven, by the 'surprise shock' ending. To achieve this Subotsky favoured 'getting the script right', and then leaving his directors alone during filming, He would then resume control during the editing process:

> I like to come back on the picture when we start editing because I think of editing as a continuation of script writing. You can now take the film and use it as your base and create all sorts of new things, ... that you didn't think of when you were working on the script, that the director didn't think of when he was directing it ... You have to start changing the order to make the structure stronger. Once you've got the structure right then you can start the final editing . I think films are made in the script stage and the cutting stage. In between, there isn't an enormous variation in what different directors are going to do with that film.[73]

Although *Asylum* is one of Baker's favourite films, because 'it all fits together so neatly, with terrific pace',[74] his two portmanteau films represented, in terms of their moral context, a substantial deviation from his earlier films. This was probably due more to the tone and structure developed by Subotsky who made films that, as Peter Hutchings argues, 'do not expect us to take them seriously as "morality plays"'. If, he continues, 'they shock us into a momentary awareness of anything (and I think they do), it is of the contingency and arbitrariness of everyday life'.[75]

The overall tenor of the Amicus portmanteau films was cruel, broad and generally searching for that moment of black humour with which to end the episode. While *The October Man, Paper Orchid, Don't Bother to Knock, A Night to Remember* and *Flame in the Streets* may have challenged or questioned various aspects of British society, they did not repudiate its basic tenets. His portmanteau films, on the other hand, did. The inherent nihilism in 'Frozen Fear' and 'Lucy Comes to Stay' in *Asylum*, or 'Midnight Mass' and 'Neat Job' in *The Vault of Horror*, is uncharacteristic of Baker. In 'Neat Job', for example, Critchit (Terry-Thomas) drives his wife Eleanor (Glynis Johns) to murder because of his obsession with neatness. She kills him and keeps his body parts in neatly labelled jars. There is no such thing, as Peter Hutchings points out, 'as family unity or solidarity ... the family is just a social structure and nothing else'.[76]

Morality in these films, unlike Baker's earlier films, merely comprises a set of laws – 'they do not connect with or express transcendent notions of good and evil'.[77] In 'Midnight Mass', for example, Rogers (Daniel Massey), after murdering his sister, is punished and finds himself hanging upside down with a tap in his neck in a restaurant patronised only by vampires. While the punishment is inevitable, the film is less concerned with the moral basis of his actions and more its function in justifying the closing 'joke'. This view is confirmed by Subotsky, and when he was asked whether the vampire's 'obviously false fangs' were deliberate: 'Oh yes. This is the last shot in the picture – it's a gag or it's nothing. It's quite deliberate and I think it works. These films are a kind of comic strip on film'.[78]

A recurring aspect of these films also involved the use of the direct address to the camera/audience. It generally occurred at the end of the film.[79] *Asylum* closes with Reynolds/Dr Starr welcoming the next applicant, and as he closes the door he looks straight into the camera lens and says: 'Better keep the door closed and keep out the draughts – as Dr Starr used to say'. At the end of *The Vault of Horror* Rogers, Maitland (Michael Craig), Moore (Tom Baker) and Critchit leave the subterranean room for their graves. Alex (Curt Jürgens) waits behind and addresses the audience: 'That's how it is. And how it always will be. Night after night we have to retell the evil things we did when we were alive. Night after night for all eternity.' The effect was, as Hutchings points out, 'to put the audience at a distance from the drama. This goes hand in hand with in-jokes and moments of self-reflexivity'.[80] It also worked against Baker's stated aim of involving the audience in these films.

The reviews for *Asylum* were mixed, although considering it was a horror film they were better than expected. Clive Hirschhorn in the *Sunday Express* (30 July 1972) described it as 'the most effective horror film for years', thanks 'to Roy Baker's atmospherically eerie direction'. Similarly, Margaret Hinxman in the *Sunday Telegraph* (30 July 1972) thought it was 'stylish horror' and praised Baker's direction for relying 'on imagination rather than brutality' for effect. The *Daily Mirror* (29 July 1972) was more guarded ('predictable shocker but it is acted throughout in a nice deadpan style') while John Coleman in the *New Statesman* (4 August 1972) was less impressed ('You may not guess the denouement: you may not even stay for it'). George Melly's headline, 'Hokum in the nuthouse', in the *Observer* (30 July 1972) captured the tone of his review: 'a good strong cast all cackling their heads off, and for those with a taste of the Grand Guignol, it's perfectly acceptable' and Margaret Hamsworth in the *Sunday Mirror* (30 July 1972) also thought it was 'pure hokum' whilst providing a warning that easily 'frightened people should not go unaccompanied'. Jan Dawson (*Financial Times*, 29 July 1972) was not impressed with the film's 'plodding pace and creakingly old-fashioned style' and Ian Christie in the *Daily Express* (28 July 1972) concluded his review by arguing that the 'tales vary in quality from the ridiculous to the grotesque but have a few genuinely blood-curdling moments'. John Russell Taylor in *The Times* (28 July 1972) expressed the majority viewpoint that *Asylum* was a 'foolish but reasonable film' and praised Baker for his 'nice, glossy job on the direction'.

And Now the Screaming Starts! (1972)

And Now the Screaming Starts! was based on the Gothic novel by David Case called *Fengriffen*. The film's working title, *The Bride of Fengriffen*, confirmed that this was to be Gothic horror rather than the usual Amicus mixture of contemporary comedy and horror. Subotsky, however, rejected this title as he felt that it was not 'strong' enough and 'wouldn't get the audience'.[81] Instead, he preferred 'I Have No Mouth and I Must Scream' but as this was already the title of a story by Harlan Ellison, and as Ellison refused to give Amicus permission to use it, Subotsky replaced it with *And Now the Screaming Starts*. His partner, Max Rosenberg, provided the punctuation.[82] Subotsky, ever aware of the need to attract international audiences to his films, maintained that *And Now the Screaming Starts!* as a title, 'translates well into other languages.'[83] The inspiration for Subotsky's choice may have been the fact that the 1969 Amicus film *Scream and Scream Again!*, with Vincent Price as an insane scientist who creates a race of humanoids, fared well at the box office.

The Gothic basis of Baker's film is established by Catherine's (Stephanie Beacham) pre-credit voice-over that is reminiscent, in its tone, in the opening minutes of *Rebecca* (1940) and the 1944 version of Charlotte Brontë's *Jane Eyre*. This tone is sometimes linked to the 'Du Maurier tradition',[84] although in an earlier era it would have been associated with novelists such as Ann Radcliffe. This pre-credit moment is one of the few happy moments in the film, as Catherine and her husband-to-be Charles Fengriffen (Ian Ogilvy) travel by coach through a sunny woodland, although her words foreshadow the sense of dread that lies ahead: 'In my dreams I go back to the year 1795 to a time when I was happy. I was on my way to be married. I was going to the house in which I was to find my days filled with fear, my nights filled with horror.'

Catherine's fears, and paranoia, gradually escalate and, in keeping with conventions of the genre, are dismissed by her husband, her doctor and most of the servants. They begin during her first tour of Fengriffen house, built 300 years before by Charles's ancestors (Catherine: 'Is there a ghost?'). After Catherine becomes fixated on the portrait of Henry Fengriffen (Herbert Lom), a bloodied hand shoots out from it toward her and this action, in various forms, is repeated throughout the film. On her wedding night, for example, she is raped by the hand while waiting in bed for Charles and this sequence is expertly filmed by Baker. In his customary style, he invests key objects, such doors and locks, with meaning as they combine with the wind and close-ups of Catherine's face to convey the terror of her ordeal – without a graphic presentation of violence or sex.

Catherine's mental condition deteriorates and during sexual intercourse with Charles she sees a hideous, scarred face outside her bedroom window. This violation is accompanied by a series of mysterious murders involving servants, the family lawyer Maitland (Guy Rolfe), Dr Whittle (Patrick Magee) and Catherine's Aunt Edith (Gillian Lind). Catherine, on the other hand, keeps meeting Silas (Geoffrey Whitehead), a woodsman with a large red birthmark on the right cheek of his face. When she fails to convince Charles of the existence of the severed hand, he brings in Pope (Peter Cushing), a doctor interested in mental illness. Pope learns that his patient is severely aggravated by her discovery that she is pregnant.

After Catherine claims that she could smell the graveyard on her wedding night, Pope forces Charles to recount the story of Henry Fengriffen who, fifty years earlier, invoked his ancient *prima nocta* rights to the virginity of any bride on his estate. When the woman's husband (Silas's father) objected to the rape of his wife, Henry cuts off the man's hand. The woodsman then vowed: 'The evil you did this day will be revenged. The next virgin bride to come to Fengriffen will be violated, but then shall come the true vengeance on the house of Fengriffen and death shall fall on anyone who tries to prevent it.' Catherine overhears Charles telling this story to Pope and she takes a large knife back to the bedroom. As she brings it down towards her stomach the dismembered hand suddenly appears to protect the unborn baby.

After the birth, Charles, who is first to see the baby, runs out of their bedroom, kills Silas (Jr), ransacks Henry's grave and smashes his uncle's skeleton against the gravestone. Pope, who witnesses this, returns to the Fengriffen house and tells the servants to get the authorities as Charles is dangerous and armed with an axe. He then passes the baby over to Catherine who sees the large red birthmark on his right cheek. The camera moves away from the demented mother, and slowly tracks through the house to confirm the success of Silas' vengeance on the

House of Fengriffen. The camera finally stops on the Fifth Commandment in the Bible as Pope's voice-over reads one portion of it: 'For I the LORD thy God am a jealous God, visiting the iniquity of the fathers upon the children unto the third and fourth generation.'

Both Peter Hutchings[85] and Phil Hardy[86] group *And Now the Screaming Starts!* with other late 1960s and early 1970s British horror films such as *Taste the Blood of Dracula*, *Demons of the Mind* (1971) and *Hands of the Ripper*. This group is linked by the theme of 'the sins of the fathers'. While this is part of Baker's film it does not exhaust the significance of the film's bleak ending. To appreciate the full extent of the final scene one has to read the entire Commandment as it is shown on the screen – not just listen to Pope's narration. The Commandment goes beyond Pope's voice-over and it ends with the 'fathers upon the children unto the third and fourth generation *of them that hate me*' [my italics]. The final line is significant as it modifies, or extends, the 'sins-of-the-father' theme and it points to a world in which God exists – not as a moral principle eliciting love, worship, and respect – but as an interdiction, a primitive force within nature that strikes fear into the hearts of humans. The ending confirms a universe where there is no longer an operable idea of the Sacred or Holy, but rather a set of supernatural forces that must be acknowledged, combated, propitiated and conjured with. 'God', in this universe, is simply one figure in a 'manichaeistic daemonology'.[87]

Silas, and the bloodied hand, is not just an evil sign but also a victim of the class system. The early part of the film seem to be an elemental melodrama with Virtue (Catherine) constantly threatened by Evil (the hand). After the flashback, which occurs late in the film, there is a dramatic shift in this simple dichotomy and the ending is a logical manifestation of this change – Charles, having murdered Silas Jr, is last seen smashing Henry Fengriffen's skeleton against his gravestone while his wife's fragile mental state finally disintegrates at the sight of her baby's birthmark. Even the rationalist Pope, who had earlier discounted the basis of the book *Malleus Maleficarum*, which claimed the existence of sexual relations between humans and demons, is forced to acknowledge the victory of the supernatural over the rational.

Notes

1. See Chapter 1 for the reasons for the name change.
2. Baker did, however, direct genre films, such as spy and detective films, for American and British television. This included an excellent Sherlock Holmes World War mystery, *The Masks of Death*. See Chapter 1 for details.

HAMMER AND AMICUS 183

3 In Kneale's television version the discovery was made whilst working on Roman excavations.
4 Quoted in Marcus Hearn, 'Rocket Man', *Hammer Horror*, Number 7, September 1995, p. 20. Brian Donlevy played Quatermass in the first two films, *Quatermass Xperiment* and *Quatermass II*, both directed by Val Guest. Guest, on the other hand, was more than happy with Donlevy in these films as he gave 'a down-to-earth feel to a very off-the-earth subject'. See Adam Jezard, 'Reel Life', *Hammer Horror*, Number 7, 1995, p. 9.
5 John Baxter, *Science Fiction in the Cinema*, New York, A.S. Barnes & Co, 1970, p. 98.
6 J. Sheridan Le Fanu, 'Carmilla', in Alan Ryan (ed.), *The Penguin Book of Vampire Stories*, London, Bloomsbury Books, 1987 [1871], p. 90.
7 Author interview with Roy Ward Baker, September 2000.
8 See Chapter 1 for the development of *The Vampire Lovers*.
9 Baker, *The Director's Cut*, p. 129.
10 *The Vampire Lovers* is often grouped with *Lust For a Vampire* (1971), starring Danish model Yutte Stensgaard as Mircalla/Carmilla, and *Twins of Evil* (1971), where Mircalla (Katya Wyeth) was relegated to a minor role.
11 Reprinted in *Little Shoppe of Horrors*, Number 4, May 1984, p. 46.
12 See David Pirie, *The Vampire Cinema*, London: Galley Press, 1977, p. 6.
13 See Syndy McMillan Conger, 'Gothic Romance', in Jack Sullivan (ed.), *The Penguin Encyclopedia of Horror and the Supernatural*, New York: Viking Penguin, 1986, p. 179.
14 *Ibid.*, p. 180.
15 *Ibid.*, p. 181.
16 Quoted in *ibid*.
17 Le Fanu, 'Carmilla', p. 89.
18 *Ibid.*, p. 74.
19 *Ibid.*, p. 134.
20 *Ibid*.
21 *Ibid.*, p. 137.
22 Brooks, *The Melodramatic Imagination*, p. 29.
23 *Ibid.*, p. 29.
24 The motif of the vampire's inability to live in the sunlight was developed by Bram Stoker, who was familiar with Le Fanu's 'Carmilla'. In Stoker's 1897 novel, *Dracula*, the vampire is weakened, but not killed, by the sunlight. Jimmy Sangster developed this motif even further in his script for *Dracula* (1958).
25 Such as *The Masque of the Red Death*, which was filmed in Britain in 1964.
26 David Sanjek, 'Twilight of the Monsters: The English Horror Film 1968–1975', in Wheeler Winston Dixon (ed.), *Reviewing British Cinema, 1900–1992: Essays and Interviews*, New York: State University of New York Press, 1994, p. 200.
27 Ian Conrich, 'Traditions of the British Horror Film', in Murphy (ed.), *The British Cinema Book*, p. 230.
28 Phil Hardy (ed.), *The Encyclopedia of Horror Movies*, London: Octopus Books, 1986, p. 227.
29 Harvey Fenton and David Flint (eds), *Ten Years of Terror: British Horror Films of the 1970s*, Surrey: FAB Press, p. 64.
30 Hallenbeck, 'The Karnstein Trilogy', p. 31.
31 Jack Sullivan, 'Joseph Sheridan Le Fanu', in Sullivan (ed.), *The Penguin Encyclopedia of Horror and the Supernatural*, p. 258.
32 Le Fanu, 'Carmilla', p. 106.
33 See Fenton and Flint (eds), *Ten Years of Terror*, p. 223.
34 Another scene shows the doctor examining two puncture marks on Laura's left breast.

35 Pirie, *The Vampire Cinema*, p. 120.
36 Le Fanu, 'Carmilla', p. 89.
37 *Ibid.*, p. 90.
38 Jack Sullivan, 'Vampires', in Sullivan (ed.), *The Penguin Encyclopedia of Horror and the Supernatural*, p. 435.
39 Author interview with Roy Ward Baker, September 2000.
40 Baker, *The Director's Cut*, p. 131.
41 See Hearn and Barnes, *The Hammer Story*, p. 136.
42 See Baker, *The Director's Cut*, p. 93.
43 *Ibid.*
44 See 'Roy Ward Baker Interviewed by John Stoker', p. 115.
45 Baker adopted the same practice on *Moon Zero Two* for almost the same reasons – poor script and inadequate budget.
46 See Hallenbeck, 'Scars of Dracula', p. 113.
47 Pirie, *The Vampire Cinema*, p. 26.
48 The BBFC insisted on the deletion of the shot showing Dracula actually drinking the blood pouring from her chest. The scene now ends with him leaning over her. See Hearn and Barnes, *The Hammer Story*, p. 139.
49 Baker, *The Director's Cut*, p. 131.
50 See Chapter 1.
51 'Roy Ward Baker Interviewed by John Stoker', p. 116.
52 *Ibid.*
53 Author interview with Roy Ward Baker, September 2000.
54 Hallenbeck, 'Scars of Dracula', p. 111.
55 Hearn and Barnes, *The Hammer Story*, p. 139.
56 Hallenbeck, 'Scars of Dracula', p. 111.
57 Amicus also released *I, Monster*, another version of Stevenson's story, in 1971.
58 See Hutchings, 'Authorship and British Cinema', p. 184.
59 Quoted in Richard Dalby, 'Robert Louis Stevenson', in Sullivan (ed.), *The Penguin Encyclopedia of Horror and the Supernatural*, p. 403.
60 *Ibid.*
61 *Ibid.*
62 Harper, *Women in British Cinema*, p. 116.
63 Richard Corliss, *Village Voice*, 7 July 1972.
64 See *ibid.*
65 *Ibid.*
66 See *ibid.*
67 Hearn and Barnes, *The Hammer Story*, p. 149.
68 Chris Knight, 'And Now the Screaming Starts!', *Cinefantastique*, Volume 2, Number 4, summer 1973, p. 6.
69 *I, Monster* (1970) was the only other single-plot period horror film produced by Amicus between 1964 and 1974.
70 Knight, 'The Amicus Empire', p. 9.
71 *Ibid.*
72 Quoted in Hutchings, 'The Amicus House of Horror', pp. 135–6.
73 Knight, 'The Amicus Empire', p. 12.
74 See Baker, *The Director's Cut*, p. 137.
75 Hutchings, 'The Amicus House of Horror', p. 141.
76 *Ibid.* Hutchings is referring to the 'And all Through the House' segment from *Tales From the Crypt* but it also applies to episodes in *Asylum* and *The Vault of Horror*.
77 *Ibid.*
78 Quoted in Knight, 'The Amicus Empire', p. 17.

79 Hutchings, 'The Amicus House of Horror', p. 139.
80 *Ibid.*
81 Knight, 'The Amicus Empire', p. 16.
82 *Ibid.*
83 *Ibid.*
84 See Joanna Russ, 'Somebody's Trying to Kill Me and I Think It's My Husband', *Journal of Popular Culture*, Volume VI, Number 4, spring 1973, p. 666.
85 Hutchings, 'The Amicus House of Horror', p. 134.
86 Hardy (ed.), *The Encyclopedia of Horror Movies*, p. 275.
87 Peter Brooks reached the same conclusion in his essay on *The Monk*. See 'Virtue and Terror: *The Monk*', *English Literary History*, Volume 40, Number 2, summer 1973, p. 251.

Conclusion:
The One That Got Away

I have never been the sort of director who deliberately makes films with messages but I came close to it with *The One That Got Away*.¹

The British prisoner-of-war story was popular in the 1950s. Although there were sporadic examples in the 1940s, such as *The Captive Heart* (1946), Basil Dearden's excellent film for Ealing, the cycle gained impetus in the early 1950s with Jack Lee's *The Wooden Horse* (1950), Lewis Gilbert's *Albert RN* (1953) and, especially, Guy Hamilton's *The Colditz Story* (1954). By the end of the 1950s the formula had lost some of its box-office appeal, although Hammer tried to reinvigorate it by switching the setting from Europe to Asia and focusing on Japanese atrocities, in Val Guest's *Camp on Blood Island* (1958). British Lion produced, and Don Chaffey directed, one of the last 'traditional' POW films, *Danger Within* (1959), although it differs from the earlier films due to its emphasis on the hostility and distrust between the British prisoners.

While Jack Lee, Lewis Gilbert, Don Chaffey *et al.* were showing how Leo Genn, Jack Warner, Richard Todd and Richard Attenborough could outsmart the Germans, Roy Baker in *The One That Got Away* was returning the favour by tracing the adventures of a charismatic German, Oberleutnant Franz Von Werra (Hardy Krüger). He was the only German POW to escape from British authorities and successfully return to Germany. Baker's motivation in making the film, aside from the fact that it was an exciting story, was his desire to rectify what he perceived as an incorrect, or incomplete, screen stereotype of Germans as 'homosexual, Prussian officers, Gestapo torturers or beer-swilling Bavarians, all presented in ridiculously hammy performances'.² Although the image of the German in the POW films was shifting before *The One That Got Away* – the Kommandant (Frederick [Fritz] Valk) in *The Colditz Story*, for example, is presented as an essentially humane man determined to avoid needless bloodshed in his camp – Baker's film represented a quantum leap in this regard. Hardy Krüger – with his youth, blonde hair and cherubic face – is physically different from the conventional British depiction of the sadistic Nazi.[3] Krüger's Von Werra exudes charm and energy and he provides a strong contrast to the polite, passive demeanour of the British officers. In fact, Krüger's charisma easily overwhelms the quiet, underplaying of actors such as Michael Goodliffe (RAF Interrogator), Colin Gordon (Army Interrogator), Terry Alexander (RAF Intelligence Officer), Jack Gwillim (the Commandant at Grizedale) and Alec McCowen (Duty Officer Hucknall).

Krüger's appeal, plus the basic structure of the story, ensured that the film would encounter problems in Britain. The film's 'structure of sympathy', to borrow from Murray Smith's thesis on the emotional relationship between screen characters and spectators,[4] is loaded in Von Werra's favour. He does not, for example, kill or physically hurt British soldiers or civilians. There are very few signs of his Nazi ideology, or allegiance to Hitler, and the presentation of different cultural values between Britain and Germany is minimised – unlike Michael Powell and Emeric Pressburger's 1941 propaganda film, *49th Parallel*. 'The only thing Von Werra believes in', as his Army interrogator (Colin Gordon) explains to a colleague, 'is Von Werra'.

The film's moral dimension, or what Smith calls the allegiance of the spectator to the character,[5] does not weaken audience support for Von Werra. While the British are presented in a positive manner, so is Von Werra. We learn early in the film that he is a daring pilot with thirteen aircraft shot down in combat and six destroyed on the ground. He also carries a photo of a young woman in his wallet. There is, unlike most POW films, no villain, and audience interest is maintained by the use of suspense in his attempts to escape. The first occurs at Camp Grizedale in the Lake District when he is spotted running from a group of Germans. It takes, however, a large number of British soldiers to finally corner him. The Duty Officer at Hucknall exposes his next attempt when he poses as a Dutch airman in order to steal a British Hurricane. Success comes when he jumps out of a train heading towards Lake Superior in Ontario. After finding the St Lawrence River not totally frozen he steals a small boat and drags it across the ice to the water before collapsing on American soil. His last action in the film is to send a postcard, with the Statue of Liberty on the front, to his RAF interrogator (Michael Goodliffe) informing him that he owes him [Von Werra] a packet of cigarettes. This follows a bet between the two men early in the film. The British interrogator, however, does not appear to be overly concerned by Von Werra's success: 'We might have to revise the system of interrogation a little'.

Baker was bemused, and irritated, by the reaction of some of his colleagues to the film. He objected to Basil Dearden's complaint that the film glorified the Germans and depicted the British as 'cripples'.[6] Instead, he argued, the film celebrated the British system of treating enemy prisoners 'firmly but properly'.[7] Others, such as Anthony Carthew in the *Daily Herald* (November 1957), disagreed. Carthew, under the heading 'Laugh! Laugh! Laugh!, wrote:

> I am not particularly psychic but I had a vision this week which I'm sure will come true. The vision was of thousands of Germans laughing their square heads off at the expense of the British.
>
> Their Teutonic chests will swell with pride when they pay some of that good, hard German currency to see a new film **THE ONE THAT GOT AWAY** (Odeon, Marble Arch) ...
>
> Why will the Germans be proud? Because the film eulogises the exploits of a young fighter pilot in escaping from a British prisoner of war camp.
>
> I don't say it sets out to deliberately glorify the blond ober-leutnant. But it can't help itself: he is the hero, his is the daring, and the British are the people who have the wool pulled over their eyes ...
>
> 'The One That Got Away' is a vastly exciting film. But it leaves a nasty taste since it is based on the kind of forgive-and-forget morality which many people will not find to their liking.[8]

Philip Oakes in the *Evening Standard* (10 November 1957) was less worried about the audience reaction to a German hero and praised Baker's film as 'exciting'. Oakes, however, thought it was 'ironic that the only tribute to a dead Nazi should come from a British studio'. Both critics praised the execution of the film as 'exciting', taut and well acted – Oakes makes a point of acknowledging that the film has 'no fat' and contains 'good performances'. Even Carthew thought that Hardy Krüger was 'very good' and both men praise the performances of Alec McCowen and Michael Goodliffe. Forty-five years later Australian critic and filmmaker Peter Thompson, when introducing the film on the pay television channel 'Encore', also praised it while noting that even though 'Von Werra might represent an odious, indefensible regime, you can't help identifying with him and sharing his determination to somehow shake loose his endlessly polite jailers'.

The One That Got Away was one of Baker's best films and it sums up the paradoxical nature of his career as a feature film director. The film, described by Carthew, Oaks and Thompson as 'exciting' and 'entertaining', was conventional, or classical, in its dramatic structure and presentation. It is, as the critics note, a fine example of this mode of cinema. It is also, within the context of the British cycle of POW films, strange in celebrating the triumph of a Nazi pilot over the British authorities when the Second World War was little more than a decade old.[9] No such sympathy was offered by Hollywood to the Nazis in the 1958 production of Irwin Shaw's novel *The Young Lions*. Hence credit must go to Baker, and John Davis, for making *The One That Got Away*. It did not represent a formal or moral challenge to the tenets of the classical cinema – as did some of the British New Wave films. But it holds, as Thompson notes, a 'special fascination' within the cycle of British POW films.

For an artist who received little attention when he was making feature films, Baker's career is an impressive one. He directed the best version, by far, of the *Titanic* story, *Quatermass and the Pit* is the superior film in Nigel Kneale's series of Quatermass stories, and *The Vampire Lovers* is the finest, and most faithful, adaptation of Sheridan Le Fanu's novella. Baker easily adapted to the production methods of Twentieth Century-Fox and he legitimised Marilyn Monroe's career as a dramatic actress and made the best 3D film (*Inferno*) in the history of the cinema. His contribution to film noir was substantial, with *The October Man*, *Paper Orchid* and *Night Without Sleep*, and the delirious, idiosyncratic qualities of *The Singer Not the Song* will ensure that this film will always be remembered. *Passage Home*, on the other hand, might just be, in terms of its depiction of repression, the quintessential British film of the 1950s. Above all else, Baker's skill, adaptability and intense work ethic meant that he survived in the British film and television industry for nearly 60 years – despite Dirk Bogarde's leather trousers.

Notes

1. Baker, *The Director's Cut*, p. 99.
2. Ibid.
3. See, for example, Anton Diffring in *Albert RN*.
4. See Murray Smith, *Engaging Characters: Fiction, Emotion, and the Cinema*, Oxford: Clarendon Press, 1995.
5. Ibid., Chapter 6.
6. Baker, *The Director's Cut*, p. 99.
7. Ibid.
8. Hardy Krüger reported in 1957 that when he came to promote the film he expected 'only friendly faces' and he was surprised at the hostility expressed towards him by some people.
9. *The One That Got Away* was a profitable film so Baker and Davis must have been correct. See Baker, *The Director's Cut*, pp. 99–100.

Filmography

Islington, Gainsborough Studios, 15 February 1934–15 February 1940

Roy Ward Baker was employed by Gainsborough from February 1934 to February 1940. He began as a 'gofer' and tea boy and was promoted to Assistant Production Manager, Production Manager, Location Manager, and Second Assistant Director during this period. Except for *Oh Daddy!*, *Band Waggon* and *Night Train to Munich*, all of the films that he worked on during this period were produced at Gainsborough's Islington studio. During a lull in production at Islington he asked to work in the editing room at Shepherd's Bush and he assisted Charles Frend, who was cutting *Oh Daddy!*. Baker disliked the experience and soon returned to Islington. In early 1936 *Pot Luck* was transferred from Shepherd's Bush to Islington and Baker worked on the last few weeks of the production. In 1938 he took a second unit and filmed people leaving work, and this was used in the opening scene in *Bank Holiday*. In 1939 he worked on the Twentieth Century Fox production of the Gracie Fields musical *Shipyard Sally*, which was shot at Islington. In August that year the Arthur Askey musical *Band Waggon* began shooting at Islington but at the end of the first week Gainsborough decided to close the studio down and the production was shifted to Shepherd's Bush. Baker accompanied the film and during the production of his next film at Shepherd's Bush, *Night Train Munich*, he was called up into the Army. During this period from 1934 to 1940 he never worked as a First Assistant Director.

'Gofer' and Production Assistant

Chu Chin Chow, 1934. Dir. Walter Forde. Leading players: George Robey, Anna May Wong, Fritz Kortner.

My Old Dutch, 1934. Dir. Sinclair Hill. Leading players: Betty Balfour, Gordon Harker, Florrie Ford.

The Camels Are Coming, 1934. Dir. Tim Whelan. Leading players: Jack Hulbert, Anna Lee, Hartley Power.

Assistant Editor

Oh Daddy!, 1935. Dirs Graham Cutts, Austin Melford. Leading players: Leslie Henson, Frances Day, Robertson Hare.

Production Assistant

Heat Wave, 1935. Dir. Maurice Elvey. Leading players: Albert Burdon, Cyril Maude, Les Allan.
Fighting Stock, 1935. Dir. Tom Walls. Leading players: Tom Walls, Ralph Lynn, Robertson Hare.
The Clairvoyant, 1935. Dir. Maurice Elvey. Leading players: Claude Rains, Fay Wray, Mary Clare.
Boys Will Be Boys, 1935. Dir. William Beaudine. Leading players: Will Hay, Gordon Harker, Jimmy Hanley.
Stormy Weather, 1935. Dir. Tom Walls. Leading players: Tom Walls, Ralph Lynn, Robertson Hare.
Jack of All Trades, 1936. Dirs Jack Hulbert, Robert Stevenson. Leading players: Jack Hulbert, Gina Malo, Robertson Hare.
Foreign Affaires, 1936. Dir. Tom Walls. Leading players: Tom Walls, Ralph Lynn, Robertson Hare.

Second Assistant Director

First Offence (also known as *Bad Blood* in the United Kingdom), 1936. Dir. Herbert Mason. Leading players: John Mills, Lilli Palmer, Bernard Nedell.
Tudor Rose, 1936. Dir. Robert Stevenson. Leading players: Nova Pilbeam, Cedric Hardwicke, John Mills, Felix Aylmer, Frank Cellier.
Pot Luck, 1936. Dir. Tom Walls. Leading players: Tom Walls, Ralph Lynn, Robertson Hare, Diana Churchill.
Where There's A Will, 1936. Dir. William Beaudine. Leading players: Will Hay, Gina Malo, Hartley Power, Graham Moffatt.
The Man Who Changed His Mind, 1936. Dir. Robert Stevenson. Leading players: Boris Karloff, Anna Lee, John Loder, Frank Cellier.

Location Manager/Second Assistant Director

Everybody Dance, 1936. Dir. Charles Reisner. Leading players: Cicely Courtneidge, Ernest Truex, Percy Parsons.
Windbag the Sailor, 1936. Dir. William Beaudine. Leading players: Will Hay, Moore Marriott, Graham Moffatt, Gina Malo.
Good Morning, Boys, 1937. Dir. Marcel Varnel. Leading players: Will Hay, Lilli Palmer, Graham Moffatt, Charles Hawtrey, Will Hay Jr.
Okay for Sound, 1937. Dir. Marcel Varnel, Leading players: Bud Flanagan, Chesney Allen, Jimmy Nervo, Teddy Knox, Charlie Naughton, Jimmy Gold.

Said O'Reilly to McNab, 1937. Dir. William Beaudine. Leading players: Will Mahoney, Will Fyffe, Ellis Drake.
Dr Syn, 1937. Dir. Roy William Neill. Leading players: George Arliss, Margaret Lockwood, John Loder.
Oh, Mr Porter!, 1937. Dir. Marcel Varnel. Leading players: Will Hay, Moore Marriott, Graham Moffatt, Sebastian Smith.
Owd Bob, 1937. Dir. Robert Stevenson. Leading players: Will Fyffe, John Loder, Margaret Lockwood, Graham Moffatt, Moore Marriott.

Second Assistant Director

Bank Holiday, 1938. Dir. Carol Reed. Leading players: Margaret Lockwood, John Lodge, Hugh Williams, René Ray, Merle Tottenham, Wally Patch, Kathleen Harrison.
Alf's Button Afloat, 1938. Dir. Marcel Varnel. Leading players: Bud Flanagan, Chesney Allen, Jimmy Nervo, Teddy Knox, Charlie Naughton, Jimmy Gold, Alastair Sim.
Convict 99, 1938. Dir. Marcel Varnel. Leading players: Will Hay, Moore Marriott, Graham Moffatt, Googie Withers.
The Lady Vanishes, 1938. Dir. Alfred Hitchcock. Leading players: Margaret Lockwood, Michael Redgrave, Paul Lukas, Dame May Whitty, Cecil Parker, Linden Travers, Naunton Wayne, Basil Radford.
Hey! Hey! USA, 1938. Dir. Marcel Varnel. Leading players: Will Hay, Edgar Kennedy, David Burns.
Old Bones of the River, 1938. Dir. Marcel Varnel. Leading players: Will Hay, Moore Marriott, Graham Moffatt, Robert Adams.
A Girl Must Live, 1939. Dir. Carol Reed. Leading players: Margaret Lockwood, Renée Houston, Lilli Palmer, George Robey, Hugh Sinclair, Naunton Wayne, Moore Marriott.
Ask a Policeman, 1939. Dir. Marcel Varnel. Leading players: Will Hay, Graham Moffatt, Moore Marriott, Charles Oliver.
Where's That Fire?, 1939. Dir. Marcel Varnel. Leading players: Will Hay, Moore Marriott, Graham Moffatt, Peter Gawthorne.
Shipyard Sally, 1939. Dir. Monty Banks. Leading players: Gracie Fields, Sydney Howard, Morton Selden, Norma Varden, Tucker McGuire.
The Frozen Limits, 1939. Dir. Marcel Varnel. Leading players: Bud Flanagan, Chesney Allen, Jimmy Nervo, Teddy Knox, Charlie Naughton, Jimmy Gold, Moore Marriott, Eileen Bell, Anthony Hulme, Bernard Lee.
Band Waggon, 1939. Dir. Marcel Varnel. Leading players: Arthur Askey, Richard Murdoch, Moore Marriott, Patricia Kirkwood, Jack Hylton.
Night Train to Munich, 1940. Dir. Carol Reed. Leading players: Margaret Lockwood, Rex Harrison, Paul von Henreid, Basil Radford, Naunton Wayne.

FILMOGRAPHY 193

Director

Army Kinematograph Service 1943–1945, Wembley Studios

Home Guard Town Fighting Series (1943)
According to Our Records ... (1943/44)
Technique of Instruction in the Army (1944)
What's the Next Job? (1944)
Warner's Warnings (1945)
A Letter From Home (1945)
Read All About It (1945)
Think It Over (1945)

Feature films

The October Man, 1947, 98 min., b/w

Production company: Two Cities
Distributors: General Film Distributors (UK), Eagle Lion (1948 – USA)
Studio: Denham
Producer: Eric Ambler
Screenplay: Eric Ambler
Photography: Erwin Hillier
Editing: Alan L. Jaggs
Art director: Alex Vetchinsky
Music: William Alwyn
Music director: Muir Mathieson
Sound recordists: W.H. Lindop, L.E. Overton
Sound editor: Harry Miller
Leading players: John Mills (Jim Ackland), Joan Greenwood (Jenny Carden), Edward Chapman (Mr Peachey), Kay Walsh (Molly Newman), Joyce Carey (Mrs Vinton), Catherine Lacey (Miss Selby), Adrianne Allen (Joyce Carden), Felix Aylmer (Dr Martin), Frederick Piper (Detective Inspector Godby), John Boxer (Detective Inspector Troth), Patrick Holt (Harry Carden), George Benson (Mr Pope), Jack Melford (Wilcox), Esme Beringer (Miss Heap), Ann Wilton (Miss Parsons), James Hayter (Garage Man), Juliet Mills (Child), John Salew (Ticket Inspector)

The Weaker Sex, 1948, 89 min., b/w

Production company: Two Cities
Distributors: General Film Distributors (UK), Eagle Lion (1949 – USA)
Studio: Denham
Producer: Paul Soskin

Screenplay: Esther McCracken, Paul Soskin, and Val Valentine (additional scenes). Based on the play *No Medals* by Esther McCracken
Photography: Erwin Hillier
Editing: Michael Chorlton and Joseph Sterling
Art direction: Alex Vetchinsky
Music: Arthur Wilkinson
Music director: Muir Mathieson
Sound recordists: John Cook and Desmond Drew
Sound editors: Dennis Gurney and K. Heeley-Ray
Leading players: Ursula Jeans (Martha Dacre), Cecil Parker (Geoffrey Radcliffe), Joan Hopkins (Helen Dacre), Derek Bond (Nigel), Lana Morris (Lolly Dacre), Thora Hird (Mrs Gaye), Bill Owen (Soldier), John Stone (Roddy), Marian Spencer (Harriet Lessing), Digby Wolfe (Benjie Dacre), Kynaston Reeves (Captain Dishart), Dorothy Bramhall (Mrs Maling), Eleanor Summerfield (Clippie)

Paper Orchid, 1948, 86 min., b/w

Production company: Ganesh and Columbia-British
Distributor: Columbia Pictures
Studio: Nettlefold Studios
Producer: John R. Sloan
Executive producer: William Collier
Screenplay: Val Guest. Based on the novel by Arthur La Bern
Photography: Basil Emmott
Art direction: Bernard Robinson
Music: Robert Farnon
Leading players: Hugh Williams (Frank McSweeney), Hy Hazell (Stella Mason), Sidney James (Freddy Evans), Garry Marsh (Johnson), Ivor Barnard (Eustace Crabb), Vida Hope (Jonquil Jones), Andrew Cruickshank (Inspector Clement Pill), Ella Retford (Lady Croup), Hughie Green (Harold Croup), Walter Hudd (Briggs), Frederick Leister (Walter Wibberley), Ray Ellington and his Quartet

Morning Departure, 1950, 102 min., b/w

Production company: Jay Lewis Independent Productions
Distributors: General Film Distributors (UK), as *Operation Disaster* by Universal International in the United States, January 1951
Studio: Denham
Producer: Jay Lewis
Screenplay: William E.C. Fairchild. Based on the play *Morning Departure* by Kenneth Woollard
Photography: Desmond Dickinson
Editing: Alan Osbiston

Art director: Alex Vetchinsky
Music: William Alwyn
Sound: George Croll, Peter Davies, John W. Mitchell, Jack Slade
Administrator: Leslie Parkyn
Leading players: John Mills (Lieutenant Commander Armstrong), Richard Attenborough (Stoker Snipe), Nigel Patrick (Lieutenant Manson), James Hayter (Able Seaman Higgins), Helen Cherry (Helen Armstrong), Lana Morris (Rose Snipe), Bernard Lee (Commander Gates), Peter Hammond (Sub Lieutenant Oakley), Andrew Crawford (Sub Lieutenant McFee), George Cole (E.R.A. Marks), Michael Brennan (C.P.O. Barlow), Victor Maddern (Leading Telegraphist Hillbrook), Kenneth More (Lieutenant Commander James), Wylie Watson (Able Seaman Nobby Clark), Roddy McMillan (Leading Seaman Andrews), Frank Coburn (Leading Seaman Brough), Zena Marshall (The Wren)

Highly Dangerous, 1950, 88 min., b/w

Production company: Two Cities Films
Distributor: General Film Distributors (UK), Lippert Pictures (1951 – USA)
Studio: Pinewood
Producer: Anthony Darnborough
Screenplay: Eric Ambler
Photography: Reginald Wyer
Editing: Alfred Roome
Art direction: Alex Vetchinsky
Music: Richard Addinsell
Sound recordist: John Cook
Sound mixer: Gordon McCallum
Leading players: Margaret Lockwood (Frances Gray), Dane Clark (Bill Casey), Marius Goring (Commandant Anton Razinski), Naunton Wayne (Mr Hedgerley), Wilfred Hyde-White (Mr Luke), Eugene Deckers (Alf), Michael Horden (Owens), Olaf Pooley (Detective), Gladys Henson (Sandwich Stand Attendant), George Benson (Sandwich Stand Customer), Eric Pohlmann (Joe), Ernest Butcher (Tom), John Horsley (Customs Officer), Patric Doonan (Customs Man), Paul Hardtmuth (Priest), Anthony Newley (Operator), Noel Johnson (Voice of Frank Conway)

The House on the Square, 1951, 90 min., b/w and col.

Production company: Twentieth Century Fox
Distribution: Released as *I'll Never Forget You* on 7 December 1951 in the United States
Producer: Sol C. Siegel
Screenplay: Ranald MacDougall. Based on the play *Berkeley Square* by John L. Balderston

Photography: Georges Périnal
Editing: Alan Osbiston
Art direction: C.P. Norman
Music: William Alwyn
Music director: Muir Mathieson
Sound: Buster Ambler
Costume: Margaret Furse
Leading players: Tyrone Power (Peter Standish), Ann Blyth (Helen Pettigrew/ Martha Forsyth), Michael Rennie (Roger Forsyth), Dennis Price (Tom Pettigrew), Beatrice Campbell (Kate Pettigrew), Kathleen Byron (Duchess of Devonshire), Raymond Huntley (Mr Throstle), Irene Browne (Lady Anne Pettigrew), Felix Aylmer (Sir William), Robert Atkins (Dr Samuel Johnson), Victor Maddern (Geiger Man), Ronald Adam (Ronson), Alex McCrindle (James Boswell)

Don't Bother to Knock, 1952, 76 min., b/w

Production company: Twentieth Century Fox
Producer: Julian Blaustein
Screenplay: Daniel Taradash. Based on the novel *Mischief* by Charlotte Armstrong
Photography: Lucien Ballard
Editing: George A. Gittens
Art direction: Richard Irvine, Lyle Wheeler
Music: Lionel Newman, Jerry Goldsmith. Also music from *Panic in the Streets*, 1950, by Alfred Newman is included
Sound: Bernard Freericks, Harry M. Leonard
Costume: Travilla
Leading players: Richard Widmark (Jed Towers), Marilyn Monroe (Nell Forbes), Anne Bancroft (Lyn Lesley), Donna Corcoran (Bunny Jones), Jeanne Cagney (Rochelle), Lurene Tuttle (Ruth Jones), Elisha Cook Jr (Eddie Forbes), Jim Backus (Peter Jones), Verna Felton (Mrs Ballew), Don Beddoe (Mr Ballew), Willis Bouchey (Joe), Gloria Blondell (Photographer), Michael Ross (Pat), Grace Hayle (Mrs McMurdock)

Night Without Sleep, 1952, 77 min., b/w

Production company: Twentieth Century Fox
Producer: Robert Bassler
Screenplay: Frank Partos and Elick Moll. Based on a story by Elick Moll
Photography: Lucien Ballard
Editing: Nick DeMaggio
Art direction: Addison Hehr, Lyle Wheeler
Music: Cyril Mockridge
Musical director: Lionel Newman

Lyricist: Ken Darby
Music director: Lionel Newman. Songs 'Too Late for Spring', music: Alfred Newman, words: Haven Gillespie. 'Look At Me', music: Alfred Newman, words: Ken Darby
Sound: Arthur Kirbach, Harry M. Leonard
Costume: Renie
Leading players: Linda Darnell (Julie Bannon), Gary Merrill (Richard Morton), Hildegarde Kneff (Lisa Muller), June Vincent (Emily Morton), Joyce Mackenzie (Laura Harkness), Donald Randolph (Dr Clarke), Hugh Beaumont (John Harkness), Louise Lorimer (Mrs Carter), William Forrest (Mr Carter), Steven Geray (George), Beverly Tyler (Singer), Mae Marsh (Maid)

Inferno, 1953, 83 min., col., stereoscopic/3D

Production company: Twentieth Century Fox
Producer: William Bloom
Screenwriter: Francis Cockrell
Photography: Lucien Ballard
Editing: Robert L. Simpson
Art direction: Lewis H. Creber, Lyle Wheeler
Music: Paul Sawtell
Musical supervision: Lionel Newman
Sound: Arthur Kirbach, Roger Heman
Costume: Dorothy Jeakins
Leading players: Robert Ryan (Donald Carson), Rhonda Fleming (Geraldine Carson), William Lundigan (Joseph Duncan), Larry Keating (Emory), Henry Hull (Sam Elby), Carl Betz (Lieutenant Mike Platt), Robert Burton (Sheriff)

Passage Home, 1954, 102 min., b/w

Production company: Rank
Distribution: General Film Distributors
Studio: Pinewood
Producer: Julian Wintle
Screenwriter: William Fairchild. Based on the novel *Passage Home* by Richard Armstrong
Photography: Geoffrey Unsworth
Editing: Sidney Hayers
Art direction: Alex Vetchinsky
Music: Clifton Parker
Musical director: Muir Mathieson
Sound mixers: Gordon K. McCallum, C.C. Stevens
Sound editor: Harry Miller

Costumes: Phyllis Dalton
Leading players: Peter Finch (Captain 'Lucky' Ryland), Anthony Steel (First Mate Vosper), Diane Cilento (Ruth Elton), Geoffrey Keen (Ike), Duncan Lamont (Llewellyn), Michael Craig (Burton), Cyril Cusack (Bohannon), Hugh Griffith (Pettigrew), Gordon Jackson (Burne), Patrick McGoohan (McIssacs), Bryan Forbes (Shorty), Robert Brown (Shane), Martin Benson (Guiterres), Sam Kydd (Crew)

Jacqueline, 1955, 92 min., b/w

Production company: Rank
Studio: Pinewood
Producer: George H. Brown
Screenwriters: Patrick Kirwan and Liam O'Flaherty. Additional dialogue by Patrick Campbell and Catherine Cookson. Based on the novel *A Grand Man* by Catherine Cookson
Photography: Geoffrey Unsworth
Editing: John D. Guthridge
Art direction: John Maxsted
Music: Cedric Thorpe Davie
Music conductor: Muir Mathieson
Sound editor: Jim Groom
Sound recordists: Gordon K. McCallum, Dudley Messenger
Costumes: Eleanor Abbey
Leading players: John Gregson (Mike McNeil), Kathleen Ryan (Elizabeth McNeil), Jacqueline Ryan (Jacqueline McNeil), Noel Purcell (Mr Owen), Cyril Cusack (Mr Flannagan), Tony Wright (Jack McBride), Maureen Swanson (Maggie), Liam Redmond (Mr Lord), Maureen Delaney (Mrs McBride), Richard O'Sullivan (Michael), Maire Kean (Mrs Flannagan), Rita Begley (Sarah Flannagan), Josephine Fitzgerald (Mrs McMullen), Barry Keegan (Bob Quinton), James Devlin (Mr Lord's Servant), Harold Goldblatt (Schoolmaster), Jack McGowran (Campbell), Sam Kydd (Foreman), Christopher Steele (Mr Pike)

Tiger in the Smoke, 1956, 94 min., b/w

Production company: Rank
Distribution: General Film Distributors
Studio: Pinewood
Producer: Leslie Parkyn
Screenwriter: Anthony Pelissier, Roy Ward Baker (uncredited). Based on the novel *Tiger in the Smoke* by Margery Allingham
Photography: Geoffrey Unsworth
Editing: John D. Guthridge
Art direction: Jack Maxsted

Music: Malcom Arnold
Sound editor: Roger Cherrill
Sound recordists: Geoffrey Daniels, Gordon K. McCallum
Costumes: Joan Ellacott
Leading players: Donald Sinden (Geoffrey Levett), Muriel Pavlow (Meg Elgin), Tony Wright (Jack Havoc), Bernard Miles (Tiddy Doll), Laurence Naismith (Canon Avril), Alec Clunes (Assistant Commissioner Oates), Christopher Rhodes (Chief Inspector Luke), Charles Victor (Will Talisman), Thomas Heathcote (Rolly Gripper), Sam Kydd (Tom Gripper), Kenneth Griffith (Crutches), Beatrice Varley (Mrs Cash), Gerald Harper (Duds Morrison), Wensley Pithey (Detective Sergeant Pickett), Stanley Rose (Uncle), Stratford Johns (Police Constable Perkins), Hilda Barry (Mrs Talisman), Dandy Nicholls (Stall Attendant)

The One That Got Away, 1957, 106 min., b/w

Production company: Rank
Studio: Pinewood
Producer: Julian Wintle
Screenwriter: Howard Clewes. Based on the book *The One That Got Away* by Kendall Burt and James Leasor
Photography: Eric Cross
Editing: Sidney Hayers
Art direction: Edward Carrick
Music: Hubert Clifford
Sound editors: Ray Fry, Arthur Ridout
Sound recordists: Gordon K. McCallum, C.C. Stevens
Costumes: Anthony Mendleson
Leading players: Hardy Krüger (Franz Von Werra), Michael Goodliffe (RAF Interrogator), Colin Gordon (Army Interrogator), Alec McCowen (Duty Officer, Hucknall), Terence Alexander (RAF Intelligence Officer), Jack Gwillim (Commandant, Grizedale), Andrew Faulds (Lieutenant, Grizedale), Julian Somers (Booking Clerk), John Van Eyssen (German Prisoner)

A Night to Remember, 1958, 123 min., b/w

Production company: Rank
Producer: William MacQuitty
Screenplay: Eric Ambler. Based on the book *A Night to Remember* by Walter Lord
Photography: Geoffrey Unsworth
Editing: Sidney Hayers
Art direction: Alex Vetchinsky
Music: William Alwyn. Played by the Sinfonia of London
Music conductor: Muir Mathieson

200 FILMOGRAPHY

Sound editor: Harry Miller
Sound recordists: Geoffrey Daniels, Gordon K. McCallum
Special effects: Bill Warrington
Special effects photography: Skeets Kelly
Costumes: Yvonne Caffin
Leading players: Kenneth More (Second Officer Charles Herbert Lightoller), Ronald Adam (Mr Clarke), Robert Ayres (Major Arthur Peuchen), Honor Blackman (Mrs Lucas), Anthony Bushell (Captain Arthur Rostron), John Cairney (Murphy), Jill Dixon (Mrs Clarke), Jane Downs (Mrs Sylvia Lightoller), James Dyrenforth (Colonel Archibald Gracie), Michael Goodliffe (Thomas Andrews), Kenneth Griffith (John Phillips), Harriette Johns (Lady Richard), Frank Lawton (Chairman), Richard Leech (First Officer William Murdoch), David McCallum (Harold Bride), Alec McCowen (Harold Cottam, *Carpathia*), Tucker McGuire (Molly Brown), John Merivale (Robert Lucas), Ralph Michael (Jay Yates), Laurence Naismith (Captain E.J. Smith), Russell Napier (Captain Stanley Lord, *Carpathia*), Redmond Phillips (Hoyle), George Rose (Charles Joughin, baker), Joseph Tomelty (Dr William O'Loughlin), Patrick Waddington (Sir Richard), Jack Watling (Fourth Officer Joseph Boxhall), Geoffrey Bayldon (Wireless Operator Harold Evans, *Californian*), Michael Byrant (Sixth Officer James Moody), Cyril Chamberlain (Quartermaster George Rowe), Richard Clarke (Martin Gallagher), Bee Duffell (Mrs Farrell), Harold Goldblatt (Benjamin Guggenheim), Gerald Harper (Third Officer, *Carpathia*), Richard Hayward (Victualling Officer), Thomas Heathcote (Third Steward), Danuta Karell (Polish Mother), Andrew Keir (Second Engineer James Hesketh), Christina Lubicz (Polish Girl), Barry MacGregor (Apprentice James Gibson, *Californian*), Edward Malin (Fifth Steward), Helen Misener (Mrs Ida Strauss), Mary Monaghan (Kate), Howard Pays (Fifth Officer Harold Lowe), Philip Ray (Reverend Anderson, *Carpathia*), Harold Siddons (Second Officer Herbert Stone, *Californian*), Julian Somers (Mr Bull), Theresa Thorne (Edith Russell), Tim Turner (Third Officer Charles Groves, *Californian*), Meier Tzelniker (Isador Strauss), Bernard Fox (Look-out Frederick Fleet), Desmond Llewelyn (*Titanic* seaman), Norman Rossington (Steerage Steward), Stuart Wagstaff (Steward), Rosamund Greenwood (Mrs Bull)

The Singer Not the Song, 1960, 132 min., col., Cinemascope

Production company: Rank
Distribution: Rank (UK), Warner Bros (US – May 1962)
Location: Filmed in the mountains near Malaga in southern Spain
Producer: Roy Baker
Associate producer: Jack Hanbury
Screenplay: Nigel Balchin. Based on the novel *The Singer Not the Song* by Audrey Erskine Lindop

Photography: Otto Heller
Editing: Roger Cherrill
Art direction: Alex Vetchinsky
Music: Philip Green
Sound: Gordon K. McCallum
Costumes: Yvonne Caffin
Leading players: Dirk Bogarde (Anacleto), John Mills (Father Keogh), Mylene Demongeot (Locha), Laurence Naismith (Old Uncle), John Bentley (Police Captain), Leslie French (Father Gomez), Eric Pohlmann (Presidente), Roger Delgado (Locha's Father), Selma Vaz Dias (Chela), Serafino Di Leo (Jasefa), Jacqueline Evans (Dona Marian), Philip Gilbert (Phil Brown), Nyall Florenz (Vito), Lee Montague (Pepe), Laurence Payne (Pablo)

Flame in the Streets, 1961, 93 min., col., Cinemascope

Production company: Rank
Distribution: Rank (UK), Atlantic Releasing Corp. (US – 1962)
Producer: Roy Baker
Associate producer: Jack Hanbury
Screenplay: Ted Willis, based on his original story
Photographer: Christopher Challis
Editing: Roger Cherrill
Art direction: Alex Vetchinsky
Music: Philip Green
Sound: Gordon K. McCallum
Leading players: John Mills (Jacko Palmer), Sylvia Syms (Kathie Palmer), Brenda de Banzie (Nell Palmer), Earl Cameron (Gabriel Gomez), Johnny Sekka (Pete Lincoln), Ann Lynn (Judy Gomez), Wilfred Brambell (Jacko's father), Meredith Edwards (Harry Mitchell), Michael Wynne (Les), Newton Blick (Visser), Glyn Houston (Hugh Davies), Dan Jackson (Jubilee), Cyril Chamberlain (James Dowell), Gretchen Franklin (Mrs Bingham), Harry Baird (Billy), Barbara Windsor (Girlfriend)

The Valiant, 1962, 100 min., b/w, Cinemascope

Production companies: BHP, Euro International Film
Studio: Shepperton Studios
Distribution: United Artists
Location: Filmed on location in Italy
Producer: Jon Penington
Screenplay: Keith Waterhouse and Willis Hall. Based on the play *L'Equipage au complet* by Robert Mallett
Photography: Wilkie Cooper
Editing: John Pomeroy

Art direction: Arthur Lawson
Music: Christopher Whelen
Second unit direction: Giorgio Capitani
Underwater photography: Egil Woxholt
Special effects: Wally Weevers
Costumes: Giannina Giurati
Leading players: John Mills (Captain Morgan), Ettore Manni (Luigi Durand de la Penne), Roberto Risso (Emilio Bianchi), Robert Shaw (Lieutenant Field), Liam Redmond (Surgeon Commander Reilly), Ralph Michael (Commander Clark), Colin Douglas (Chief Gunner's Mate), Dinsdale Landen (Norris), John Meillon (Bedford), Patrick Barr (Reverend Ellis), Moray Watson (Captain Turnbull), Charles Houston (Medical Orderly), Gordon Rollings (Payne), Laurence Naismith (Admiral)

Two Left Feet, 1962 (released 1965), 93 min., b/w

Production companies: British Lion/RBP
Producer: Leslie Gilliat
Screenplay: Roy Baker, John Hopkins. Based on the novel *In My Solitude* by David Stuart Leslie
Photography: Wilkie Cooper, Harry Gillam
Editing: Michael Hark
Art directors: Maurice Carter, Jack Maxsted
Music: Philip Green
Music played by: Sandy Brown, Judd Proctor, Kenny Baker and Bob Wallis and his Storeyville Jazzmen. 'Two Left Feet' sung by Tommy Bruce. 'Where Were You' sung by Susan Maughan
Animals trained by: John Holmes
Costume: Jackie Cummins
Sound: Norman Bolland, Red Law
Leading players: Michael Crawford (Alan Crabbe), Nyree Dawn Porter (Eileen), David Hemmings (Brian), Michael Craze (Ronnie), Julia Foster (Beth Crowley), Dilys Watling (Mavis), Bernard Lee (Mr Crabbe), David Lodge (Bill), Cyril Chamberlain (Miles), Hazel Coppen (Mrs Daly), Douglas Ives (Joe), Neil McCarthy (Ted), Howard Pays (Peter), Michael Ripper (Uncle Reg), Anthony Sheppard (Policeman)

Quatermass and the Pit, 1967, 97 min., col.

Production companies: Hammer Films, Seven Arts
Distribution: Hammer (UK – November 1967), Released in the United States as *Five Million Years to Earth* by Twentieth Century Fox in 1968
Studio: MGM British
Producer: Anthony Nelson Keys
Screenplay: Nigel Kneale, based on his story

Photography: Arthur Grant
Editing: Spencer Reeve
Art direction: Bernard Robinson
Music: Tristram Cary
Music supervisor: Philip Martell
Sound recordist: Sasha Fisher
Sound editor: Roy Hyde
Special effects: Les Bowie
Leading players: James Donald (Dr Matthew Roney), Andrew Keir (Professor Bernard Quatermass), Barbara Shelley (Barbara Judd), Julian Glover (Colonel Breen), Duncan Lamont (Sladden), Bryan Marshall (Captain Potter), Edwin Richfield (Minister of Defence), Peter Copley (Howell), Maurice Good (Sergeant Cleghorn), Grant Taylor (Police Sergeant Ellis), Noel Howlett (Abbey Librarian), Thomas Heathcote (Vicar), Robert Morris (Jerry Watson)

The Anniversary, 1967, 95 min., col.

Production companies: Hammer Films, Twentieth Century Fox, Seven Arts
Distribution: Warner-Pathé (UK – January 1968), Twentieth Century-Fox (US – February 1968)
Studio: ABPC Elstree
Producer: Jimmy Sangster
Screenplay: Jimmy Sangster. Based on the play *The Anniversary* by Bill MacIlwraith
Photography: Harry Waxman
Editing: Peter Weatherly
Art direction: Reece Pemberton
Music: Philip Martell. Title music played by The New Vaudeville Band
Sound editor: Charles Crafford
Sound recordist: Les Hammond
Leading players: Bette Davis (Mrs Taggart), Sheila Hancock (Karen Taggart), Jack Hedley (Terry Taggart), James Cossins (Henry Taggart), Elaine Taylor (Shirley Blair), Christian Roberts (Tom Taggart), Timothy Bateson (Mr Bird), Arnold Diamond (Headwaiter), Sally-Jane Spencer (Florist)

Moon Zero Two, 1969, 100 min., col.

Production companies: Hammer Films, Warner Bros-Seven Arts
Distribution: ABC (UK – October 1969), Warner Bros-Seven Arts (US – March 1970)
Studios: ABPC Elstree and Bray
Producer: Michael Carreras
Screenplay: Michael Carreras. From an original story by Gavin Lyall, Frank Hardman and Martin Davison

Photography: Paul Beeson
Editing: Spencer Reeve
Art direction: Scott MacGregor
Music: Don Ellis
Musical supervision: Philip Martell
Sound editor: Roy Hyde
Special effects: Les Bowie
Special effects photography: Kit West, Nick Allder
Costumes: Carl Toms
Choreography: Jo Cook
Leading players: James Olson (Bill Kemp), Catherina Von Schell (Clementine Taplin), Warren Mitchell (J.J. Hubbard), Adrienne Corri (Liz Murphy), Ori Levy (Karminski), Dudley Foster (Whitsun), Bernard Bresslaw (Harry), Neil McCallum (Space Captain), Joby Blanshard (Smith), Michael Ripper (First Card Player), Robert Tayman (Second Card Player), Sam Kydd (Barman), Keith Bonard (Junior Customs Officer), Leo Britt (Senior Customs Officer), Carol Cleveland (Hostess)

The Vampire Lovers, 1970, 91 min., col.

Production companies: Hammer Films, American International Pictures
Distribution: EMI (UK – September 1970), American International Pictures (US – October 1970)
Studio: ABPC Elstree
Producers: Harry Fine, Michael Style
Screenplay: Tudor Gates. Based on J. Sheridan Le Fanu's story *Carmilla*
Photography: Moray Grant
Editing: James Needs
Art direction: Scott MacGregor
Music: Harry Robinson
Music supervisor: Philip Martell
Sound editor: Roy Hyde
Sound recordist: Claude Hitchcock
Costumes: Brian Cox
Leading players: Ingrid Pitt (Carmilla/Mircalla/Marcilla), George Cole (Roger Morton), Kate O'Mara (Mme Perrodot), Peter Cushing (General Spielsdorf), Ferdy Mayne (Doctor), Douglas Wilmer (Baron Joachim von Hartog), Madeline Smith (Emma Morton), Dawn Addams (The Countess), Jon Finch (Carl Ebhardt), Pippa Steele (Laura Spielsdorf), Kirsten Betts (First Vampire), John Forbes-Robertson (Man in Black), Harvey Hall (Renton), Graham James (Young Man), Shelagh Wilcocks (Housekeeper), Janet Key (Gretchin), Olga James (Village Girl), Charles Farrell (Landlord), Joanna Shelley (Woodman's Daughter)

The Scars of Dracula, 1970, 96 min., col.

Production companies: Hammer Films, EMI Films
Distribution: EMI (UK – October 1970), American Continental Films (US – December 1970)
Studio: Elstree
Producer: Aida Young
Screenplay: John Elder (Anthony Hinds)
Photography: Moray Grant
Editing: James Needs
Art direction: Scott MacGregor
Music: James Bernard
Musical supervision: Philip Martell
Sound: Roy Hyde
Special effects: Roger Dicken
Leading players: Christopher Lee (Dracula), Dennis Waterman (Simon Carlson), Jenny Hanley (Sarah Framsen), Christopher Matthews (Paul Carlson), Patrick Troughton (Klove), Michael Gwynne (Priest), Wendy Hamilton (Julie), Anouska Hempel (Tania), Delia Lindsay (Alice), Michael Ripper (Landlord), Bob Todd (Burgomaster), David Leland (First Policeman), Richard Durden (Second Policeman)

Dr Jekyll and Sister Hyde, 1971, 97 min., col.

Production companies: Hammer Films, EMI Films
Distribution: EMI (UK – October 1971), American International Films (US – April 1972)
Studio: EMI-MGM Elstree
Producers: Brian Clemens, Albert Fennell
Screenplay: Brian Clemens. Based on Robert Louis Stevenson's story, *The Two Faces of Dr Jekyll*
Photography: Norman Warwick
Editing: James Needs
Art direction: Robert Jones
Music: David Whitaker
Musical supervision: Philip Martell. Song 'He'll Be There' with words and music by Brian Clemens
Special effects: Michael Collins
Costumes: Rosemary Burrows
Leading players: Ralph Bates (Dr Jekyll), Martine Beswick (Sister Hyde), Gerald Sim (Professor Robertson), Lewis Fiander (Howard Spencer), Susan Brodrick (Susan Spencer), Dorothy Alison (Mrs Spencer), Ivor Dean (Burke), Philip Madoc (Byker), Irene Bradshaw (Yvonne), Neil Wilson (Older Policeman), Paul Whitsun-Jones (Sergeant Danvers), Tony Calvin (Hare), Julia Wright (Street Singer), Geoffrey Kenion (First Policeman), Jackie Poole (Margie), Rosemary Lord (Marie), Jeannette

Wild (Jill), Petula Portell (Petra), Liz Romanoff (Emma), Anna Brett (Julie), Virginia Wetherell (Betsy), Pat Brackenbury (Helen), Dan Meaden (Town Crier)

Asylum, 1972, 92 min., col., Scope

Production companies: Amicus Productions, Harbour Productions
Distribution: Cinema International Corporation. The film was re-released as *House of Crazies* in the United States in 1980 and it was reduced to 88 minutes.
Producers: Milton Subotsky, Max J. Rosenberg
Executive producer: Gustave Berne
Screenplay: Robert Bloch. The film was subsequently novelised by William Johnston
Photography: Denys Coop
Editing: Peter Tanner
Art direction: Tony Curtis
Music: Douglas Gamley
Sound: Norman Bolland, Clive Smith, Robert Jones,
Special effects: Ernie Sullivan
Leading players: Peter Cushing (Smith), Britt Ekland (Lucy), Herbert Lom (Dr Byron), Patrick Magee (Dr Rutherford), Barry Morse (Bruno), Barbara Parkins (Bonnie), Robert Powell (Dr Martin), Charlotte Rampling (Barbara), Sylvia Syms (Ruth), Richard Todd (Walter), James Villiers (George), Geoffrey Bayldon (Max Reynolds), Megs Jenkins (Miss Higgins), Ann Firbank (Anna), John Franklyn-Robbins (Stebbins)

And Now the Screaming Starts!, 1972, 87 min., col.

Production company: Amicus Productions
Distribution: Cinerama
Producers: Milton Subotsky, Max J. Rosenberg
Executive producer: Gustave Berne
Screenplay: Roger Marshall. Based on the novel *Fengriffen* by David Case
Photography: Denys Coop
Editing: Peter Tanner
Art direction: Tony Curtis
Music: Douglas Gamley
Leading players: Peter Cushing (Dr Pope), Herbert Lom (Henry Fengriffen), Patrick Magee (Dr Whittle), Stephanie Beacham (Catherine Fengriffen), Ian Ogilvy (Charles Fengriffen), Geoffrey Whitehead (Silas Jr/Silas Sr), Guy Rolfe (Maitland), Rosalie Crutchley (Mrs Luke), Gillian Lind (Aunt Edith), Sally Harrison (Sarah), Janet Key (Bridget), John Sharp (Henry's Friend), Norman Mitchell (Constable), Lloyd Lamble (Sir John Westcliff), Frank Forsyth (Servant)

The Vault of Horror, 1972, 87 min., col.

Production companies: Amicus Productions, Metromedia Producers Corporation

Distribution: Cinerama. Also released as *Further Tales from the Crypt* in 1973 and *Tales from the Crypt II* in 1974.

Producers: Milton Subotsky, Max J. Rosenberg

Executive producer: Charles W. Fries

Screenplay: Milton Subotsky. Based on the stories by Al Feldstein and William Gaines in *The Vault of Horror* and *Tales From the Crypt*. The film was subsequently novelised by Jack Oleck

Photography: Denys Coop

Editing: Oswald Hafenrichter

Art direction: Tony Curtis

Music: Douglas Gamley

Leading players: Dawn Massey (Inez), Tom Baker (Moore), Michael Craig (Maitland), Denholm Elliott (Diltant), Glynis Johns (Eleanor), Edward Judd (Alex), Curt Jürgens (Sebastian), Daniel Massey (Rogers), Anna Massey (Donna), Terence Alexander (Breedley), Terry-Thomas (Critchit), Robin Nedwell (Tom), Geoffrey Davies (Jerry), Michael Pratt (Clive), Erick Chitty (Old Waiter), Jerold Wells (Waiter), Marianne Stone (Jane), John Forbes-Robertson (Wilson), Jasmina Hilton (Indian Girl), Ishaq Bux (Fakir), Arthur Mullard (Gravedigger), John Witty (Gaskill)

The Legend of the Seven Golden Vampires, 1973, 89 min., col., Panavision

Co-directed by Roy Ward Baker and Chang Cheh

Production companies: Hammer Films, Shaw Brothers

Distribution: Released in August 1974 in London, it was not released in the United States until 1979 in a severely re-edited form as *The Seven Brothers Meet Dracula* by Dynamite Entertainment. The film was re-released by Warner Bros Television in 1984 as *The Legend of the Seven Golden Vampires*

Producers: Don Houghton, Vee King Shaw

Executive producers: Run Run Shaw, Michael Carreras

Screenplay: Don Houghton

Photography: Roy Ford, John Wilcox

Editing: Chris Barnes

Art direction: Johnson Tsau

Music: James Bernard

Musical supervision: Philip Martell

Martial arts sequences: Tang Chia, Liu Chia-Liang

Sound: Les Hammond

Special effects: Les Bowie

Leading players: Peter Cushing (Professor Van Helsing), David Chiang (Hsi Ching), Julie Ege (Vanessa Buren), Robin Stewart (Leyland Van Helsing), Shih Szu (Mai Kwei), John Forbes-Robertson (Dracula), Robert Hanna

(British Consul), Chan Sen (Kah), James Ma (Hsi Ta), Liu Chia Yung (Hsi Kwei), Feng Ko An (Hsi Sung), Chen Tien Loong (Hsi San), Wong Han Chan (Leung Hon)

The Monster Club, 1980, 97 min., col.

Production company: Amicus
Distribution: ITC Entertainment. The film was never released for theatres in the United States
Producer: Milton Subotsky
Photography: Peter Jessop
Screenplay: Edward Abraham, Valerie Abraham based on the stories of R. Chetwynd-Hayes
Editing: Peter Tanner
Art direction: Tony Curtis
Music: Douglas Gamley
Sound: Norman Bolland, Russ Hill, Richard Dunford, Bill Barringer
Leading players: Vincent Price (Erasmus), John Carradine (R. Chetwynd-Hayes), Anthony Steel (Busotsky), Donald Pleasence (Pickering), Stuart Whitman (Sam), Richard Johnson (Busotsky's Father), Britt Ekland (Busotsky's Mother), Barbara Kellerman (Angela), Anthony Valentine (Mooney), James Laurenson (Raven), Simon Ward (George), Patrick Magee (Innkeeper), Geoffrey Bayldon (Psychiatrist), Roger Sloman (Werewolf Secretary), Fran Fullenwider (Buxom Beauty), Neil McCarthy (Watson), Warren Saire (Busotsky as a child)

Films made for television

The Spy Killer, 1969, 74 min., col.

Production companies: American Broadcasting Company (ABC), Halsan Productions
Distribution: Made for American television
Studio: Pinewood
Producer: Jimmy Sangster
Executive producer: Harold Cohen
Screenplay: Jimmy Sangster, based on his novel *Private I*
Photography: Arthur Grant
Editing: Spencer Reeve
Art direction: Scott MacGregor
Music: Johnny Pearson
Musical director: Philip Martell
Sound: Wilfred Thompson, Robert MacPhee

Leading players: Robert Horton (John Smith), Sebastian Cabot (Max), Jill St John (Mary Harper), Barbara Shelley (Danielle), Eleanor Summerfield (Mrs Roberts), Lee Montague (Igor), Philip Madoc (Gar), Douglas Sheldon (Alworthy), Robert Russell (Police Sergeant), Harvey Hall (Agent), Donald Morley (Dunning), Kenneth J. Warren (Diaman)

Foreign Exchange, 1970, 75 min., col.

Production companies: American Broadcasting Company (ABC), Halsan Productions
Distribution: Made for American television
Studio: Pinewood
Producer: Jimmy Sangster
Executive producer: Harold Cohen
Screenplay: Jimmy Sangster, based on his novel
Photography: Arthur Grant
Editing: Spencer Reeve
Art direction: Scott MacGregor
Music: Johnny Pearson
Musical director: Philip Martell
Sound: Wilfred Thompson, Robert MacPhee
Leading players: Robert Horton (John Smith), Sebastian Cabot (Max), Jill St John (Mary Harper), Eleanor Summerfield (Mrs Roberts), Dudley Foster (Leo), Clive Graham (Johns), George Roubicek (Karkov), Eric Pohlmann (Borensko), Eric Longworth (Boreman),

The Masks of Death, 1984, 76 min., col.

Production company: Tyburn
Distribution: Made for television. Distributed by Karl-Lorimar Video, Also released as *Sherlock Holmes and the Masks of Death*
Producer: Norman Priggen
Executive producer: Kevin Francis
Screenplay: N.J. Crisp. The story by John Elder (Anthony Hinds) based on the characters created by Sir Arthur Conan-Doyle
Photography: Brendan J. Stafford
Editing: Chris Barnes
Art direction: Geoffrey Tozer
Music: Malcolm Williamson
Sound: Jonathan Andrews, Otto Snel
Leading players: Peter Cushing (Sherlock Holmes), John Mills (Dr John H. Watson), Anne Baxter (Irene Adler), Ray Milland (Home Secretary), Anton Diffring (Graf Udo Von Felseck), Gordon Jackson (Inspector Alec Mac-Donald), Susan Penhaligon (Miss Derwent), Jenny Laird (Mrs Hudson), Russell Hunter (Alfred Coombs), James Cossins (Frederick Bains), Eric Dodson (Lord Claremont), Georgina Coombs (Lady Cynthia Claremont)

Television series/mini-series (year of production)

1961
Zero One (MGM/BBC)

1963
The Saint (New World/ITC)

1964
The Saint
The Human Jungle (Independent Artists/ABC)
Gideon's Way (New World/ITC)

1965
The Avengers (Telemen/ABC)

1966
The Saint
The Baron (Filmakers/ITC)

1968
The Champions (Scoton/ITC)
Randall & Hopkirk (Deceased) (Scoton/ITC)
Department S (Scoton/ITC)
Journey to the Unknown (Hammer/Twentieth Century Fox)
The Avengers
The Saint

1970
The Persuaders (Tribune/ITC)

1971
Jason King (Scoton/ITC)

1972
The Protectors (Group Three/ITC)

1977
The Return of the Saint (Tribune/RAI/ITC)

1978
Danger UXB (Euston Films/Thames)

1979
Sherlock Holmes and Doctor Watson (Polish Television)

Minder (Euston Films/Thames)
The Flame Trees of Thika (Euston Films/Thames)

1980
Minder

1981
Minder

1982
Q.E.D. (Consolidated Productions)
The Irish RM (Channel 4/Ulster)

1983
The Irish RM

1984
The Irish RM
Minder

1985
Fairly Secret Army (Video Arts/Channel 4)
Minder

1988
Minder

1989
Saracen (Central)

1990
The Good Guys (Havahall/LWT)

1992
The Good Guys

Treatments/screenplays

1983   Screenplay: ***Jane the Quene***
1986   Treatment: ***Lovers on the Nile***
1986/87   Screenplay: ***Whiteout***
1988   Screenplay: ***Doctor Frigo***
1990   Treatment: ***Ghost from the Grand Banks***
1991   Television script: ***In the Bees and Honey***

Select bibliography

Ashby, Justine and Andrew Higson (eds), *British Cinema, Past and Present*, London: Routledge, 2001.
Baker, Roy, 'Discovering Where the Truth Lies', *Films and Filming*, Number 7, May 1961.
Baker, Roy Ward, *The Director's Cut*, London: Reynolds & Hearn, 2000.
Bargainnier, Earl F., 'Melodrama as Formula', *Journal of Popular Culture*, Volume 9, Number 3, 1975.
Baxter, John, *Science Fiction in the Cinema*, New York: A.S. Barnes & Co, 1970.
Bentley, Eric, *The Life of the Drama*, New York: Athenaeum, 1964.
Booth, Michael, *English Melodrama*, London: Herbert Jenkins, 1965.
Bordwell, David, 'Happily Ever After, Part Two', *The Velvet Light Trap*, Number 19, 1982.
Bordwell, David, Janet Staiger and Kristin Thompson, *The Classical Hollywood Cinema: Film Style and Mode of Narration to 1960*, London: Routledge, 1985.
Brooks, Peter, 'Virtue and Terror: *The Monk*', *English Literary History*, Volume 40, Number 2, summer 1973.
Brooks, Peter, *The Melodramatic Imagination: Balzac, Henry James, Melodrama, and The Mode of Excess*, New Haven: Yale University Press, 1995.
Brosnan, John, *The Horror People*, London: MacDonald & Janes, 1976.
Conger, Syndy McMillan, 'Gothic Romance', in Jack Sullivan (ed.), *The Penguin Encyclopedia of Horror and the Supernatural*, New York: Viking Penguin, 1986.
Conrich, Ian, 'Traditions of the British Horror Film', in Robert Murphy (ed.), *The British Cinema Book*, London: BFI Publishing, 2001.
Corliss, Richard, *Village Voice*, 7 July 1972.
Dalby, Richard, 'Robert Louis Stevenson', in Jack Sullivan (ed.), *The Penguin Encyclopedia of Horror and the Supernatural*, New York: Viking Penguin, 1986.
Dixon, Wheeler Winston, 'Twilight of the Empire: The Films of Roy Ward Baker. An Interview', *Classic Images*, Volume 234, December 1994.
Dixon, Wheeler Winston, 'Twilight of the Empire', Part II, *Classic Images*, Volume 235, January 1995.

Durgnat, Raymond, 'Saturnalia in Cans', *Films and Filming*, November 1961.
Durgnat, Raymond *A Mirror for England: British Movies from Austerity to Affluence*, London: Faber & Faber, 1970.
Ellis, John, 'British Cinema as Performance Art: *Brief Encounter, Radio Parade of 1935* and the Circumstances of Exhibition', in Justine Ashby and Andrew Higson (eds), *British Cinema, Past and Present*, London: Routledge, 2001.
Elsaesser, Thomas, 'Tales of Sound and Fury: Observations on the Family Melodrama', *Monogram*, Number 4, 1972.
Everson, William, 'British Film Noir', *Films in Review*, Volume 38, Numbers 5 and 6.
Fenton, Harvey and David Flint (eds), *Ten Years of Terror: British Horror Films of the 1970s*, Surrey: FAB Press, 2001.
Gledhill, Christine, 'Rethinking Genre', in Christine Gledhill and Linda Williams (eds), *Reinventing Film Studies*, London: Arnold, 2000.
Gow, Gordon, *Hollywood in the Fifties*, New York: A.S. Barnes & Co., 1971.
Grimsted, David, *Melodrama Unveiled: American Theater and Culture, 1800–1850*, Chicago: University of Chicago Press, 1968.
Hallenbeck, Bruce G., 'Tudor Gates Interviewed by Bruce G. Hallenbeck', *Little Shoppe of Horrors*, Number 4, May 1984.
Hallenbeck, Bruce G., 'The Karnstein Trilogy', *Little Shoppe of Horrors*, Number 4, May 1984.
Hallenbeck, Bruce G., 'Scars of Dracula', *Little Shoppe of Horrors*, Number 13, November 1996.
Hardy, Phil. (ed.), *The Encyclopedia of Horror Movies*, London: Octobus Books, 1986.
Hardy, Phil (ed.), *The BFI Companion to Crime*, Berkeley: University of California Press, 1997.
Harper, Sue, *Women in British Cinema: Mad, Bad and Dangerous to Know*, London: Continuum, 2000.
Hearn, Marcus, 'Rocket Man', *Hammer Horror*, Number 7, September 1995.
Hearn, Marcus, and Alan Barnes, *The Hammer Story*, London: Titan Books, 1997.
Hedling, Erik, 'Lindsay Anderson and the Development of British Art Cinema', in Robert Murphy (ed.), *The British Cinema Book*, London: BFI Publishing, 2001.
Heilman, Robert, *Tragedy and Melodrama: Versions of Experience*, Seattle: University of Washington Press, 1968.
Higson, Andrew, 'Space, Place, Spectacle: Landscape and Townscape in the "Kitchen Sink" Film', in Andrew Higson (ed.), *Dissolving Views: Key Writings on British Cinema*, London: Cassell, 1996.
Hill, John, *Sex, Class and Realism: British Cinema, 1956–1963*, London: British Film Institute, 1986.
Howells, Richard, 'Atlantic Crossings: Nation, Class and Identity in *Titanic* (1953) and *A Night to Remember* (1958)', *Historical Journal of Film, Radio and Television*, Volume 19, Number 4, 1999.

Hunter, I.Q. (ed.), *British Science Fiction Cinema*, London: Routledge, 1999.
Hunter, I.Q., 'The Legend of the Seven Golden Vampires', *Postcolonial Studies*, Volume 3, Number 1, 2000.
Hutchings, Peter, 'Authorship and British Cinema: The Case of Roy Ward Baker', in Justine Ashby and Andrew Higson (eds), *British Cinema, Past and Present*, London: Routledge, 2000.
Hutchings, Peter, 'Beyond the New Wave: Realism in British Cinema, 1959–1963', in Robert Murphy (ed.), *The British Cinema Book*, London, BFI Publishing, 2001.
Hutchings, Peter, *Terence Fisher*, Manchester: Manchester University Press, 2001.
Hutchings, Peter, 'The Amicus House of Horror', in Steve Chibnall and Julian Petley (eds), *British Horror Cinema*, London: Routledge, 2002.
Jarlett, Franklin, *Robert Ryan: A Biography and Critical Filmography*, Jefferson, NC: McFarland and Company, 1990.
Jezard, Adam, 'Reel Life', *Hammer Horror*, Number 7, September 1995.
Johnson, Tom and Deborah Del Vecchio, *Hammer Films: An Exhaustive Filmography*, Jefferson, NC: McFarland and Company, 1996.
Klemensen, Richard, 'Harry Fine Interviewed by Richard Klemensen', *Little Shoppe of Horrors*, Number 4, May 1984.
Klinger, Barbara, *Melodrama and Meaning, History, Culture, and the Films of Douglas Sirk*, Bloomington: Indiana University Press, 1994.
Knight, Chris, 'The Amicus Empire', *Cinefantastique*, Volume 2, Number 4, summer 1973.
Knight, Chris, 'And Now the Screaming Starts!', *Cinefantastique*, Volume 2, Number 4, summer 1973.
Knight, Chris, interview with Roy Baker, *Cinefantastique*, Volume 2, Number 4, summer 1973.
Krutnik, Frank, *In a Lonely Street: Film Noir, Genre, Masculinity*, London: Routledge, 1991.
Laws, Stephen, 'Andrew Keir Interviewed by Stephen Laws', *Little Shoppe of Horrors*, Number 12, April 1994.
Le Fanu, J. Sheridan, 'Carmilla', in Alan Ryan (ed.), *The Penguin Book of Vampire Stories*, London: Bloomsbury Books, 1987.
Lindop, Audrey Erskine, *The Singer Not the Song*, London: The Reprint Society, 1954.
Lord, Walter, *A Night to Remember*, London: Longmans, Green and Co, 1956.
MacQuitty, William, *Titanic Memories: The Making of A Night to Remember*, London: National Maritime Museum, 2000.
Maltby, Richard, 'Film Noir: The Politics of the Maladjusted Text', in Ian Cameron (ed.), *The Movie Book of Film Noir*, London: Studio Vista, 1992.
Mayer, Geoff 'The Liberation of Virtue. The Cinema, Melodrama and Lizzie Borden', *Metro*, Number 95, spring 1993.
Mayer, Geoff, 'Jeffrey Richards, *A Night to Remember: The Definitive Titanic Film*, reviewed in *Screening the Past*, Issue 15, 2002. www.latrobe.edu.au/screeningthepast. Updated 2 July 2003.

SELECT BIBLIOGRAPHY 215

McConachie, Bruce A., *Melodramatic Formations: American Theater and Society, 1820–1870*, Iowa City: University of Iowa Press, 1992.
McFarlane, Brian, *An Autobiography of British Cinema: By the Actors and Filmmakers who made it*, London: Methuen, 1997.
Murphy, Robert, *Realism and Tinsel: Cinema and Society in Britain 1939–1948*, London: Routledge, 1989.
Murphy, Robert, *Sixties British Cinema*, London: BFI Publishing, 1992.
Murphy, Robert (ed.), *The British Cinema Book*, Second Edition, London: BFI Publishing, 2001.
Naremore, James, *More Than Night: Film Noir in its Contexts*, Berkeley: University of California Press, 1998.
Neale, Steve, 'Questions of Genre', *Screen*, Volume 31, Number 1, spring 1990.
Neale, Steve, 'Melo Talk: On the Meaning and Use of the Term "Melodrama" in the American Trade Press', *The Velvet Light Trap*, Number 32, autumn 1993.
Neale, Steve, *Genre and Hollywood*, London: Routledge, 2000.
Pines, Jim, 'British Cinema and Black Representations', in Robert Murphy (ed.), *The British Cinema Book*, London: BFI Publishing, 2001.
Pirie, David, *A Heritage of Horror: The English Gothic Cinema*, London: Gordon Fraser, 1973.
Pirie, David, *The Vampire Cinema*, London: Galley Press, 1977.
Rahill, Frank, *The World of Melodrama*, Philadelphia: University of Pennsylvania Press, 1967.
Richards, Jeffrey, *A Night to Remember: The Definitive Titanic Film*, London: I.B. Tauris, 2003.
Russ, Joanna, 'Somebody's Trying to Kill Me and I Think It's My Husband', *Journal of Popular Culture*, Volume VI, Number 4, spring 1973.
Sangster, Jimmy, *Do You Want It Good or Tuesday? From Hammer Films to Hollywood! A Life in the Movies*, Baltimore: Midnight Marquee Press, 1997.
Sanjek, David, 'Twilight of the Monsters: The English Horror Film 1968–1975', in Wheeler Winston Dixon (ed.), *Reviewing British Cinema, 1900–1992: Essays and Interviews*, New York: State University of New York Press, 1994.
Shelley, Barbara, in *Little Shoppe of Horrors*, Number 12, April 1994.
Singer, Ben, 'Female Power in the Serial-Queen Melodrama: The Etiology of an Anomaly', *Camera Obscura*, Number 22, winter 1990.
Singer, Ben, *Melodrama and Modernity*, New York: Columbia University Press, 2001.
Smith, Murray, *Engaging Characters: Fiction, Emotion, and the Cinema*, Oxford: Clarendon Press, 1995.
Spicer, Andrew, *Film Noir*, Essex: Longman, 2002.
Stoker, John, 'Roy Ward Baker Interviewed by John Stoker', *Little Shoppe of Horrors*, Number 13, November 1996.
Strachey, J. (ed.), *The Complete Psychological Works of Sigmund Freud, Volume XVII (1917–1919)*, London: The Hogarth Press, 1978.

Sullivan, Jack, 'Joseph Sheridan Le Fanu', in Jack Sullivan (ed.), *The Penguin Encyclopedia of Horror and the Supernatural*, New York: Viking Penguin, 1986.
Sullivan, Jack, 'Vampires', in Jack Sullivan (ed.), *The Penguin Encyclopedia of Horror and the Supernatural*, New York: Viking Penguin, 1986.
Turnbull, Greg, 'Ingrid Pitt by Greg Turnbull', *Little Shoppe of Horrors*, Number 4, May 1984.
Turner, Frederick Jackson, *The Frontier in American History*, New York: Holt, Rinehart and Winston, 1962.
Williams, Linda, 'Melodrama Revised', in Nick Browne (ed.), *Refiguring American Film Genres: Theory and History*, Berkeley: University of California Press, 1998.
Williams, Linda, *Playing the Race Card: Melodramas of Black and White from Uncle Tom to O.J. Simpson*, Princeton: Princeton University Press, 2001.
Williams, Tony, *Structures of Desire: British Cinema, 1939–1955*, Albany: State University of New York, 2000.
Young, Aida, 'Three's a Crowd: SCARS OF DRACULA', *Little Shoppe of Horrors*, Number 13, November 1996.

Index

Note: page numbers in **bold** refer to the main entries.

According To Our Records 18
Addams, Dawn 50
Aird, Holly 15, 16
American International Pictures (AIP) 48, 50, 51, 174
'Aldwych Farces' 4
Alexander, Terence 187
Allingham, Margery 29, 124, 126
Alwyn, William 97, 100
Ambler, Eric 6, 7, 17, 18, 19, 22, 32, 79, 84, 86, 97–8, 109, 112, 155
Amicus 1, 3, 10, 11, 54, 55, 56, 57, 152, 170, 175, 176, 177, 178, 180
Amis, Kingsley 69
And Now the Screaming Starts! 10, 11, 56–7, 175, 176, **180–2**
Anderson, Lindsay 70
Anniversary, The 11, 24, **40–3**, 45, 152
Anniversary, The (play) 41
Armstrong, Charlotte 112
Armstrong, Richard 28
Army Kinetograph Service Film Production Unit (AKS) 6, 17, 18, 27, 70
Askey, Arthur 16
Associated British Picture Corporation (ABPC) 39, 41, 50, 51
Asylum 3, 11, **55–6**, **176–80**
Atlantic 90
Attenborough, Richard 106, 108, 186
Avengers, The 3, 38, 53, 170
Aylmer, Felix 15, 99

Backus, Jim 25, 113
Baker, Robert S. 38, 61
Baker, Roy (sound editor) 39, 62
Baker, Tom 57, 179
Balchin, Nigel 103
Balderston, John 23
Ballard, Lucien 24, 27, 116, 118
Bancroft, Anne 26, 112
Band Waggon 16
Bank Holiday 16
Banzie, Brenda de 36, 77
Barnard, Ivor 104
Baron, The 3, 38
Barron, Keith 63
Bates, Ralph 53, 54, 171, 172, 173
Baxter, Anne 63
BBC *see* British Broadcasting Corporation
Beacham, Stephanie 180
Beaudine, William 15, 17, 170
Beaumont, Hugh 116
Belafonte, Harry 35
Benson, George 99
Bentley, John 130
Beringer, Esme 99
Berkeley Square 23
Berman, Monty 38
Bern, Arthur La 20, 21, 104
Beswick, Martine 54, 171, 172, 173
Big Clock, The 105
Black Angel 117
Black Angel (novel) 116
Blackman, Honor 83
Blaustein, Julian 24, 26
Bloch, Robert 55, 176, 177
Blondell, Gloria 113
Blood and Roses (*Et Mourir de Plaisir*) 156

218 INDEX

Blood from the Mummy's Tomb 54, 174
Bloom, William 24
Blyth, Ann 23, 24
Bogarde, Dirk 1, 30, 33, 35–6, 128–30, 133–6, 189
Boulting, Roy 109
Boxer, John 100
Boys Will Be Boys 15
Bresslaw, Bernard 44
Brief Encounter 4
Brighton Rock 96
British Board of Film Censors (BBFC) 49, 164
British Broadcasting Corporation (BBC) 153, 155, 170
Broderick, Susan 171
Brontë, Charlotte 180
Brooks, Peter 8, 71, 81–2, 89, 158–9
Buñuel, Luis 136
Burton, Richard 35
Burton, Robert 118

Cabot, Sebastian 46
Cain, James M. 124
Camels Are Coming, The 14
Cameron, James 85, 90
Camp on Blood Island, The 186
Campbell, Beatrice 23
Captive Heart, The 186
Carlson, Veronica 166
Carey, Joyce 99
Carey, Tristum 154
Carmilla (novella) 47–8, 155–7, 163
Carradine, John 62
Carreras, James 48, 49, 50, 51, 53, 54, 58, 156
Carreras, Michael 43, 44, 58, 62
Case, David 56, 180
Cassavetes, John 35
Castle of Otranto, The (novel) 157
Cavalcanti, Alberto 80
Caves of Steel, The 170
Chaffey, Don 186
Champions, The 39, 61
Chandler, Raymond 124
Chase, James Hadley 124
Cheh, Chang 59
Cherry, Helen 107
Chetwynd-Hayes, R. 62
Cheyney, Peter 124
Chia-Liang, Liu 59
Chiang, David 59
Chu Chin Chow 14

Cilento, Diane 1, 28, 122
City of the Dead 54
Clair, René 13
Clairvoyant, The 15
Clarke, Dane 22, 110
classical style 1, 3, 4, 76, 97, 188, 189
Clemens, Brian 53, 54, 170, 174
Clunes, Alec 127
Cockrell, Francis 27
Cohen, Harold 45
Colditz Story, The 186
Cole, George 50, 109, 158
Collier Jr, William 104
Collinson, Madeline 161
Collinson, Mary 161
Columbia Studios 20, 39, 104
Comfort, Lance 96
Cook Jr, Elisha 25, 113
Cookson, Catherine 28
Corcoran, Donna 113
Corridor of Mirrors 96
Cossin, James 41, 42
Courtneidge, Cicely 16
Craig, Michael 57, 179
Crawford, Michael 37
Creasey, John 124
Crisp, N.J. 62
Crossfire 118
Cruickshank, Andrew 21
Cripta e l'Incubo, La (Terror in the Crypt) 156
Cusack, Cyril 29, 122
Cushing, Peter 50, 53, 55, 59, 60, 62, 63, 158, 161, 165, 176, 181

Damned, The (1962) 43
Danger UXB 61
Danger Within 186
Darnell, Linda 26, 114, 116
Davies, Rupert 167
Davis, Bette 24, 40–3
Davis, John 30, 31, 33, 34, 35, 189
Davison, Martin 44
Daybreak 96
Dead of Night 54, 55, 177, 178
Dearden, Basil 186, 188
Deckers, Eugene 110
Del Guidice, Filippo 18
Demongeot, Mylene 36, 128, 129, 130, 134
Demons of the Mind 182
Department S 39, 61
DiCaprio, Leonardo 90

INDEX 219

Dickinson, Thorold 17, 95
Diffring, Anton 62, 63
Donald, James 153
Donlevy, Brian 39, 154
Don't Bother To Knock 24–6, 112–14, 178
Double Indemnity 117
Douglas Fairbanks Presents 55
Dr Jekyll and Sister Hyde 10, 11, 53–4, 96, **168**–75
Dr Terror's House of Horrors 54, 55
Dracula (1931) 156
Dracula (1958) 10, **164**–6, 167
Dracula (novel) 165
Dracula A.D. 1972 53
Dracula Has Risen From the Grave 166, 167
Dracula Prince of Darkness 10, 164, **166**–7
Dracula's Daughter 156
Dreyer, Carl 156
Dupont, E.A. 90
Durgnat, Raymond 95, 106, 112, 121, 124, 125, 126, 134, 135, 136
Dyrenforth, James 89

Ealing Studios 54, 178, 186
Eaton, Shirley 49
Edwards, Meredith 76
Ege, Julie 59
Eisenstein, Sergei 18
Ellison, Harlan 56, 180
Ekland, Britt 56, 177
Elder, John *see* Hinds, Anthony
Elstree Studios 21, 39, 50, 51, 70, 90
EMI 51, 58, 168
Et Mourir de Plaisir (Blood and Roses) 156
Evans, Jacqueline 131
Everybody Dance 16
Ewing, Barbara 166

Fairchild, William 21, 28, 107
Fairly Secret Army 63
Fallen Sparrow, The 96
Fantale Films 48, 50
Farmer, Suzan 166
Feldstein, Al 57
Fengriffen (novel) 56, 180
Fennell, Albert 53, 54
Fiander, Lewis 173
Field, Shirley Anne 72
Fighting Stock 14

film noir 95, 97, 112, 113, 114, 116, 134, 173, 189
Finch, Jon 50, 165
Finch, Peter 1, 28, 122
Fine, Harry 48, 49, 155
Finney, Albert 72
Fischer, O.W. 30
Fisher, Terence 10, 50, 95, 166
Five Million Years to Earth see Quatermass and the Pit
Flame in the Streets, 2, 5, 9, 10, **36**–7, 62, 70–1, 73–8, 82, 178
Flame Trees of Thika, The 15, 61
Fleming, Rhonda 27, 117
Forbes, Bryan 71
Forbes-Robertson, John 59, 60
Forbidden 97
Forde, Walter 170
Foreign Exchange 45–6
49th Parallel 187
Foster, Julia 37
Foster, Norman 98
Francis, Freddie 57, 166
Frank, Charles 19
Free Cinema Movement 70, 72
French, Leslie 131
Frend, Charles 14
From Beyond the Grave 177

Gaines, William 57
Gainsborough Studios 4, 13, 14, 16, 18, 170
Ganesh Productions 20, 104
Gates, Tudor 48, 49, 164
Gaunt, Valerie 16
Gideon's Way 3, 38
Gilbert, Lewis 186
Gilbert, Philip 130
Gilliatt, Leslie 37
Glover, Julian 153
Goldwyn Jnr, Samuel 34
Good Guys, The 63
Goodliffe, Michael 83, 187, 188
Gordon, Colin 187
Goring, Marius 110
Gothic Romance 157, 163
Gough, Michael 165
Grand Man, A (novel) 28
Grant, Moray 161
Grass is Greener, The (play) 34, 35
Great Day 96
Green, Guy 71
Green, Philip 133

220 INDEX

Greenwood, Joan 99, 100
Griffith, D.W. 18
Griffith, Hugh 122
Guest, Val 20, 39, 71, 104, 154, 186
Guillermin, John 3, 38, 71
Gwillim, Jack 187
Gwynn, Michael 167

Hakim, André 23
Hall, Harvey 159
Hamilton, Guy 10, 121, 186
Hammer Films 1, 3, 10, 11, 38, 39, 40, 41, 43, 44, 47, 48, 49, 50, 51, 52, 56, 152, 155, 156, 157, 160, 161, 162, 164, 166, 167, 168, 170, 174
Hammett, Dashiell 47, 124
Hanbury, Jack 33
Hancock, Sheila 41, 42
Hands of the Ripper 10, **168–70**, 182
Hanley, Jenny 167
Hardman, Frank 44
Hare, Robertson 14
Harper, Gerald 125
Harvey, Frank 109
Harwicke, Cedric 15
Hathaway, Henry 26
Havers, Nigel 63
Hay, Will 14, 15
Hayter, James 106
Hayward, Susan 26
Hazell, Hy 21, 104
Heatwave 14
Hedley, Jack 41, 42
Hemmings, David 37
Hempel, Anouska 166
Henson, Gladys 111
Hepburn, Audrey 23
High Treason 109
High Wall, The 96
Highly Dangerous 22, **109–12**
Hill, Sinclair 14
Hillier, Erwin 19, 97
Hinds, Anthony (also credited as John Elder) 41, 53, 62
Hitchcock, Alfred 4, 14, 16, 17, 18, 21, 70, 98, 102, 112, 170, 177
HMS Truculent 21, 107
Holt, Patrick 100
Holt, Seth 40, 41, 42
Home Guard Fighting Series 6, 17, 18, 27
Hope, Vida 104
Hopkins, John 37
Horror of Frankenstein, The 51, 52, 53, 168

Horton, Robert 46, 47
Hot Summer Night (play) 36, 74
Houghton, Don 58, 59
Hound of the Baskervilles, The 62
House, Jack 18
House Committee on Un-American Activities 109
House of Dracula 164
House of Frankenstein 164
House on the Square, The **23–4**, 112
House that Dripped Blood, The 55
Howard, Trevor 46, 121
Hudd, Walter 21
Hughes, Howard 23, 109
Hulbert, Jack 14
Human Jungle, The 3, 38
Hurst, Brian Desmond 29
Hutchings, Peter 71, 121, 178, 179, 182
Huxley, Elspeth 61

I Married a Communist 109
I'll Never Forget You see House on the Square, The
In My Solitude (novel) 37
In Which We Serve 107
Inferno 1, 6, 10, **26–8**, 95, 112, **117–21**, 189
Irish RM, The 63
Iron Curtain, The 109
Islington Studios 3, 4, 14, 15, 16, 17, 70, 170
It Always Rains on Sunday 21, 104

Jackson, Gordon 62, 123
Jacqueline 2, 3, 9, 11, **28–9**, 34, 124
James, Sidney 21, 105
Jane Eyre (1944) 180
Jane the Quene (unfilmed screenplay) 16
Janni, Joseph 71
Jason King 39, 61
Jenkin, Megs 177
Johns, Glynis 57, 178
Johns, Harriette 87
Johns, Stratford 127
Journey Into Fear 6, 98
Journey to the Unknown 39, 61
Judd, Edward 57
Jürgens, Curt 57, 179

Karloff, Boris 15
Keating, Larry 118
Keen, Geoffrey 122
Keir, Andrew 39, 40, 153, 154, 167

Keys, Anthony Nelson 39, 152
Killing of Sister George, The 164
Kimmins, Anthony 10, 102
Kiss of Death (1947) 112
Kneale, Nigel 39, 153, 154, 189
Kneff, Hildegarde 26, 114
Koerner, Charles 98
Korda, Alexander 18
Kruger, Hardy 30, 186, 187, 188
Kubrick, Stanley 44, 153
Kydd, Sam 123

Lacey, Catherine 99
Lady Vanishes, The (1938) 16, 112
Lamont, Duncan 122
Larraz, Joseph 162
Lawton, Frank 88
Le Fanu, J. Sheridan 18, 47–8, 155–64, 189
Lean, David 95
Lee, Bernard 106
Lee, Christopher 51, 52, 53, 54, 58, 60, 156, 164, 166, 167, 168
Lee, Jack 186
Legend of the Seven Golden Vampires, The 11, 53, **58–61**
Levy, Ori 44
Lewis, Jay 17, 21, 22, 23
Lewis, M.G. 157
Lind, Gillian 181
Lindop, Audrey Erskine 130, 132, 135
Lockwood, Margaret 22, 109, 112
Lom, Herbert 177, 181
Loneliness of the Long Distance Runner, The 69
Long and the Short and the Tall 1, 34, 35, 69
Look Back in Anger (play) 69
Lord, Walter 31, 84, 86
Losey, Joseph 95
Lucky Jim (novel) 69
Lundigan, William 27, 117
Lust for a Vampire 50, 53, 156
Lyall, Gavin 44
Lynn, Ann 76
Lynn, Ralph 14
Lytess, Natasha 25

MacDougall, Ranald 23
MacGregor, Scott 161
MacQuitty, William 17, 31, 32, 33, 84, 86
Magee, Patrick 176, 181
Magnificent Seven, The 60

'maladjusted veterans' 96
Maltese Falcon, The (novel) 47
Manuela 10, **121–2**
Mark of the Vampire 156
Marsh, Carol 165
Martinelli, Elsa 121, 156
Masks of Death, The **62–3**
Mason, James 96
Massey, Anna 57
Massey, Daniel 57, 179
Matthews, Christopher 166
Matthews, Francis 166
Mayne, Ferdy 162
McCowen, Alec 187, 188
McCracken, Esther 19
McGuire, Tucker 88
McIlwraith, Bill 41, 43
Melodrama 3, 7, 8, 9, 28, 30, 36, 71, 74, 75, 78, 80–3, 89–90, 95, 98, 100, 102–3, 112, 118, 124, 126, 136, 158–9, 165–6, 174
Meredith, Burgess 55, 102
Merivale, John 83
Merrill, Gary 24, 26, 114
Michael, Ralph 86
Milland, Ray 62, 63
Mills, Hayley 61, 62
Mills, John 7, 15, 35, 37, 62–3, 75, 98, 106, 107, 108, 128–30, 134, 136
Mills, Juliet 99
Minder 61
Mine Own Executioner 10, 97, **102–3**, 104
Mischief (novel) 112
Mitchell, Warren 44
Mockridge, Cyril 116
Moll, Elick 26, 117
Monk, The (novel) 157, 189
Monroe, Marilyn 24, 25, 26, 112–13
Monster Club, The 62
Moon Zero Two 2, 3, 11, 40, **43–5**
More, Kenneth 33, 40, 85
Morell, André 39
Morning Departure 2, 9, 10, 21–2, 23, 28, 29, 62, **106–9**, 124
Morris, Edna 72
Morris, Lana 108
Morse, Barry 176
My Old Dutch 14

Naismith, Laurence 126, 130, 136
Naked Spur, The 118
Nanny, The 40–1
Negulesco, Jean 90

222 INDEX

New Wave 10, 38, 69, 74, 189
Newley, Anthony 109
Newman, Alfred 116
Newman, Paul 35, 36, 136
Nicholls, Dandy 127
Night Has Eyes, The 96
Night to Remember, A 1, 2, 9, 10, 17, 25, 28, **31–3**, 69, 70, 71, 74, **78–91**, 105, 112, 124, 130, 178
Night Train To Munich 16
Night Without Sleep 2, 6, 9, 10, 24, 26, 95, 112, **114–17**, 135, 173, 189
No Medals (play) 19

October Man, The 6, 9, 10, 19, 28, 62, **95–103**, 106, 115, 155, 173, 178, 189
Ogilvy, Ian 180
Oh! Daddy 14
Olivier, Laurence 46
Olsen, James 44
O'Mara, Kate 50, 54, 159
On Dangerous Ground 118
On the Buses 54
One That Got Away, The 1, 2, 4–5, 6, 10, 16, 30–1, 135, **186–9**
Osborne, John 69

Paper Orchid 2, 3, 9, 18, **20–1**, 37, **103–6**, 115, 135, 178, 189
Parkins, Barbara 176
Parkyn, Leslie 29, 124
Partos, Frank 26, 117
Passage Home 1–2, 9, 10, 21, 28, 34, 95, **121–4**, 135, 164, 189
Passage Home (novel) 28
pathos 75, 82–4, 109
Patrick, Nigel 38, 108
Pavlow, Muriel 125
Pelissier, Anthony 30, 124
Penhaligon, Susan 62
Perkins, Anthony 35
Persuaders, The 39, 61
Pickering, Donald 61
Pinewood Studios 28, 30, 34, 46, 70, 79, 84
Piper, Frederick 100
Pithey, Wensley 125
Pitt, Ingrid 49–50, 55, 158
Pitt, Ray 18
Pleasance, Donald 121
Poe, Edgar Allan 160
Porter, Eric 170

Porter, Nyree Dawn 37
Portman, Eric 96
Portmanteau films 54–5, 176, **177–8**
Powell, Michael 95, 187
Powell, Robert 176
Power, Tyrone 23
Pressburger, Emeric 187
Price, Vincent 62, 180
Pride of the Marines 96
Pringle, Bryan 72
Protectors, The 39, 61
Psycho (1960) 177
Pudovkin, Vsevolod 18

Quatermass and the Pit 3, 11, **38–40**, **152–5**, 189
Quatermass II 39, 154
Quatermass Experiment, The 39
Quartet 55

Radcliffe, Ann 180
Radio Parade of 1935 4
Rains, Claude 15
Rakoff, Alvin 24, 41–2
Rampling, Charlotte 56, 177
Randall and Hopkirk (Deceased) 39, 61
Randolph, Donald 116
Rank, J. Arthur 3, 35, 71, 128
Rank Organization, The 1, 3, 7, 18, 21, 28, 33, 34, 35, 38, 51, 69, 70, 73, 88, 98, 128, 130, 136, 152
Ray, Nicholas 118
Read All About It 18
realism 6, 9, 10, 59, 69–71, 73–4, 78–82, 84–6, 90–1, 98–9
Rebecca 180
Reed, Carol 4, 16, 17, 70, 170
regeneration 9–10, 96, 101–2, 113–14, 118–19
Reisz, Karel 69–70, 72, 74
Rennie, Michael 23
Retford, Ella 104
Return of the Saint 61
Reynolds, Sheldon 61
Rhodes, Christopher 125
Richards, Jeffrey 17, 69, 80–1, 91, 107
Richardson, Ralph 57
Richardson, Tony 70
Richfield, Edwin 153
Robb, David 62
Roberts, Christian 42
Roberts, Rachel 72

Robson, Mark 98
Rolfe, Guy 181
Rollin, Jean 162
Rosenberg, Max 54, 56, 180
Rossington, Norman 72
Ryan, Jacqueline 29
Ryan, Robert 6, 27, 117, 118–19, 120

S.O.S. Titanic 90
Saint, The 3, 38, 39, 170
Sangster, Jimmy 40–1, 42, 45–6, 50, 53
Sasdy, Peter 10, 53, 168, 169, 170
Satanic Rites of Dracula, The 53, 58, 60
Saturday Night and Sunday Morning 1, 10, **34–5, 69–73**, 82
Saturday Night and Sunday Morning (novel) 3, 34–5, 69
Sawtell, Paul 118
Scars of Dracula 10, 11, **50–3**, 62, **164–8**
Schell, Catherina Von 44
Schenk, Joseph 24
Schofield, Paul 36
Scream and Scream Again 180
Selpin, Herbert 90
Seven Arts 39, 41, 44, 51, 53, 168
Seven Brothers Meet Dracula, The 61
   see also *Legend of the Seven Golden Vampires, The*
Seven Samurai, The 60
Seventh Veil, The 96
Shaw, Run Run 58–9
Shaw, Vee King 59
Shelley, Barbara 40, 47, 153, 166
Shen, Chan 59
Shepherd's Bush Studios 14, 16
Sherlock Holmes and Doctor Watson 61
Siegel, Sol 23
Sillitoe, Alan 3, 34, 69, 73
Sim, Gerald 171, 173
Simmons, Jean 23
Sinden, Donald 125
Singer Not The Song, The 1, 2, 9, 10, 33–6, 62, 69, 96, **128–36**, 189
Singer Not The Song, The (novel) 130, 131, 132, 134, 135
Small Back Room, The 96, 97
Small Voice, The 97
Smith, Constance 23–24
Smith, Madeline 50, 158
'social problem' films 70, 74, 84–90
Soskin, Paul 19
Spy Killer, The 45–7
S.S. Titanic 31, 32, 33, 79, 85, 86, 89, 90

St John, Earl 30, 33, 34, 35, 136
Steel, Anthony 1, 122
Steele, Pippa 50, 158
Steiger, Rod 45
Stensgaard, Yutte 50
Stevenson, Robert 4, 15, 17, 70, 170
Stevenson, Robert Louis 168, 170, 172
Stewart, Robin 59
Stoker, Bram 50, 165, 167
Strange Case of Dr Jekyll and Mr Hyde, The (novel) 168
Stranger on the Third Floor, The 26, 117
Stribling, Melissa 165
Style, Michael 48–9, 156
Subotsky, Milton 3, 54, 55, 56, 58, 62, 176, 177, 178, 179, 180
Summerfield, Eleanor 47
Syms, Sylvia 76, 176
Szu, Shih 59

Tales from the Crypt 57, 176
Taradash, Daniel 25, 112
Taste of Honey, A 69
Taste the Blood of Dracula 52, 53, 162, 166, 167, 168, 182
Taylor, Elaine 42
Terror in the Crypt 156
Terry-Thomas 57, 178
They Made Me A Fugitive 96, 97
Thomson, J. Lee 3, 38, 71
Tiger in the Smoke 4, 6, 9, **29–30, 124–8**, 164
Titanic (1943) 90
Titanic (1953) 90
Titanic (1996) 90
Titanic (1997) 25, 90–1
Todd, Ann 96
Todd, Richard 176, 186
Torture Garden 55, 176
Trelawny of the Wells 13
Trevelyan, John 49, 164
Trio 55
Troughton, Patrick 166
Tudor Rose 15
Tuttle, Lurene 113
Twelve O'Clock High 96
Twentieth Century-Fox 3, 6, 21, 22–4, 26, 28, 39, 40, 41, 44, 51, 69, 70, 109, 112, 114, 189
Twins of Evil 50, 51, 156, 161
Two Cities Productions 3, 18, 19, 70
Two Left Feet 1, 3, 11, **37–8**
2001: A Space Odyssey 44, 153

Uncle Silas 18, 19, 155
Unsworth, Geoffrey 124, 125

Vadim, Annette 156
Vadim, Roger 156
Valentine, Val 19
Valiant, The 3, 11, 37, 62, 104
Valk, Frederick 186
Vampire Lovers, The 2, 6, 9, 11, 19, 47–50, 51, 54, 60, 96, 135, **155–64**, 165, 189
Vampyr 156, 160
Vampyres 162
Van Eyssen, John 166
Varley, Beatrice 127
Vault of Horror, The 11, 57–8, 176, **178–9**
verisimilitude 73–4
Vetchinsky, Alex 22, 84
Victor, Charles 126
Villiers, James 177
Vincent, June 114, 117
Viol du Vampire, Le 162
Von Werra, Franz 30, 186, 187, 188

Waddington, Patrick 87
Walk in the Sun, A 96
Walls, Tom 4, 14, 15
Walpole, Horace 157
Walsh, Kay 21, 98
Wanted for Murder 96
Warner Brothers 44, 51, 52, 53, 61, 129, 168
Warner-Pathé 43
Washbourne, Mona 41, 43

Waterman, Dennis 167
We Are the Lambeth Boys 70, 72
Weaker Sex, The 9, 11, **19–20**, 103
Welles, Orson 6, 98
White Witch Doctor 26
Whitehead, Geoffrey 61, 181
Widmark, Richard 25, 26, 112
Wild and the Willing, The 69, 73
Williams, Hugh 21, 34, 104
Williams, Linda 7, 71, 82–3
Williams, Margaret 34
Willis, Ted 36, 74
Wilmer, Douglas 50, 160
Wilton, Ann 99
Winslet, Kate 90
Winslow Boy, The 20
Wood, William 121
Wooden Horse, The 186
Woodfall Films 69, 71
Woollard, Kenneth 21, 107
Woolrich, Cornell 116
Wray, Fay 15
Wright, Tony 30, 125, 126, 127
Wyman, Jane 25
Wynne, Michael 76

X the Unknown 43

Young, Aida 51
Young Lions, The 189

Zanuck, Darryl F. 23, 24, 25, 26, 27, 119–20
Zero One 38